The Jimmy Cook Story

The Jimmy Cook Story

A Career at the Crease

Jimmy Cook

with

Frederick Cleary

PELHAM BOOKS

PELHAM BOOKS

Published by the Penguin Group
27 Wrights Lane, London W8 5TZ, England
Viking Penguin, a division of Penguin Books USA Inc, 375 Hudson Street, New York, New York 10014, USA
Penguin Books Australia Ltd, Ringwood, Victoria, Australia
Penguin Books Canada Ltd, 10 Alcorn Avenue, Toronto, Ontario, Canada M4V 3B2
Penguin Books (NZ) Ltd, 182-190 Wairau Road, Auckland 10, New Zealand
Penguin Books, Amethyst Street, Theta Ext 1, Johannesburg

Penguin Books Ltd, Registered Offices: Harmondsworth, Middlesex, England

First published in 1993

ISBN 0 720 72028 1

Typeset, printed and bound by National Book Printers, Goodwood, Cape
Cover design and artwork by Hadaway Illustration & Design
Cover photographs by courtesy of *The Star*

For my wife Linsey
and
my sons Stephen and Ryan
always my most loyal supporters

Contents

Disinterested intellectual curiosity is the life-
blood of civilisation. If the French *noblesse* had
been capable of playing cricket with their peasants,
their châteaux would never have been burnt.

George Macaulay Trevelyan

Foreword

It is an honour and a privilege for me to write the foreword for this book about Jimmy Cook.

Books have been written about many cricketers, but none can be a more worthy subject than Jimmy because he is the epitome of what cricket is all about. The word 'gentleman' is not used too often in these days of high profile and controversial sporting personalities, but it certainly describes Jimmy Cook. He is one of the very few sports people in the modern era who has been able to reach the top, and stay there consistently, without losing the integrity of his character or the way he plays the game.

I was lucky enough to catch an early glimpse of the young Jimmy Cook as he began what has been such an illustrious career. I remember the moment as if it were yesterday: a traditional Boxing Day encounter against Natal in 1972, and as captain of Transvaal I was a worried man at 24-4. My great friend and opening partner, Brian Bath, had been telling me for some while that an outstanding cricketer was emerging from the Pirates Club and he reminded me of this as Jimmy walked to the crease, batting at number six, and hit a sound 50 to steer us into calmer waters.

Jimmy never looked back after that – for Pirates, for Transvaal, for South Africa. And then he went to Somerset and in three seasons swept the batting boards in glorious style.

Jimmy Cook has been an outstanding athlete. His fielding and catching are also superb, and they tell me that he would have played football for South Africa had there been no sporting isolation. His manner on and off the field has been an example to everyone, and he has shown conclusively that nice guys can finish first.

Cricket will always be the richer because Jimmy Cook played the game.

Ali Bacher
Managing Director, United Cricket Board of South Africa

Acknowledgements

I should like to thank Ronnie Eriksen for permission to quote from his book *A View from the Dressing Room,* and the many journalists and newspapermen whose writings have been cited in this book. Particular thanks go to Jack Bannister, the text of whose after-dinner speech appears in the Appendix, and to Frank Heydenrych and David Oldham who compiled the statistics.

My appreciation, too, to all those who gave permission for the use of their photographs. If any names have inadvertently been omitted, the authors and publishers apologise and will be pleased to make appropriate acknowledgement in future editions.

Finally, I am grateful to Alison Lowry, Pam Thornley, Siegrid Weiss and Beverley Moses of the Penguin Group for their enthusiasm and for all the hard work which made this book a reality.

Jimmy Cook

Introduction

It came as a bit of a surprise to the Somerset membership that someone called Jimmy Cook was to be the overseas player in 1989. Brian Rose, a former Club Captain and England opener, had seen a video of Jimmy batting and his judgement in recommending Jimmy to the committee was accepted. Nevertheless, very few had even heard of him including the immigration officer at Heathrow who kept Jimmy there for a few hours whilst his claim of playing for Somerset was checked out!

His first net on the Taunton County Ground had him in a bit of trouble as the ball moved about off the hailstones left on the artificial surface by the usual April showers. Wizened non-playing sages in the stands, eager to see this unknown cricketer, started to mutter. Knowledgeable cricketers started to look for opposite reasons having seen an orthodox if slightly open stance, a gun barrel straight bat, and a few crisply struck shots square on both sides of the wicket. Roy Marshall, of Hampshire and West Indian fame, declared there was no doubt about it, this man could bat.

Off the field, a few members were quite startled to find Jimmy Who shaking their hands and actually talking to them. The administrative staff were amazed to find a player who was keen to find out how they did their job and what the problems were. Jimmy Who even thanked them for what they were doing. There was no doubt about it, I thought, this man was going to be a fine ambassador for his club and country.

It was not long either before Jimmy was seen playing cricket on the outfield with his two sons at the end of a very hard day's play. Suddenly Jimmy Who became Jimmy Cook.

He came for a season and stayed three. His final match at Taunton will live long in the memory of many not for the century he scored that day but for the scores of people lining up crocodile-style during the intervals just waiting for Jimmy Cook to sign their books and shake their hands. They appreciated not only Jimmy's acknowledgement of how much the game of cricket had given to him but also the small part they actually played in that.

His playing record at Somerset speaks for itself and is recorded elsewhere in this book (p 215). There were many highlights of course, but my hair still stands on end remembering one fired-up Malcolm Marshall over to Jimmy in the middle of a limited-overs match when, to stand any chance of winning, Malcolm had to get Jimmy out. Well, Jimmy won that one four balls to two but the atmosphere was electric. That over ended with a simultaneous acknowledgement by both great men that a contest had been fairly fought and won.

It would have been easy for Jimmy to bask in his cricketing achievements to the exclusion of all else. Lesser men would have done so, but there was just the inkling that his family and friends, and a sense of fair play to life in general, were more important. There is a bench not far from Taunton which bears an inscription to a local sportsman. It says, 'Good husband, good citizen, good friend, good cricketer'. It could have been made for Jimmy Cook.

Peter Anderson
Chief Executive, Somerset County Cricket Club

1
EARLY DAYS

1

EARLY DAYS

Since I was a small child and right up until what may now be described as the 'autumn' of my first-class career, cricket – and in particular the craft of batsmanship – has been an integral part of my life. I work at it assiduously, checking my technique and correcting faults. Even after a good match, I will almost invariably go and have a strenuous workout at the nets, seeking that elusive standard of perfection.

From junior school through club, provincial and international levels, the accumulation of runs has been my goal, and if I could achieve this with style and for the benefit of whatever team I happened to represent at the time, this greatly added to my satisfaction. I am not a selfish player and my thirst for aggregates would never take precedence over other obligations. After all, cricket is a team game and I like to think that I have never put my own interests above those of my team. My passion for runs has always been tempered by this fact, and hopefully it will remain so.

As South Africans, we have been denied many opportunities to compete in international cricket, but I have been fortunate to meet and play with and against some of the finest players of my generation both at home and abroad. In this book I hope to share some memories of the hundreds of games in which I have participated and of those men of talent with whom it has been my privilege to experience magic moments on cricket grounds around the world.

Even though my 40th birthday is within sight, it would be great to think that, given continued good health and opportunity, I could carry on playing cricket for some years to come. I have always looked after my body and maintained a sensible lifestyle, and I retain the same enthusiasm I have had for the game since I was first chosen for my junior school team. Although there is a tendency for modern cricketers to retire in their early or mid-thirties, there is no reason why a batsman cannot continue for another decade or so. After all, the great Jack Hobbs of Surrey and England scored 98 of his 197 first-class centuries after the age of 40, and only retired at 52. Frank Woolley (Kent and England) retired at 51; Wilfred Rhodes (Yorkshire and England) was 53; and South African Test stars Dudley Nourse junior (Natal) was 43, and Eric Rowan (Transvaal) 42. While not trying to equate my ability with that of those great players, I am making the point that some men are blessed with a greater athletic longevity than others.

Physical standards apart, what motivates a sportsman into playing for so long a time is subjective – a state of mind which only the individual can answer. For me it is the sheer thrill of the contest with the bowler, the glorious sound of bat meeting ball, and fielders floundering as the 3 runs are duly signalled on the scoreboard – particularly if it is a Test match and on one of the famous grounds like Lord's, the Oval or, in my home country, Newlands or the Wanderers.

Of course, no matter how dedicated, no matter how hard one might work on one's chosen sport, there is no guarantee that one can rise to the occasion every time. The great American golfer Bobby Jones, a highly intelligent man who earned a handsome living as a successful lawyer, and for five months every year until he retired at 28 made a habit of winning major world amateur and professional championships, once exclaimed with all due modesty that he was puzzled as to why he did not play a perfect round every time he went out on to the course. He accepted in a matter-of-fact way that he was blessed with an enormous talent and he worked hard enough perfecting it, so why shouldn't the club hit the ball one hundred per cent correctly, go the right distance and drop into the hole as he required it?

Jones' questioning was, of course, logical only to a point. Even a sportsman of his genius is subject to human frailty. It is all a question of what we call form, being physically and mentally co-ordinated to peak level on the day or days in question, as well as opportunity and that vital and unpredictable factor, luck. How often have countless cricketers experienced an unlucky decision – a wrong LBW ruling, or a catch given when the ball went off their pads or to ground first; or perhaps hit a bad delivery for a justifiable scoring shot only to see a fielder bring off a brilliant catch in the covers, mid-wicket, slips, boundary, or whatever? Conversely, many have 'got away' with a legitimate LBW appeal, or seen an easy catch dropped early in their innings, and then gone on to score a century.

There are times when one can be in good form, collect a succession of reasonable totals, say in the 30s and 40s, but for one reason or another be unable to advance further and reach a really high score when it was badly needed. A perfect example of this occurred during the 1991/92 season when the South African selectors were looking for the 14-man team to play in the World Cup in Australasia. I had batted pretty well in three innings in the brief and hurried tour of India in the October but, in the eyes of the selectors, clearly not well enough to earn a place in the Cup team. In the few games prior to the naming of the initial 20-man squad from which the final 14 would be chosen I was again hitting the ball with confidence, yet not getting into high figures. Then one Saturday at the Wanderers I took a most comforting 88 off Eastern Province. But it was too late, being the day after the selectors had apparently made up their
4   minds on the 20. My inability to put together at least a couple of hundreds

at a vital time underlines this luck factor. I was batting well, but the gods of fortune were not smiling in my direction.

I have referred to the obvious need to be in good physical shape and my general adherence to this policy. I say 'general' for, very early on when I had set my sights on carving out a batting career, two fortuitous centuries were made in spite of the fact that I had been partying the night before. They were errors which were not to be repeated. Not all of us have the stamina, especially as we get older, of one famous Australian allrounder who so often seemed to do wonders in a match after a night on the proverbial tiles. He once arrived at Lord's still in his dinner suit and looking distinctly bleary-eyed. Yet he was still able to go out and give England hell.

But perhaps the game's greatest personality, the legendary William Gilbert ('WG') Grace put this need for physical fitness most succinctly when he wrote the following:

> Ask any player who has scored over a hundred in an innings if he felt any particular influence at work on the morning of the match, and he will probably answer in the negative. But press him and he will admit that he felt fit and well, and that the feeling was owing to a good night's rest, together with the careful training of days and weeks.
>
> I am aware that there are exceptions to this rule, and that players have been known to score largely after a night of high feasting and dancing. But in my own experience, whilst admitting the occasional freaks of this kind have been followed by moderately large scores, I cannot recall many of my big innings that were not the results of strict obedience to the rules which govern the training for all important athletic contests.
>
> Temperance in food and drink, regular sleep and exercise, I have laid down as the golden rule, from my earliest cricketing days. I have carefully adhered to this rule, and to it in a great degree, I attribute the scores that stand to my name in cricket history, and the measure of health and strength I still enjoy.

While quoting Grace, I want to include the following advice he wrote to batsmen who do achieve big scores:

> It is the first long innings that requires nerve and judgment. The hopes and fears that spring up in the young player's breast when he has scored something between fifty and a hundred make it a severe trial. And I dare say that if you and I could read his thoughts we should find that every run of the last ten was made in a mental fear, 5

accompanied by a thumping heart. But when the hundred is reached, who can describe the joy that thrills him as he hears the hand-clapping and shouting!

Then he adds this sensible word of caution:

I will not say be modest in the hour of victory, but rather be modest after it. It is after the victory, as we listen to outside praise, that conceit and its enervating influence steal in. Turn a deaf ear, and remember it was in fear and trembling that you reached the much desired score. Quiet confidence is a widely different thing from conceit. The former will help you to a run of big scores, the latter will cripple every effort to sustain your hardly earned reputation.

Yes, as Grace indicated, scoring a hundred is for a batsman the very pinnacle of his sporting life. Unless the contingencies of the game deem otherwise, it must surely be the primary personal target. After more than two decades in the game and having been fortunate enough to accumulate my fair share, that magic triple-figure mark still dominates my thinking. To get a century at club and provincial level is marvellous, but to achieve one when representing your country at Test level, and particularly for the first time, is an experience which few can fully appreciate. In a way it puts all subsequent performances in the shade.

Like so many of my South African sporting colleagues, I happened to grow up during that depressing period in our nation's history when the world did not want to know us because of our government's political policies. 'Apartheid' was an obscene word universally and, as well as avoiding us in other areas, no one wanted any sporting contact with us.

Yet I was lucky to be a cricketer, for our national administrators were among the most progressive in the country. They could not dictate political decisions, but after we were ostracised by the game's hierarchy at Lord's in 1971 they rapidly put their own house in order, eliminated all forms of discrimination, racial or otherwise, and waged an intelligent and tenacious struggle to convince the world cricketing community that their sport at least was 'clean' and that South Africa should therefore be allowed to take its place once more in the international arena. In July 1991 their hard work was rewarded when we were readmitted to the International Cricket Council after the government of President F W de Klerk had, in the February of 1990, finally set in motion legislation to expunge laws based on race from the statute books.

But all this took time, and in the intervening years, while they waited for the politicians to resolve their differences, the cricket administrators rightly believed they had a duty to both their supporters and their players regarding international competition in bringing out teams to play us, even if this action was regarded as 'illegal'. Hence the birth of the famous, or infamous, 'rebel' tours, and here I was able to register my maiden Test hundred when my 30th birthday was already looming on the horizon. It came when playing Graham Gooch's England XI at the Wanderers in Johannesburg on 12 March 1982. True, it was not against the best English team of that period. True, it was not registered in an official International, but it is in *Wisden*, which is good enough for me.

I would like to be able to record that it was a story-book début with a brilliant innings. Regrettably this was not the case. It may look good in the book, but in truth it was one of the worst hundreds of my career. Technically it was terrible. The wicket was a greentop and one on which any captain winning the toss would delight in turning his bowlers loose. But our Western Province opening bowler Stephen Jefferies told our captain Mike Procter that he had a sore throat and did not think he would be able to bowl so, much to our regret at the time, we batted first.

Those experienced seamers, the left-arm John Lever, Chris Old and Les Taylor, went to work with relish on this brute. Being the master batsman he was, my opening partner Barry Richards coped magnificently as expected, but I was abysmal. I should not have lasted ten minutes, yet somehow I did. I could not get out and the fact that it took me 35 minutes to get off the mark underlines my performance. I was dropped four times, at 5, 27, 46, and 63, nicking and scrambling my way along in a most undignified fashion. Barry, with such a splendid record behind him, rose to the challenge and together we added 117 for the first wicket, with me very much the junior partner.

After that cunning left-arm slow bowler Derek Underwood had trapped Barry for 66, Peter Kirsten carried on the good work and, much to my surprise, at the close I was still there with 114 and, incredibly on that bowler's paradise, we had accumulated 270 for the loss of only one wicket. The next day I was dismissed in the first over without adding to my score, and with Kirsten weighing in with a superb 88 and Graeme Pollock giving good support with 64, we were able to muster 400 for 7 declared. Big Vintcent van der Bijl was not one to miss an opportunity to take full advantage of a wicket ordered for him and, true to form, he whipped through the Englishmen with 5 for 25. They were bundled out for 150, did better in their second innings when Gooch (109) revealed his undoubted skills, but their 283 left us needing only 30 to win and we cruised to victory by 8 wickets.

It was a most encouraging performance and we had earned our celebratory party. On a personal level, one thing that did please me was my temperament. Looking back, I realise how fortunate I am to be blessed with patience and an emotional system that does not buckle under strain. With my co-ordination awry and the ball looking as tiny as a marble on that first day, it would have been so easy to have cracked. Certainly this aspect of my make-up is an underlying reason why I have been able to enjoy my career. No matter what the sport, sound technique is no good if one's temperament is found wanting. The history of cricket and just about every other sport is full of stories of performers of great potential who could not make the grade. Over the years any number of cricketers have shown much natural talent, have mastered the principles of batting and bowling and had all the ambition possible, but failed when put to the test at provincial or international level. Usually, they have been found wanting in temperament.

Cricket has been part of my way of life for almost as long as I can remember. Like most white South African youngsters, my elder brother Brian and I were introduced to the sport at junior school – as well as to other sports such as tennis and soccer – and, with my father an enthusiastic coach, there was every opportunity for whatever talent we possessed to be drawn out and nurtured.

As my name indicates, I am of British stock, although my father Buddy was born in Bombay, being brought along with his two sisters to South Africa by his widowed mother when he was a teenager. He also enjoyed his sport but his forte was coaching and he was engaged to teach us youngsters at Rosebank Primary School in Johannesburg. Noticing our enthusiasm for sport and that we did have 'ball sense', Dad impressed on us from a very early age that if we wanted to be successful we had to work hard. This meant practice, practice, and still more practice, which we never considered a chore. The miniature bat 'Test' matches which Brian and I played as if they were the real thing reflected our passion for the game. Playing day after day until it was too dark to see, with a tennis ball, a mini bat, a bucket as stumps, and sister Susan's dolls as fielders, was the norm.

I was fortunate to have had the benefit of my father's good advice and my hard work paid off when, at only eight, I scored my first century, playing in a school team in a 30-over-a-side game against Parkhurst School. Going in at the fall of the fifth wicket after one of our opening batsmen had scored 90, yours truly waded into the bowling as there were only about 14 overs left in which to earn my spurs. When the innings ended I was 105 not out from a total of 240 for 6, so there could not have been too many defensive shots. Naturally I was very proud of myself, and probably a little swollen-headed. I was quickly brought down to earth when, in our next game, I was bowled in the first over.

During this season the school bought 'boxes' for the team. In our innocence we wore them all over – on the knees and on the head – much to the delighted amusement of the parents!

Brian continued playing primary school cricket for a few more years, but then developed encephalitis and, as he was not able to play any strenuous sport for a year or two, furthered his interest in things mechanical, initially in go-karts and then graduating to motor cars and motor racing. Eventually he lost interest in cricket and became a motor racing driver. In the mean time I continued with soccer in winter and cricket in summer, and in the latter made steady progress at a junior representative level. Selected to play for Transvaal primary schools against Natal in Durban, and opening the batting, our captain John Gardner and I put on 125 for the first wicket. Although my contribution was only 19, a half-century followed in the next game. With this moderate success, and with tremendous support and enthusiasm from my family, friends and schoolmasters, was born in me a deep love for the game and a determination to succeed at it.

Moving from representative primary school cricket to the high school grade, we were somewhat disconcerted when we played our first game for Hyde Park High School to discover that our 'field' was a gravel pitch. This was after experiencing the lush turf of the famous Wanderers Club ground when wearing Transvaal primary school colours. Of course we got used to it and the next year we were 'promoted' to a rugby field with a mat thrown down on the grass as a wicket. It was on such an uneven and unpredictable surface that many wickets were taken simply by bouncing the ball in the right place.

My Standard 8 year was a turning-point in my game in that I was chosen for the school first team. We had good practice and match facilities, and with the seam bowling by opposition teams really good, I could feel a challenge building up inside me and I worked harder than ever on my defence. This paid dividends as I was chosen for the Transvaal under-15 schools side for an inter-provincial tournament in what was then Rhodesia. It was on this tour that we were fortunate to meet and to receive some invaluable advice from the county player Harold 'Dickie' Bird who was coaching at the time in South Africa and who went on to become one of the finest umpires in England and the world. His talks with our team and with us individually were to influence our game far more than anyone 9 perhaps realised at the time. We had a good tour and I even managed to take 102 off Eastern Province and return two other useful innings.

It was towards the end of Standard 8, when I was only 15, that my father decided I was ripe enough to get a taste of club cricket and he introduced me to the Pirates Club, not perhaps one of the most fashionable clubs in Johannesburg society but a good club nevertheless. Not only was the spirit as good as anywhere, but we were also fortunate to have Brian Bath as club captain, a fine person and sportsman who happened to be a regular opener with Ali Bacher for Transvaal. I had to work harder than ever at my game in order to survive and hold my place even in the third team. This was a great test of character for me, but the determination was there.

My other great love was soccer. I was chosen for the provincial and the South African under-16 side, and our coach talked to my father about my possibly having a trial with Wolverhampton Wanderers, the famous English Midlands club. But Dad rightly decided that my future lay in cricket and that my schooling should come first. I was to play soccer for many more years for Wits University, but any ideas of a career abroad in the Association Code were discarded.

My football career saw me through the junior ranks at Wanderers, then as a Colt at the Highlands Park Club. Later, from 1976 until my retirement in 1985, I joined the Witwatersrand University club side as a professional. Playing the Association Code was an enjoyable winter diversion from cricket, and the most memorable of many good seasons was the one in which I was a member of the team which beat Kaizer Chiefs in the Mainstay Cup final in 1978.

Although I was making steady progress through the senior school and club cricket ranks, I was unable to find a place in the Transvaal Nuffield Schools team, that splendid inter-provincial tournament which was originally sponsored by the late British car magnate, Lord Nuffield, and which has long been recognised as the nursery for many Springboks. The reason for my being overlooked is not too hard to pinpoint. You had to go to the right school: that is, if you attended one of the top cricket-playing schools like Jeppe High, King Edward or Parktown, you played against similar competition and the selectors were always in attendance looking out for potential talent. Although, ironically enough, my school, Hyde Park, is situated in one of the wealthiest areas in Johannesburg, because it was fairly new it was not considered one of the cricket élite; there was little or no tradition, so we were inclined to be afforded little more than a cursory once-over. For instance, my matric year brought me over 1 000 runs in ten completed innings, with four or five centuries, for an average of over 100, and despite not having played against the strongest schools sides in the city, the opposition was the best we were allowed to face, and that was how one should have been judged.

I was selected for the North-East Area side in the Nuffield Week trials. We played three matches. On our way to the ground for the first match our car broke down and we arrived about ten minutes after the start. I was told to go in at the fall of the next wicket, and had barely got out of the car and padded up when a wicket fell. Still somewhat stiff after the car journey and not really adjusted to the light and the conditions, I went out and was bowled first ball. A 60-odd on the second day and 15 in the third match was not good enough. My consolation was the captaincy of the Transvaal Nuffield B side. This upset me, but Dickie Bird encouraged me by advising me not to worry about it as he was certain that I would go further than any of the other players who were selected.

Meanwhile, I had been holding down a place in the lower order of the Pirates Club league team, not doing anything spectacular, but soaking up experience and polishing my technique. Apart from having the opportunity close-up of seeing the solid and dependable style of batting exemplified by Brian Bath, I also went to Currie Cup matches where, of course, I was able to study my great batting heroes, Denis Lindsay and Barry Richards. The former was one of the great swashbuckling Springbok batsmen who will always be remembered with awe by all who saw his tremendous season against Bobby Simpson's touring Australians in 1966/67, when he scored 600 runs by way of innings of 69, 182, 81, 137 and 131. Denis and his father Johnny also held the distinction of keeping wicket for their province, North-Eastern Transvaal, and for their country.

Then there was Barry Richards, surely one of the most gifted batsmen to play for South Africa or any other country. He made the batting department look so easy. Blessed with superb eyesight and reflexes, he seemed to have all the time in the world to take on any kind of bowling, and was always so technically correct. His head was always so still, his footwork so exemplary, and his bat so straight.

I partnered him in my first unofficial Test, and I could not believe we were facing the same bowlers. He was playing them as if they were throwing the ball at him under-arm and I kept saying to myself, why are they bowling so fast to me and so slowly to him? As in the case of Graeme Pollock, it is such a pity that the rest of the world did not see more of him on the international stage.

The course of my own progression took an unexpected turn when, after three years as a lower-order club batsman, Brian Bath came to me at the 11 beginning of the 1972/73 season and said that he was promoting me to number three. Then one weekend we came up against the powerful Balfour Park side, which included Ali Bacher and Lee Irvine. On the Saturday we got 9 of their wickets for just under 180, and it so happened that on that particular night I went to a friend's 21st birthday party, celebrated to the full and only got home at about 2 a.m. The next day, feeling somewhat the worse for wear, we went out to field. We soon got the last Balfour wicket, and one of our opening batsmen was dismissed in the first over; thus I was virtually opening for the first time for Pirates. Luckily for me, I finished the day with an undefeated century and, with such important men as Ali, the provincial captain, and Lee watching my every shot, this innings earned me a place in the Transvaal C side to play a districts side in Pietersburg.

We set off on a Saturday and that night our team attended the traditional party. Sure enough, the party carried on until the wee small hours. On the Sunday we fielded, dismissed the opposition fairly cheaply and, opening the batting, I scored another century, this time in about 90 minutes.

This brought immediate promotion and I was pencilled in for the senior team in the annual Christmas match against Natal at the Wanderers starting on Boxing Day, to bat at number six. We were put in to bat, and spin bowler Peter de Vaal, who was to follow me in the batting order, suggested that, as we would probably not be required before late afternoon at the earliest, we should don some shorts, relax, and watch the game from the main stand. Three-quarters of an hour later Transvaal was 24 for 4, and I was at the wicket. Until then I had prided myself on having no nerves, but when I realised it was my turn to bat I was so nervous and shaking so much that I struggled to buckle on my pads. It did not help my equilibrium to know that just itching to get to work on me on what was a responsive wicket was that marvellous pair of seamers, Vince van der Bijl and Pat Trimborn.

This was my greatest test to date. Fortunately, although I was whacked about quite a bit on the legs and felt somewhat like a fish out of water, I came through with a satisfactory 54. I walked off confident enough to feel that, although much work lay ahead, I could make the grade. A score of 27 in the second innings gave me a happy enough personal performance on début, but for the fact that I ran out Lee Irvine, our star batsman. He was playing brilliantly, going like the proverbial train, and was on about 60 when it happened. He called me for a single, I sent him back, and he was run out. He had every reason to be angry with me but, typical of him, he did not say a word, accepting it as part of the game and almost certainly appreciating that his partner was still a provincial novice.

I held my place in the team with a number of reasonable enough scores, and managed to hit 60-odd against a combined side brought out by cricket fanatic and English millionaire, the late Derrick Robins. But such is the depth of talent in the country's most populous province that inevitably I was to experience the humiliation of being dropped several times during the next few seasons. Several of us were vying for middle-order berths – Norman Featherstone, Kevin McKenzie and Duncan Lindsay-Smith, among others. We used to pass at net practice, wishing one another good luck in the A, B or C teams, wherever we were headed.

At the start of the 1977/78 season a young Old Edwardians member, Wynand van der Linden, was chosen to open with David Dyer, and I took stock of my prospects for advancement. Hovering in the middle batting order in the A and B teams, I realised that they did not look too good, especially as Graeme Pollock was due to move up from Eastern Province the following season, along with Natal's Henry Fotheringham, while we already had Clive Rice and Kevin McKenzie solidly established in the senior squad middle order. I had to do something about it, so I went to selection convener Ali Bacher and put my case to him. Having scored a few centuries from the middle order in the B team, I put it to him that I would like a chance to open the batting in the B side and, if successful, gain promotion to the A team in that position, believing that this was the only way I could stake a permanent place in the senior side. Fair-minded person that he is, he took my point and asked Willie Kerr, the B team captain, to give me an opportunity to prove myself in the next match. This happened to be against Rhodesia in Salisbury, and I did justice to myself with a score of 146. Selection for the senior team to play in the final game of the season in Rhodesia followed, this time in Bulawayo, where I managed 85 and so virtually gained my spurs.

Came the annual Boxing Day match against Natal the following season at the Wanderers, and we were bowled out for about 150. Then Natal were shot out for 70 and we were 20 for no wicket in our second innings at the close of play on the first day – so one can imagine what the wicket was like. On the second day we declared at 400 for 3, my contribution being an undefeated 179, including 100 between lunch and tea. We won the match comfortably. I think that particular performance cemented my place as a senior Transvaal opening batsman, as I was never dropped again and never missed a match through injury or for any other reason.

Runs flowed regularly from my bat as the seasons went by, with a few hundreds and half-centuries. The years of hard work were bearing fruit, and no one was more pleased than my Dad who had seen my potential so early on and had encouraged me and worked with me on my game in those formative years. Naturally, my sights were now raised to higher things. Would I ever be selected for my country? My track record was good enough, but where was the opportunity? My playing colleagues around the country all felt the same frustration. The rest of the cricketing world competed happily and regularly with one another, but we South Africans were out in the cold, isolated and all but forgotten.

Then a breakthrough of sorts occurred. The South African Cricket Union (SACU), as it was then called, decided enough was enough. Competition had to be sought and, in conjunction with a couple of businessmen, the Union persuaded the outstanding English batsman Graham Gooch of Essex to captain a team of fellow countrymen on a short tour of South Africa in March 1982. Money was a major incentive, but these brother cricketers also felt that we were being unfairly treated as prisoners of our politicians. There was universal condemnation of Gooch from the international community, the MCC, other cricketing bodies and sports organisations and, naturally, the politicians who never missed an opportunity to climb on the anti-South Africa bandwagon. But, to their lasting credit, Graham Gooch and his players honoured their contracts to the full.

It was not a great tour. The visitors did not perhaps match the high standard we expected of them, but the fact that they came at all was more important than anything else.

I should like to add here that I understood and appreciated the reasons for our universal ostracism. Like so many South Africans, I wanted the day to come when both legal and social discrimination would end. I hold political views, but my thoughts here are as a sportsman, and as such I can only repeat what has been said so often in the past – cricket had moved with the times; our administrators had eliminated all elements of racism from the game. A few years before my time our senior players had, during a match in Cape Town, staged a token walk-off in protest against discrimination. We had a clear conscience when it came to our approach to this serious and complex issue.

Therefore, I believe that the SACU, having done its job as far as it was lawfully allowed to do, was entitled to extend the invitation to the English players. I think I am right in stating that all of us who participated in,this and later series of 'unofficial' tests against Sri Lanka, the West Indies and Australia, did so in the firm belief that sport should be used as a catalyst, as a means of bringing people together, engendering a closer understanding between different races and peoples. Isolation is a negative policy, and I sincerely believed then and in subsequent years that the attitude of non-isolation towards South Africa which was adopted by the British government of Mrs Margaret Thatcher was the right one. Regrettably, the gentlemen who run world cricket from the lofty heights of Lord's took a different view. They could not ban the Gooch XI as such, because to do so would be to deprive individuals of the means of earning a living. But in good old Pontius Pilate fashion they could and did wash their hands of it.

All credit, therefore, to the editor of *Wisden*, then John Woodcock, cricket correspondent of *The Times*, for giving the Gooch tour some semblance of recognition by publishing the match results, and by allowing the Kent cricketer Graham Johnson, who came to coach non-white players in South Africa, to write an article about the subject in the 1983 issue of *Wisden*. Johnson commented:

> Tours such as that by the SAB XI [as the Gooch team was called], provided they are handled correctly, can do a great deal to further changes within South Africa. There is a valid view expressed – about the future of South Africa – that socio-economic trends and principles decree that attitudes and therefore eventually laws, will have to change, and that commercial companies and their attitudes will have a big part to play in forming the country's future . . .
>
> The idea of a cricket world split in two, comprising those with and those without contacts with South Africa is disastrous. World cricket cannot afford it and South Africa would rather avoid it.
>
> I hoped to create a [coaching] system [among non-whites] in which everybody had an equal opportunity to play the game; and in which people could meet on equal terms afterwards, learning, through contact, more about each other. Without such contact messages are misunderstood and false images built up, either within the country itself or externally.

It took much courage for Graham Johnson to write that a decade ago, but he was right.

On 6 March 1982 I was a member of the first South African team chosen in over a decade and which played the first of three one-day matches against the English team in Port Elizabeth. It was a strong side: Barry Richards, myself, Mike Procter (captain), Peter Kirsten, Graeme Pollock, Clive Rice, Garth le Roux, Vince van der Bijl, Stephen Jefferies, Ray Jennings, and Alan Kourie. The enthusiasm in the country was 15 tremendous, reflecting how much we had all missed international competition. When the Springbok team arrived at the ground at about 8.30 a.m. it was already jam-packed, and the reception we received when we went out to field was overwhelming and certainly one I will never forget. The whole crowd stood up and we walked to the pitch through a corridor of clapping and cheering fans.

The game itself was keenly contested. With Gooch scoring 114, the visitors were 240 for 5 at the end of their 50 overs, which we surpassed for the loss of only 3 wickets. Richards hit a typically polished 62, Pollock an undefeated 57, and I weighed in with 82. Regrettably, the series fell somewhat flat after that opening game. Rain spoiled chances of decisions in Durban and Cape Town, the English side did not play as well as we had hoped, and they did not win a match. As if to rub salt into the wound, although they were well paid, the tourists were suspended by the Test and County Cricket Board from playing Test cricket for three years. None seemed to mind. Several, like Geoff Boycott and Derek Underwood, were at the end of their careers while Gooch, frustrated as he must have been to have to wait so long before being considered again for his country, subsequently defended his action quite strongly, along the lines that he was not a politician but a professional sportsman entitled to earn a living where he could. And, of course, when he was finally reinstated, he went on to become the England captain and one of the most successful opening batsmen England has had in years.

2

THE SRI LANKA TOUR

2

THE SRI LANKA TOUR

From the competition aspect the Gooch tour might not have been up to expectations, but the SACU none the less decided to embark on further 'unofficial' tours, as they liked to call them. Obviously their intentions were again twofold: to help stimulate local cricket and at the same time invite players from other countries in order to show that South Africans were not the ogres they were made out to be by so much of the international community. Furthermore, for the 1982/83 season it was decided to invite sides from non-Caucasian countries – in this case, Sri Lanka and the West Indies.

When this was announced the reaction abroad was, understandably, one of incredulity. While friends of South Africa welcomed the move, detractors adopted a snide attitude, dismissing it as a cheap gimmick, and those Sri Lankan and West Indian players who accepted invitations were immediately slated in parliaments and the media for allegedly selling out to 'the cause' for thirty pieces of silver or, as some newspapers put it in derogatory terms, 'the Krugerrand'. True, the players were paid handsomely, but why not? These days there is no distinction between professional and amateur cricketers, and if some are fortunate enough to be able to capitalise on their talent, good luck to them.

The Sri Lanka tour was the brain-child of the then SACU president Joe Pamensky and Tony Opatha, who had played for some seasons in Holland and would be player/manager of the Sri Lanka side. Some of the better players from that country opted not to come and those who did were banned by their board of control for 25 years – a ban that was, however, rescinded a few years later.

Sri Lanka is not a strong cricketing nation and the side that came to South Africa proved to be of little more than moderate provincial standard, particularly among the bowlers. They had no one above medium pace level, and it was almost a Roman holiday for the batsmen. I took four centuries off them in various matches, and although always delighted to hit any hundred, I regarded this success in the right perspective.

After a few warm-up matches the visitors faced the Springboks at the Wanderers in the first of the one-day Test series. Batting first, Barry Richards and I gave an indication of how comparatively easy it was against their attack by registering a first-wicket stand of 150. We were both in sailing along on a good batting wicket when Barry did an astonishing thing. He had scored 71 brilliant runs when he walked down the wicket and said to me: 'Enjoy the rest of your innings.' Puzzled, I asked him what he meant. He said he had had enough, and promptly hit the next ball gently to mid-off and walked off. Taking runs off such a mediocre attack was providing no thrill or challenge for this great batsman, not a real test of his mettle. He was bored.

I could not believe what I had witnessed and frankly disagreed with Barry's decision. This was Test cricket, we were representing our country and were obliged to give of our best, irrespective of the strength, or weakness, of the opposition. It reminded me of the famous story about Keith Miller, the legendary Australian allrounder, when he toured England in 1948 with Sir Donald Bradman's all-conquering side. Playing Essex, not then a strong county, the tourists rattled up 721 in one day at Southend, with the home bowlers being torn apart by the likes of century-makers Bill Brown, Bradman, Sam Loxton and Ron Saggers. Miller saw from the start that Essex were no great shakes and asked Bradman to declare early and so make a game of it. But the latter, who was a ruthless, win-at-all-times kind of captain, did not agree. Miller objected to being asked to participate in this slaughter of the innocents, but his captain insisted that he do his duty. Miller promptly walked to the wicket, hung out his bat, and allowed Trevor Bailey to bowl him first ball.

Scoring 120 in this first one-day Test against Sri Lanka was none the less very satisfying for me. We totalled 291 for 4, with Graeme Pollock enjoying himself with an undefeated 76, and we bundled them out for 102, winning by 189 runs. Two days later we moved on to Berea Park, Pretoria, where again our batsmen had a field day, this time scoring 281 for 5, my contribution again being a century, this time 131, and Peter Kirsten having a particularly good innings of 77. The Sri Lankans fought hard but could only total 174 for 5 at the end of their allotted 55 overs, their opening batsman Hettiaratchi managing a half-century and their stylish left-hander Aponso hitting 35. And so we cruised to our second successive victory.

They were shot out for 140 in the third match at Durban, with Vince van der Bijl, on his home turf, taking 4 for 12 in 8 overs. They had no real answer to this gifted fast-medium paced bowler, who was well supported by that hostile Cape Town duo of Garth le Roux and Stephen Jefferies. Our visitors knew they were up against a team above their level, but to their credit they ploughed on with spirit and determination. With Barry Richards scoring 74, we totalled 143 for 2 with 17 overs to spare, winning this time by 8 wickets.

Following the defeat of Sri Lanka in the first of the two four-day Internationals, it was back to the final one-day game, this time at Port Elizabeth. And the tourists gave their best performance, achieving a total of 276 for 9. Ranasinghe hit exactly 100 by way of several enormous sixes, one of which landed on the grandstand roof. Aponso weighed in with 48 and Devapriya with 44, and perhaps for the first time on the tour they saw the prospect of recording a victory. But it was not to be. The tide turned again in our favour with the second wicket putting on 220. Lawrence Seeff hit 142 and Peter Kirsten also got a century, and we ended up with 278 for 4. Again it was a case of the opposing bowlers not matching up to their batsmen and being unable to contain the rampaging Springboks.

We had returned to the Wanderers for the first four-day International, where the visitors batted first and totalled 213. The fiery Garth le Roux was on top form, helping himself to six scalps for 55 runs. Only Da Silva (70) and Woutersz (51) put up any real resistance. The Sri Lankan seamers were simply not equipped to take advantage of a wicket tailor-made for them, and we rattled up 378, and should have done even better as at one stage we were 260 for 3. I almost carried my bat, going near the end for 169, my highest Test score to date.

Normally in a Test match one is not at all sympathetic towards any member of the opposition and if a batsman or bowler is having a hard time then it is simply unfortunate. After all, it is sporting war. That said, however, one could not help but sympathise with the left-arm slow bowler G R Da Silva. He had arrived with the reputation of bowling out an Australian side, but against us he performed like a highly strung schoolboy in his first match against a junior second eleven. He was so nervous that, in his first over to me on the afternoon of the second day, he was so bathed in perspiration that he bowled two wides outside the off-stump, followed by two wides outside the leg-stump. Every other ball was either a wide, a full toss, or one that bounced half-way down the wicket. One was unsure how to deal with him. He ended by bowling 5 overs for 33, with 10 probable wides – and this in a Test match.

In contrast, our left-arm spinner Alan Kourie was world-class, and he showed it when he bewitched the visitors in their second innings with his sustained accuracy and well-flighted deliveries on what was by now a turning wicket, taking 5 for 54 and bundling them out for 141, giving us victory by an innings and 24 runs.

We went to Cape Town for the second and final Test and found our-selves playing on a really good batting wicket. Taking first strike, Sri Lanka were dismissed for 282, with Aponso getting 81 and Ranasinghe 54. Even though this was obviously not a winning total, it was easily their most impressive batting performance of the tour. But, on this batsman's delight of a wicket, the Springboks in their turn went on the rampage, accumulating 663 for 6. Barry Richards was absent because of injury, and Lawrence Seeff and I set the pattern of things to come with an opening stand of 250, my contribution being 112 and Lawrence scoring 188. 21

Adrian Kuiper enjoyed himself with a typically forceful 66, while Graeme Pollock was in one of those moods which made one feel sorry for any bowler anywhere. He simply toyed with the bowling with consummate ease, racing to 197 by way of a devastating display of power batting, hitting the ball at will and consistently to all quarters of the beautiful Newlands ground. Even allowing for the poor quality of the bowling, this was indeed a sight to behold. The off-spinner Kaluperuma had a particularly rough time. In one over, when Graeme was around the hundred mark, he saw his first delivery sail straight back over his head for six; the second soared out to mid-off for another six; the next to mid-on for six; and the next straight again for six. Utterly bewildered, the poor man then whipped down the leg side the fastest delivery I have ever seen from a slow bowler, which Graeme promptly left alone. He had had his fun.

Facing an enormous 381-run deficit, Sri Lanka again played with spirit and accumulated 281, of which the diminutive Perera scored 102, thus losing by an innings and 100 runs.

So ended a very one-sided series, but we made no apology for the ruthless way we had played, even though we realised from the outset that we were not going to be tested to our limits. In our early team talks we decided that we owed it to ourselves and our country to play to the very best of our ability and not to help our visitors save face by conjuring up close finishes. Apart from Barry Richards' 'retirement' in the first one-day Test, we did just that. To have played any other way would have been an insult to our visitors, and I believe that they understood and appreciated this fact.

After what had been a pleasant series against a nice bunch of players, an unfortunate note was struck when, asked by a reporter about the umpiring, player/manager Tony Opatha said it was the worst in the world. Referring to me in particular, he said that if ever I played outside South Africa I would not score many runs as I would be dismissed pretty quickly leg before wicket in every innings. He said I was hit numerous times on the pads but denied an LBW decision by biased umpires. On reflection, I could hardly recall ever being hit on the pads or any bowler coming close enough to be able to appeal for a leg-before decision. Indeed, few of their bowlers were actually good enough to find anyone's pads. I had scored four centuries in six innings against them, and to this day believe Opatha's comment was a case of sour grapes. Having subsequently gone to England and scored runs for Somerset, I like to think I have made Mr Opatha eat his words.

We had now played to visiting teams in successive seasons and done very well, and my Springbok colleagues and I were thirsting for new opponents. We knew we had a good squad, but we were anxious to meet a team which could really stretch us. We did just this in Lawrence Rowe's West Indians.

3

THE WEST INDIANS

3

THE WEST INDIANS

The West Indies is a truly remarkable cricketing region. Comprising a few scattered Caribbean states, it has for decades managed to produce more gifted cricketers in relation to the size of its population than any other nation. From George Headley and Learie Constantine in the pre-World War Two era, through the post-war period, an almost endless stream of great players have displayed their skills at home and around the world .. . . Frank Worrell, Everton Weekes, Clyde Walcott, who were the 'Three Ws' of the 1950 side that shook England (not forgetting those superb spinners Sonny Ramadhin and Alf Valentine), Garfield Sobers, Clive Lloyd, Viv Richards, Joel Garner, Wes Hall, Andy Roberts, Malcolm Marshall . . . and so it goes on, name after name . . .

Natural athletes with an incredible flair for the game which they inherited from their former colonial masters, the British, they have been world champions for years. They have been criticised for packing their teams with batteries of fast bowlers who delight in bombarding the opposition with bumper after bumper, trying to frighten them into submission. Critics say that this tactic is not in the spirit of the game, and I am inclined to agree. But one cannot help note the view of Clive Lloyd, who introduced this 'panzer' approach. He maintains, in effect, that a side has to use its resources to the best of its ability, and if the West Indies have the best fast bowlers, then it is tough on the opposition. Would not any other team do the same?

In my three seasons with Somerset I faced these famed Windies pacemen several times, but in 1983 they were just names I had read about. Like my Springbok colleagues, I was itching to test whatever skill I might have against them. To prove myself as a world-class batsman I wanted to take on the best. Well, we came pretty close.

When the SACU first put out feelers in an attempt to achieve a dramatic breakthrough in our isolation and bring a side out from the Caribbean, most of the West Indies Test squad either were not interested personally, or were warned off by their respective boards of control. The money offered must have been tempting, but politics plays an open role in Caribbean cricket and it was made quite clear that any top player who might, in a rash moment, put his bank balance before 'government wishes' was kissing his career goodbye. But such is the depth of talent that the SACU representative and Gregory Armstrong from Barbados had no difficulty in gathering an extremely powerful team containing many world-class performers.

The Sri Lankans had no sooner returned home to enjoy their substantial financial rewards and digest what they had learned on the field of play than in flew the West Indian 'rebels', captained by Lawrence Rowe, for 27 their five-week itinerary of matches through January and February. The tour was the culmination of several months of secret negotiations between Joe Pamensky and Ali Bacher and Armstrong. Armstrong had slipped into the country earlier in order to satisfy himself that what he knew would be a highly controversial tour would be run smoothly and not in any way be embarrassing for the players. The thought that they might be insulted or afforded inferior treatment because of their colour must almost certainly have crossed his mind, such was the image portrayed abroad of the attitude of all white South Africans to those of another race. Armstrong made it clear that each man in his squad was opposed to apartheid and was coming on the tour with the hope that it would lead to an improvement in race relations and in some way help to better the lot of non-whites in the country.

As far as I know, there were no 'incidents'. The team had no sooner flown into Johannesburg's Jan Smuts airport than the pattern was set. The players got a tremendous welcome, not only from cricket lovers but from a broad spectrum of the public. Social invitations were extended and it was made clear that they were to have a tour to remember. They produced some memorable performances before capacity crowds and they seemed to enjoy themselves so much that several – Collis King, Sylvester Clarke, Emmerson Trotman, Ezra Moseley, Hartley Alleyne and Franklyn Stephenson – were to return and sign on for provincial sides, joining batsman Alvin Kallicharran who was already with Transvaal.

What a different playing proposition they were after the Sri Lankans. No amiable trundlers or nervous spinners this time. No batsman with little more to offer than courage. Of the 16, 12 had between them worn the famous red cap of their national side over 200 times, and this collective experience was heavily drawn on as they delved into a crowded schedule of no fewer than ten one-day games and two four-day Tests in 30 days of criss-crossing our vast country. I know this tour cost a fortune, but in retrospect I wonder if it was fair to demand so much cricket in such a short space of time. So popular was Rowe's team that a peculiar thing happened as the tour progressed. Normally South African crowds can be as partisan as those in any other country, but this time they (and even some of our officials) seemed to go out of their way to support the tourists – so much so that our captain for the series, Peter Kirsten, had to appeal for some support for his players. Has this ever happened anywhere before? As players we felt that, while the West Indians had shown admirable courage in defying the opprobrium that was being heaped on them at home, they were being handsomely rewarded. Surely, we felt, our efforts deserved some recognition, particularly as we won the one-day series 4-2 and drew the full Internationals on that first visit.

After winning three successive one-day games against Western Province, Border and Eastern Province, the tourists returned to Cape Town for the first four-day game. And for the first time in my career I got the taste of what West Indian fast bowlers can do. Traditionally Newlands has a low bouncing wicket, and those of us who saw them on television in action against Western Province were quick to notice how their fast men were generating enough pace to make the ball fly quite high. So when Barry Richards and I went out to face them in the first innings, we had some idea of what to expect, particularly from Clarke, Moseley and Stephenson. Until then I had never worn a helmet and disdained advice to wear one now as it did not feel comfortable and I felt confident enough to dodge the 'bullets'.

Those first two overs from Clarke and Moseley were frightening. Garth le Roux was pretty quick, but nothing like this pair. However, we played on until, after about ten overs, I mentioned to Barry that I was becoming accustomed to the pace and felt that it might not be too bad after all. Having faced some of the best pacemen in the world, he agreed and assured me that one did get used to it. My confidence was growing when suddenly Moseley sent down a ball that was just short of a length. I was just coming across to get into line with it when it took off like a rocket, miraculously just missing my face. I swayed horribly to the off side, my arms, legs and body twisting and turning like some gyrating puppet. A press photographer caught my actions superbly and my picture was plastered all over the country, much to the amusement of everyone. Whatever sun tan I had acquired that summer vanished beneath the sheet of grey which enveloped my face. I could not believe any bowler could generate such venom – and at Newlands of all places. Barry walked down the wicket and said I had played the ball brilliantly and would never again get another like that. That made me feel good, the remark coming as it did from such a master batsman. My confidence was restored and my face returned to its normal colour.

Despite that taste of what we could expect, we settled down and between us played well and put on 85 for the first wicket before Barry fell to Moseley just one short of his half-century. One thing I did notice and remember was that Barry did not hesitate to hook any ball that might have been short and warranted such treatment, no matter how fast. I simply got out of the way. It is somewhat ironic that, despite this marvellous pace battery, in the end their most successful bowler of the innings turned out to be the off-spinner Derek Parry, who finished with 5 for 117.

I should add, though, that Kirsten, Rice and McKenzie were trapped leg-before on the front foot and stretching well forward – and this from a man who turned the ball quite a lot. Lawrence Rowe also got a most questionable decision, and at the end of the match the quality of umpiring generated a heated discussion.

With Graeme Pollock contributing a typical masterly hundred, my 73, a 69 from Alan Kourie – who always enjoyed plonking his burly frame on the crease and staying around as long as possible – and a last-wicket stand of 67 between Stephen Jefferies and Garth le Roux, we totalled a handsome 449. Our seamers picked up the challenge and the West Indies were soon in terrible trouble, with six men back in the pavilion for only 89.

With 7 West Indies wickets down for 129, overnight our officials did a strange thing. They came into our dressing-room and said the 200-run follow-on rule for a four-day match was being changed and they wanted us to bat again after this first West Indian innings. They were told quite forcibly by our senior players that this was not on and that the follow-on rule would be enforced. The rules could not be changed mid-match. Obviously this proposal had been made in order to stretch the match out for the full four days and so ensure that it was a financial success. But we were not having it. In the end they were dismissed for 246, 3 runs short of the figure they needed to escape the follow-on. Only Richard Austin (93) and Stephenson (56) batted with any real merit and we duly enforced the follow-on. But they atoned for themselves somewhat in the second innings, ten of them reaching double figures, with Kallicharran hitting 89, and they were all out for 309. Kallicharran was out in an unusual way – a delivery from Kourie shooting through, which wicket-keeper Ray Jennings missed but which bounced off the inside of his legs and on to the stumps with Kallicharran well out of his ground. He was most upset, thinking that Jennings had cheated him, but I do not believe this to have been the case. We needed only 107 for victory, and this we achieved for the loss of 5 wickets, throwing our bats at the ball in the final two-hour session of the match.

Naturally, we were thrilled with our success and celebratory drinks flowed freely in the Springbok dressing-room. We may not have beaten the official West Indies side, but it was a darned good second eleven. Normally after a team has done well its dressing-room is soon filled with well-wishers but, strange to relate, on this occasion not a single South African official came in to congratulate us for at least half an hour. Then only one deigned to do so, popping his head round the door and saying 'Well done', and then retreating in haste. What had we done to be cold-shouldered in such fashion?

It transpired that our board members had gone into the West Indies dressing-room to commiserate with them on their defeat and had promised to produce a wicket which would suit them in the next Test at the Wanderers in Johannesburg. When these officials eventually remembered us and came to our dressing-room the damage had been done and we told them they were not welcome. That night I was having a drink with Graeme Pollock and one of the officials, and Graeme spoke his mind on the matter in no uncertain manner. The official saw his point of view and had the good grace to apologise.

We had heard a lot about the batting prowess of Collis King, and he unwrapped his full array of shots at the Wanderers in the second Test, scoring a thrilling 101 in the West Indies first innings on a typical Wanderers wicket that gave encouragement to the seamers. But apart from Greenidge (42) and Kallicharran (37), the other batsmen could not handle the home bowling although, surprisingly on such a wicket, it was Alan Kourie who did the main damage with 6 for 55 in 29 overs. As his record for South Africa and Transvaal showed, Kourie was an exceptionally good slow left-arm specialist, the best slow bowler in the country for years, and another South African who would have won international recognition had he been able to display his skills abroad. He did not spin the ball prodigiously, like Hugh Tayfield a generation before him, relying more on accuracy and flight, a subtle change of pace, and intelligent reading of the opposing batsman's weaknesses.

We were happy to curtail them for 267, but we made a disastrous start on our innings. In the single over before the close on that first day, Richards went for a duck; the next morning both overnight watchman Ray Jennings and I also went without scoring, and South Africa had lost 3 for only 8 runs. But then skipper Kirsten (56) and Pollock (73) began hauling us back into respectability, and with the other middle-order men also pulling their weight, we managed 233, a 34-run deficit. Batting again, the visitors found it heavy-going against our seam attack of Van der Bijl, Le Roux and Jefferies and could only muster 176, their top scorers being Alvin Greenidge (48) and Collis King who got out of a sick bed to score a brave 39. We were now looking for 211 for victory, and again we faced one over before the close. This time we did not lose a wicket and thus went into the last day facing what seemed to be a reasonable target to achieve in plenty of time. At lunch we were 85 for no wicket and already we could taste that champagne. Two victories in a row, winning a home series against the famous West Indies . . . we felt good.

But we had omitted from our calculations the talent of a certain Sylvester Clarke, who had already given us an example of his skills with 5 for 66   31 in the first innings. He wound himself up and, whipping the ball into the batsmen with sustained pace and accuracy and then, for variety, moving it away with his leg-cutter, he proceeded to scatter the confident Springboks to the four winds with an incredible spell of bowling, arguably one of the finest ever seen on that ground.

And yet but for Alvin Kallicharran this magnificent performance might never have been. During the lunch interval Sylvester saw that we needed to score only 126 in the two remaining sessions of play, resigned himself to the inevitability of defeat and put on a pair of tackies. Kallicharran went to his friend and asked him to don his boots and give one more sustained burst. He agreed reluctantly, came out, and took 7 for 34 in 22 overs. South Africa managed only 181, despite a fighting tail-end (55-run) partnership between Kevin McKenzie (26 not out) and Stephen Jefferies (31), and lost by 29 runs. With 12 for 100 Clarke was unquestionably man of the match.

Of all the overseas players who came out to South Africa to coach and play for provincial sides in the last decade, Sylvester Clarke was undoubtedly the finest and Transvaal was indeed fortunate to sign him for a few seasons. Not only was he a bowler of the highest calibre, compared by many to the legendary Alec Bedser of England in skill, build and style of delivery but he was also a fine team-mate and a warm-hearted personality. In England he played for Surrey and, later in his career when he was past his peak, he had some contractual problems which eventually led to his fading from the scene. As far as I know, his 'downfall' – if one can use a rather harsh-sounding term – resulted more from his inability to say 'No' than from any histrionics. He found himself contracted to play for too many teams at the same time, which led to all kinds of difficulties.

Sylvester confined his aggression to the field of play and I will always regard him as one of the greatest bowlers I have ever faced. As our series against Lawrence Rowe's team progressed over the two seasons during which they visited South Africa the more experienced batsmen did learn to play him with greater confidence, but he terrified the life out of most of us.

From the squared Test series we plunged into the six one-day Tests, all in the space of eight days: South Africa won by 91 runs in Port Elizabeth; by 43 runs in Cape Town; 12 runs in Pretoria; and 57 runs in the second match in Johannesburg. The West Indies won by 7 wickets in the first

Johannesburg match, and by 84 runs in Durban.

There were some enthralling encounters between our leading batsmen and the aggressive West Indian pacemen. For instance, the highlight of that first match was undoubtedly Graeme Pollock's duel with Clarke in our total of 250 for 7. Barry Richards was top scorer with a customary polished 102, but the crowd will long savour the last over with Clarke bowling to Pollock. Here were two giants of the game, two proud and well-matched gladiators duelling in the hot Port Elizabeth sun. Pollock square-cut the first delivery to the boundary, the next was pulled to mid-wicket for four, the third crashed through the covers for four, and the fourth raced to the mid-wicket boundary. He did not touch the last two deliveries and was unbeaten with 66. It was the Pollock genius at its very best. The visitors could only muster 159.

The Western Province players (Ken McEwan 61, Peter Kirsten 50, and Garth le Roux 34 not out) pleased their home supporters at Newlands with our 194-8, and the tourists replied with 151. It was a close encounter in Pretoria with the West Indies squad getting 167 to our 179-9. We were now dormy 3-0 and much of the pressure was off us. Now desperately anxious to win at least one of these games, Rowe's men really turned on the pressure in a day/night match at the Wanderers and found success at last, bundling us out for a miserly 139 and replying with 141 for the loss of only 3 wickets. We got our revenge the next day, a Saturday, totalling 228-6, while they managed only 171, with my Transvaal team-mate Rupert Hanley notching a hat-trick.

The series ended on a high note for the West Indies who won comfortably on the Sunday in Durban, thanks largely to Collis King who added 60 to their 155, and the long-legged Franklyn Stephenson blasting our batsmen out of the ground with 6 for 9 runs as we struggled to a miserable 71. We were all exhausted from too much cricket in too short a space of time and battered and shell-shocked after facing such sustained fast bowling. Sure, we had the satisfaction of winning, but no thanks to the tour planners.

On a personal level I was reasonably pleased with my showing in the series, but at our team inquest we all agreed that the batsmen were still too tentative and were not making enough of the shots of which we were capable and were producing in domestic competition. For example, our most successful batsmen were Pollock and Kirsten, and they never hesitated to cut and hook, often with productive results. I was not doing this, preferring more often than not to duck out of the way of those scorching deliveries. The outcome was that at times I would be in for a longish time, was just beginning to get among the runs, and then fell. As an opener I knew I was obliged to do better and help to lay a more solid foundation   33 on which the later batsmen could build the innings. I had to be more aggressive and I resolved to correct this matter in the return series the following summer.

Rowe and his men came back determined to win that second series. They reflected this mood at the beginning of the first Test over Christmas in Durban when they rattled up 529 for 7, this after starting moderately with 3 down for 87. Kallicharran (103) and Rowe (157) pulled them round and then the lower-order men went on the rampage and we could not stem the run flow. They declared at tea on the second day and Henry Fotheringham of Natal, playing in his first Test, had the unfortunate experience of falling leg before wicket to the very first delivery he received. With rain interrupting play a great deal, we totalled 333, of which I scored a satisfactory 69, Kirsten hit 84, and Pollock 62. We followed-on, but with so much time lost because of the rain there were only two or three hours of play left, during which we were 59 for no wicket, and the match was drawn.

We went to the Cape, where we had never lost to them, and bowled them out for 252, King slamming 83. Kourie again had a good time, tying them up for long periods and ending with 5 for 66. Poor Kallicharran was unfortunate in the way he went out 'caught'. He swept a Kourie delivery in the meat of the bat straight towards Fotheringham at short-leg, and the ball lodged between the latter's legs for a remarkable dismissal. We replied with 404, most batsmen getting among the runs. Pollock registered yet another century, Kirsten 88, Rice an unbeaten 71, myself 45, and McEwan 32. Clarke was again their best bowler with 5 for 92. Without anyone getting a big score, the West Indies mustered 268, leaving us needing only 117 to win. We knocked this off without loss in only 83 minutes. Fotheringham had long forgotten his inauspicious Test début, thumping the bowling mercilessly as he could on his day, ending with 71, and I managed to hit 40. As far as my game was concerned, it was evident that my decision to be more aggressive was paying dividends. I even found myself hooking Clarke, something I would not have dared to do the year before.

Off, then, to Wanderers for the third encounter and, yes, the wicket was again a greentop and laid on for the seamers. So it was no surprise when South Africa was dismissed for only 160, with only the old reliables Kirsten (67) and Pollock (41) shaping to any degree against the fearsome quartet of Clarke, Stephenson, Moseley, and Hartley Alleyne who had missed the first series. The West Indies decided that aggression was the best policy, and throwing their bats at everything from the start of their innings they reached a total of 193. We managed a respectable 236 in our second innings (Kirsten 61, Rice 47, and Pollock 46 coming out best), and the visitors needed 204 for victory, which they achieved, but only just.

With the last pair at the wicket and needing 5 to win, Clarke hit a boundary, to level the scores. Then he hit one towards mid-off. In typical terrier fashion, Kirsten rushed in and cut the ball off before it had travelled very far. Clarke was stranded. Kirsten threw at the stumps, but missed. Had he connected it would have been a tie. As it was they scrambled home for that vital run. It was a tremendous finish to a fine match.

The deciding Test was at Port Elizabeth. South Africa made a disastrous start, losing 3 for only 16, this time Kirsten and Pollock for once failing. I went cheaply for 26, but then Ken McEwan, one of the most fluent stroke-makers of his day who did so well for Essex in England, came into his own and scored a superb 120, making amends for his 'pair' at the Wanderers. Reliable Kourie weighed in with an unbeaten 63 and we came up with a respectable 277 and then whipped them out for 199. Then came our second innings, and with it one of the most sustained periods of fast bowling one is ever likely to encounter.

How that quartet got to work on us! Clarke, Alleyne, Stephenson and Moseley seemed to compete with one another as to who could send them down faster. The St George's ground usually favours the batsman, but not this time. The wicket had been shaved closely and the ball sizzled through at an uneven level. Not a ball from Clarke in those opening overs passed me without being chest-high. Because of the extra bounce I made the mistake of constantly gloving the ball high down the leg side when trying to flick it off my body, instead of playing it lower off my hips, and as a result I went early. They went through us like the proverbial knife through butter for only 127.

Nerves were strained to the utmost in the Springbok camp, particularly after the remaining batsmen saw Pollock struck on the helmet by a delivery from Alleyne and having to retire for a while – although he did end up with the top score of 42. If Graeme could be hit, everyone wondered, how could they possibly cope? I should add that, having previously disdained a helmet, I wore one after the first innings of the first Test of the series when Moseley nearly pole-axed me, and I have usually worn one ever since. They needed 206 to win, which they got for the loss of four wickets, and so won this second series 2-1. Nevertheless, we felt we had played pretty well, having shared the first game, won the second with ease, and lost the third only by a hairsbreadth. Only in this last game at Port Elizabeth had they won handsomely – and deservedly so.

We played six one-day games, losing by four games to two, but again it   35 was a closer contest than the final figure suggests. We won by 4 wickets at Port Elizabeth, and by 173 runs in Pretoria, while they triumphed by 2 wickets and 3 wickets (on run-rate) in the two Johannesburg games, 6 wickets in Durban (on run-rate), and 8 wickets in Cape Town.

I must confess that pleased though we were to have had a chance to play the West Indians, to have enjoyed their company and overall to have acquitted ourselves pretty well against them, we were glad to see them fly off home. We were exhausted after the almost non-stop torrent of hostile seam bowling. Mandy Yachad of Northern Transvaal came to me after playing in only one International and admitted that he had had enough. I reminded him that we had faced them for two years, and he said he did not know how we had withstood the strain. Such is modern cricket.

The one consolation was that I for one returned to the relative calm of Currie Cup competition knowing that, good though they were speedwise, whatever Van der Bijl, Le Roux, Jefferies and others threw at me, it would not be as bad as what I had encountered at the hands of the West Indies. My one regret about those West Indian tours was that I never took a hundred off them, even though generally I had played well enough. One technical flaw in my game was underlined and that was, as I have already explained, a tendency to play the ball high off my body down the leg side. Often I was getting too far inside the flight of the ball coming into me, so often resulting in my flicking the ball fine to leg, resulting in my being out caught by the wicket-keeper, leg gully or leg-slip. It is a particularly annoying way of getting out, and on reflection was happening probably because I was too keen to get in line with the ball. In later years the problem was eradicated, but it hurt me very badly on those two West Indies tours.

4

THE AUSTRALIANS

The Australians came to South Africa for the 1985/86 and 1986/87 seasons, but the visits had been conceived years before. To give the background to the secret way the SACU officials had to go about arranging these unofficial tours in those days, I am taking the liberty of quoting journalist Colin Bryden's article in the 1986 *Protea Cricket Annual* based on his knowledge as public relations man close to the SACU:

Plans for the tour had been hatched in 1982 and continued in 1983 when Dr Ali Bacher, and the former Australian opening batsman Bruce Francis operated from an apartment in an exclusive area in London at the time of the Prudential World Cup. It was clear that many leading Australians were in favour of touring South Africa, but plans had to be kept on ice because of the West Indies tours which took place in 1982/83 and 1983/84. Dr Bacher flew to Singapore in October 1984 to conclude agreement with a number of players – and the tour was on.

The big prize was the capture of Kim Hughes. He had been approached by the SACU but turned down the initial offer. Events within Australian cricket led him to make contact again and he agreed to tour after making a trip to South Africa with his wife. The tour issue came to a head when three players selected for the official Australian tour of England in 1985, Terry Alderman, Rod McCurdy and Steve Rixon, refused to sign contracts which restricted their movements after the English tour. They had, of course, already signed to play in South Africa.

The Australian Cricket Board instituted action against Bruce Francis and the SACU for inducement to breach contract, and their own contracted players for breach of contract. Geoff Dakin, Joe Pamensky and Ali Bacher flew to Australia to defend the action and an out-of-court settlement was reached. The players contracted by the SACU were entitled to tour South Africa and the SACU was entitled to recruit replacements for injured players, provided they did not approach ACB-contracted players. The team that finally arrived in South Africa boasted a total of 230 Test caps and 353 appearances in official one-day internationals.

There had been a season's break between the last West Indies and the first Australian tour for the obvious sensible reasons: the SACU did not want the domestic Currie Cup and one-day tournaments to fade in importance, as they might have done if foreign teams came every year; there was the need to guard against both players and public losing their appetites   39 through too many tours; and, finally, the companies which sponsored or underwrote so much of these costly ventures also needed a financial respite.

And, sure enough, by the time Kim Hughes and his team flew in, those of us who were to play them were all too eager for combat, particularly as the Springboks had soundly thrashed the last official team to visit us from that country, Bill Lawry's side of 1970. Hughes, the boyish-looking captain, was their most experienced player, with 70 full International caps and 97 for one-day games. He had the reputation of being a dashing batsman who relished getting after the bowling from the start with his fancy footwork and flashing blade, an approach which had earned him a name as a real crowd pleaser. It was a tour I was to enjoy immensely.

The visitors won or drew several warm-up matches against moderately strong sides, which gave them time to acclimatise. But, surprisingly, they lost a three-day fixture against Eastern Province by 2 wickets although, to be fair, this was thanks mainly to a sporting second-innings declaration by Hughes. Then they were beaten by 7 runs by an eager Northern Transvaal side in a one-day game, and again in another one-day encounter with an extremely powerful Transvaal side which had dominated the domestic scene through most of the 1980s and which enjoyed the sobriquet 'The Mean Machine'. The strength of Transvaal was reflected in the number chosen for the Springbok side for the first Test over the Christmas holidays in Durban – seven in all, the other four hailing from Western Province. It must have been a long time since a South African side was drawn from only two provinces.

I did not wear a helmet when we won the toss and batted first because Rod McCurdy, whom we thought was their fastest bowler, was injured and not playing, and their other frontline bowler, Rodney Hogg, had not impressed with any appreciable pace in the Transvaal match. Indeed, his opening over was rather tame, so much so that I walked down the wicket to my partner Henry Fotheringham and said that if this was the best they could serve up we were likely to reach 600. Carl Rackemann sent down an equally average-paced over, and Hogg repeated the pattern at the other end. Again I walked down to Fotheringham and said that it was unbelievable; we could be in line for a feast day. But little did we know Rodney Hogg. In he breezed to deliver the first ball of his third over. I shaped up confidently enough – but what a difference! He sent down a screamer which sizzled past my head. A helmet was duly sent for, and for the next four or five overs we experienced the fury that this man could unleash when it suited him. No one had told us that it was his pattern to get a sighting with a couple of warm-up overs before getting down to serious business. He never aimed to sustain his pace for longer than half a dozen overs and, having done so, he would often retire to the country and rest until the next spell.

However we survived, and on a good batting wicket Fotheringham and I put together a sound opening stand of 124 and then, returning from the lunch break, Hogg and Rackemann broke through, getting Henry (70) after a fine innings, myself (52), Peter Kirsten (2), and Ken McEwan (4). We had thus lost 4 wickets for 24 runs and were in serious trouble. The ball with which Hogg trapped me leg-before was a beauty. He had sent down several out-swingers at just above medium pace and I was getting the measure of him. Then he let me have a ball which was at least a foot outside the off-stump, which I ignored. I paid the penalty, for it swung back sharply on to my pads. I could not believe what had happened, and neither could my colleagues who were watching the TV monitor. It was a superb delivery.

Bad light curtailed play, and with Clive Rice and Alan Kourie going cheaply on the second day, South Africa might have been shot out for a modest score indeed. But, fortunately for us, Graeme Pollock was again in one of his masterly moods. With Garth le Roux content to prop up one end, their seventh-wicket stand realised 51 in 74 minutes. Having taken a patient 171 minutes for his half-century, Graeme opened up to play havoc with the Australian attack as only he could, disdaining anything they threw at him and needing only 41 balls to get his second 50 and the 62nd century of his career. It was fitting he should return to this ground for yet another century in this hour of need, for it was here 16 years before that he recorded his highest Test innings, 274 against Bill Lawry's team. The Springbok tail wagged feverishly, Ray Jennings and Stephen Jefferies reaching their forties, and we finally emerged with a satisfactory 393. Hogg (5-83) and Rackemann (5-112) shared the wickets.

Australia started well enough, but it was left to Mike Taylor to build respectability into the innings with an impressive century, aided by half-centuries from Tom Hogan and Greg Shipperd. The latter was a most likeable little man and quite a character. To paraphrase what American writer Dorothy Parker once wrote about Katharine Hepburn's acting, his range of strokes ran the full gamut from A to B. Never seen without a sweater, no matter how hot the weather, he was like the proverbial limpet – his sole purpose in life seemed to be devoted to keeping his wicket, with runs being of secondary importance.

With Australia all out 34 behind on 359, we went in again merely to see out time; because so much time had been lost through rain and bad light, a result was now out of the question. Suddenly we were 30 for 5 as Hogg and Rackemann went to town with a glorious display of sustained fast bowling. Only Henry Fotheringham (100) and, to a lesser extent, Alan Kourie (44) and Garth le Roux (28) held out against them. Without wishing to detract one iota from the performance of the Australian bowlers, there is no doubt that our dramatic collapse was a perfect example of batsmen not adopting the right mental strategy. Unconsciously, perhaps, we had our eyes on the clock and not on the game. In so many sports played at the highest level, much of the secret of success is in the mind. We slipped up and could have paid the price.

The merit of Henry Fotheringham's undefeated century is even more creditable when it is remembered that he batted with a badly damaged right thumb, an injury he sustained in the first innings. He was only down to bat in an emergency, and with such a situation at hand he rose superbly to the challenge, coming in low down in the innings and showing complete indifference for what had gone before him by slamming Rackemann's first delivery after lunch for six. How his home supporters roared with approval! Lifting his right hand on impact, he slammed boundary after boundary with his left hand doing most of the work. No wonder, with his first innings 70, he was adjudged the batsman of the match. With 7 down for 203 Rice closed the innings and Australia were 32 for 2 at the close. Drawn though it was, it was an absorbing game, and bearing in mind that they were without Terry Alderman, Graham Yallop, Rod McCurdy and Steve Smith, the tourists did exceedingly well and set the tone for what promised to be a wide-open series.

I had not managed to reach three figures against the West Indies and so I was looking hard for a century when we flew to Cape Town a few days later for the second Test over the New Year holidays. Fotheringham failed this time, but on a pitch not all that conducive to strokeplay, I battled on and with Peter Kirsten (72) and Graeme Pollock (79) laid the foundation for our potentially match-winning total of 430. With only 9 needed for that elusive 100, I was trapped leg before wicket. The *Protea Cricket Annual* records that I was 'plumb' to McCurdy but, with respect, this was far from the case. The ball was going far down the leg side and I went to flick it off my legs and it hit me on the back of my right foot. Even one of the fielders admitted to me later that the ball would never have hit the stumps. But that is how it goes. For every bad decision that goes against one, there are those which go the other way.

My score was nevertheless pleasing enough, with Kim Hughes and his bowlers aiding and abetting me by bowling constantly down my leg side. Earlier in my innings I miscued a bouncer when going for a hook and was nearly caught at fine-leg. This they seemed to interpret as my weak area and directed the attack accordingly, constantly dropping the ball short. Some indifferent hook shots and some solid hitting resulted, but in between the 'indifferent' deliveries I was sailing along and was around 70 by lunch. Shrewd and experienced captain though he was, I am afraid Kim Hughes slipped up this time. Is not cricket indeed at times a form of chess under the sun?

Australia made a poor start to their first innings, but opening batsman John Dyson was patience personified, selecting his shots with great discrimination against a Springbok attack in which Garth le Roux was bowling with perfect line and length on a Newlands wicket which usually does not favour seamers but which he knew how to exploit to the full. His usual tactic was to pitch the ball just short of a length, eight to twelve inches outside the off-stump, which so often the batsman would leave alone. Then he would bring one a fraction closer. Many a time the batsman would lose patience then and go for a shot to find himself being pulled across the stumps and trapped leg-before or bowled.

After batting most patiently Dyson (95) fell just short of his hundred to a Kirsten off-break, having been at the wicket for 304 minutes. Half-centuries by Hughes and Graham Yallop saw them finish with 304, thus avoiding the follow-on.

Going into the third evening and batting again we found the Australians playing the slow motion tactic, bowling at a rate of about 11 overs an hour. Carl Rackemann would field at long-on and then amble up to bowl his overs from the other end. A message was sent to us to get on with the scoring, but this was easier said than done. It was clear they had decided they could not win, so would drag the match out. In the last two hours of play they bowled about 23 overs. After the game they were warned that another attempt at such tactics would entail a heavy fine. To this day I remain surprised and disappointed at Kim Hughes, as this attitude was so uncharacteristic of him. Throughout his career he was noted for his sportsmanship and sense of fair play. His own positive batting style reflected his natural desire to get on with the game.

Both Kirsten and Pollock went cheaply, mainly by losing their patience and having a go. With my contribution being a satisfactory 70 to string along with my 91, we declared at 202 for 5, setting the visitors a target of 329 for victory. With three men gone for only 106 they had no real chance, although for a while Hughes and Taylor indulged in some glorious strokeplay. But once Taylor went Hughes shut up shop, saved the match and ended with an unbeaten 97 out of a total of 224 for 4.

Now it was back to Johannesburg for the third and deciding International and for the R30 000 winner-takes-all final. Such was the excitement and interest in the deciding third game at the Wanderers in Johannesburg that it was decided to play it over five days, and what an incredible tussle it turned out to be. It had everything – heroism, pathos, drama, and records galore.

The Australians, anxious to win this decider and make amends for humiliating defeats in successive Test series by Bobby Simpson's and Bill Lawry's official Test teams in South Africa in previous decades, had serious problems in the bowling department. Carl Rackemann developed a chest ailment and was confined to bed but courageously – or foolishly – ignored it and opted to play. Then seamer Terry Alderman, playing in his first International, put his back out: he too carried on with indomitable courage. As if that were not enough, Rodney Hogg damaged a hamstring after only 4 overs and took no further part in the proceedings.

This last drama occurred during the first half hour. For once Hughes won the toss and sent us in on a wicket that had plenty of grass and on which he hoped his seam attack would enjoy themselves. Hogg set out to do just that. He opened up at a blistering pace, scattered my stumps when I had only scored 5, and then pulled up lame. Off he went, his contribution over. The pain in his leg was probably bad enough, but nothing like the pain of frustration he must'have endured: a wicket made for him, a wicket captured, and then sidelined. No wonder Hughes was a worried man. He had omitted Rod McCurdy for allrounder Peter Faulkner, thus finding himself with only two far-from-well seamers to take on the powerful Springbok batting machine in fiery summer heat. Could they last out, never mind take wickets?

He need not have worried, as in Carl Rackemann he had the man for the occasion. First Alderman trapped Henry Fotheringham in front of his stumps, leaving us rocky at 21 for 2, and then the burly Queensland farmer got to work. Bowling on a perfect line and length, he whipped through the top order, Kirsten, Pollock and Rice going cheaply. Only Kevin McKenzie of the recognised batsmen held out. With Alan Kourie and Garth le Roux giving him support, he relished the challenge, playing vintage shots round the ground to the delight of his home fans and taking the total from a disastrous 86 for 5 to 166 before he too became a Rackemann victim when on 72, giving wicket-keeper Steve Rixon his third catch. Bad light ended play with South Africa on 184 for 8, not a happy situation. The next day Rackemann was at it again, but even this giant of a man finished exhausted – not, however, before he had seen South Africa dismissed for a miserable 211. He had chalked up a personal tally of 8 for 84 in 26,6 overs.

After Australia had lost an early wicket, Steve Smith, returning to the side after an injury, set out to enjoy himself with a full range of telling shots, and the home bowlers were unable to contain him. He was the second man out, but not before he had scored 116 out of 159. His century came from only 145 deliveries in 188 minutes, and when he had reached that landmark he raised his arms in delight and acknowledgement of the massive applause from the appreciative crowd. The scene was set for skipper Hughes to ram home the advantage against a tired and frustrated attack, but the Free Stater Corrie van Zyl, making his International début, had other ideas and trapped him in front of his stumps with his first delivery. That limpet Greg Shipperd (44) stayed around in typically stubborn fashion, but the Australians had lost the opportunity to capitalise on the situation and ended up with only 267, a lead of a bare 56 runs.

At first Alderman and Rackemann picked up where they had left off when we batted again, seeing Fotheringham, Kirsten and myself off cheaply, and then it was the familiar pattern of the menacing left-hander Graeme Pollock striding purposefully to the wicket to take charge of proceedings. How often had he done so on his home grounds in South Africa, and in England and Australia? How the stomachs of even the best bowlers of his era must have churned at the sight of him coming to do battle, to challenge their effrontery in trying to tame him. The world has known some great left-handers – Frank Woolley, Bert Sutcliffe, Clem Hill, Clive Lloyd, Gary Sobers, Arthur Morris and Neil Harvey, to name but a few – and Robert Graeme Pollock ranks proudly alongside them. He did not score his usual century in this innings, but it was a memorable display of controlled, aggressive batsmanship, and dramatic too. After rushing to 51 off only 41 balls, he was struck on the right hand by a vicious, lifting delivery from Rackemann which X-rays subsequently revealed had broken a bone just above the knuckles and he was forced to retire.

Australia's fortunes also took a bad turn in this incredible game. With Hogg sidelined, Rackemann, Alderman and Faulkner had no option but to continue for marathon spells in the tremendous heat. It was no wonder that the heavy Rackemann, who had been ill prior to the game, began to hyperventilate and had to leave the field. This left only Alderman and Faulkner to bowl for the remainder of the day, a task they performed commendably. Kim Hughes admitted to us after the match that he literally did not have another man who could bowl. I wonder when last an international side was so depleted?

After a rest day on the Sunday, Rackemann came back on the Monday, quite recovered and full of fire, and early on he slammed Clive Rice on the helmet with a bouncer. Eventually he got Rice after he had made   45

50. With the lower order collapsing, and at 273 for 8 at lunch on the fourth day, not even some sparkling batting by Kevin McKenzie looked good enough to save South Africa. But rain washed out further play that day. When, at the fall of the ninth wicket on the final day Pollock, disdaining his injury, joined McKenzie the home crowd let out a tremendous cheer, although they must have been apprehensive about their team's chances. This pair decided on a policy of aggression and added a further 31. McKenzie recorded a brilliant 110 to add to his earlier 72 (by far his best Test performance), and Pollock slammed Alderman for successive boundaries for his undefeated and most gallant 65. South Africa ended with 305, and Australia needed 250 for victory.

This was not a huge total, but we remembered that McKenzie had noted how, during his second innings, the ball had still seamed appreciably, even though the ball was old and the wicket worn. He believed our fresh seam attack using a new ball still had a good chance of pulling us through. Good chance? We pulverised them. They were shot out for a miserable 61. Not only were our bowlers fired up but, with rain about, new shoots of grass had begun to peep through a wicket which now invited seamers to do their worst. And they did just that. Garth le Roux tore in like a man possessed and got himself a hat-trick. After Corrie van Zyl had removed Smith at 24, the fair-haired Capetonian first sent Shipperd's off-stump reeling, had Hughes caught-behind first ball, and then trapped Taylor leg before wicket. This last delivery was a beauty, without doubt one of the finest ever in his distinguished career. As Taylor made his way sadly to the pavilion, we knew we had the match and the series in the bag. It was an exhilarating moment. Rice and Kourie grabbed 3 wickets apiece. Rice, having dismissed Rackemann and Hogg with the last two balls of the first innings, bowled Yallop first ball after lunch and thus was also able to claim a hat-trick. Australia lost by 188 runs, and if it is any consolation for their opening batsman John Dyson, by being undefeated on 18, he is still the only player to carry his bat in a first-class match at the Wanderers.

Steve Rixon's ten catches equalled both the official Test record held by Bob Taylor of England against India at Bombay, and the unofficial one set by West Indian David Murray against South Africa in 1983/84 in Port Elizabeth. Garth le Roux's hat-trick was his second, and Clive Rice's was his first. The last man to take a hat-trick spanning two innings was in fact a batsman, the former Springbok captain and opening batsman Jack McGlew, against Transvaal in the 1963/64 season.

Six one-day Internationals were scheduled, and for the first three
46 matches the South African selectors decided to include in the Springbok

squad several promising provincial players, namely Rob Bentley (Natal), Roy Pienaar and Lee Barnard (Northern Transvaal), Eric Simons (Western Province), and Tim Shaw (Eastern Province). Graeme Pollock was out for the season with his broken hand, and this selection policy handicapped us further as Peter Kirsten and Ken McEwan, among others, were ignored. I am all for blooding youngsters, and it would have been fine had we already sewn up the one-day series, but surely not before it had even started. Apart from anything else, overlooking some of our best players for the sake of experimentation seemed insulting to the visitors. And so it was not surprising that the tourists won this first match at the Wanderers by 46 runs, scoring 197 to our 151. Having made only a couple in Johannesburg, my indifferent form followed me in the next game in Durban where I went for only 10, but Clive Rice (91) and Henry Fotheringham (71) were in form and we totalled 221 for 6, to which the Australians responded by hitting 224, also for 6, with Steve Smith leading the way with 70, and with good support from Dyson (41), Haysman (37) and Taylor (22).

We went into the third one-day International knowing, firstly, that we needed to win it to keep the series alive and, secondly, that we could re-select the side for the final three games. Luckily we managed to win.

I regained my touch in Port Elizabeth with 45, but apart from Rice (78 not out) and Kevin McKenzie (62), no one else could cope with the fiery Australian pace attack and we lost 9 for 223 at the end of our allotted period. Was it enough? Perhaps Garth le Roux was not too sure, so he whipped through them, taking 5 for 13 off only 8,1 overs, to see them out for 151 and victory for us by 72 runs. With Kirsten and McEwan reinstated after that costly experiment with the inexperienced players, we went on to level the series in Cape Town. Again we batted first, making 234, but the tourists could only manage 210, giving us the match by 24 runs.

Anton Ferreira, the beefy Northern Transvaal allrounder, had a good début in the fifth game at the Wanderers, breaking the top Australian order with his 3 for 31 and they could only muster a moderate 185-7. The Australians somewhat tarnished his man-of-the-match award by claiming that Anton had taken all 3 wickets with no-balls that had gone uncalled. We replied with 189 for 5, winning by 5 wickets.

The last match at Berea Park, Pretoria, was a thriller. On a superb batting wicket, Australia's opening batsman John Dyson set the tone of things to come by hitting the first ball of the day for six. (When was that last done in any game?) Smith went for 29, but then Dyson and his captain really got to work, slamming 93 runs in only 73 minutes in their second-wicket partnership. After Hughes (46) went, Taylor picked up the 47 tempo with Dyson and a further 72 runs flowed in 41 minutes. The latter fell for 49, but Dyson richly deserved his 115 when Australia ended on 272-6, a potentially winning total. But we would have none of it.

We made a horrible start, losing 3 for 69. And when Rod McCurdy struck Clive Rice on the foot, breaking a bone, things were indeed bleak for us. But this was a situation made for Clive, a man for all crises. It was great to be part of this partnership, and with Peter Kirsten running for him, Rice lashed out with growing confidence. I went for 76, and Kevin McKenzie took over my role, lashing out fiercely for an unbeaten 57. We reached 273 for the loss of four men, winning by 6 wickets. Rice was still there with a courageous 95 and there was no argument as to who was the man of the match. He was also named the man of the series, having scored 344 runs for an average of 86, and his 13 wickets were the most taken by a bowler on either side. As Kim Hughes remarked in typically blunt Australian fashion: 'What a bloody fine player.'

Following our victory in the major series, this 4-2 success was sweet indeed, particularly as the selectors had denied us our strongest combination for the first three games.

With Test series completed against Gooch's Englishmen, Sri Lanka, the West Indies twice, and this one Australian side, South Africa now had a seasoned and cohesive combination. We did not yet consider ourselves world-beaters, but we felt we were at least maintaining as high an international level as circumstances permitted. We had broken out of the confines of provincialism and had, overall, done pretty well. True, Barry Richards and Mike Procter had retired and Graeme Pollock, although still a potent force, was in the autumn of an illustrious career. But numerous young players like Daryll Cullinan, Mike Rindel, Louis Vorster, Brian McMillan, Craig Matthews, Corrie van Zyl, Allan Donald, Philip Amm and Mark Rushmere were fast making their mark. We yearned to go abroad, but had to be patient. In the mean time, a return series against Kim Hughes' side was on the cards for the 1986/87 season.

He brought back much the same team, with the additional and important inclusion of Kepler Wessels. A Free Stater by birth, he had emigrated to Australia in search of official international Test experience, did wonderfully well – even scoring a century in his first Test – then, surprisingly, he turned his back on his adopted country, returned home and settled in Port Elizabeth, where his solid technique, wide range of shots and unquenchable thirst for runs in the Boycott fashion moved him once more to the forefront of the domestic ranks. He was a proven international and worthy of inclusion in the coming series, but for whom? A man of firm convictions, he attracted controversy and there were many South Afri-

48

cans who felt he did not deserve to be considered for the country he had 'deserted'. As it was, he elected to be eligible for Australia – and were Kim Hughes and his colleagues glad to have him.

The Australian tour started with four day/night Tests, the first encounter being at the impressive new Centurion Park in Verwoerdburg outside Pretoria. Kepler Wessels immediately proved his worth when Australia batted first, slamming 75 out of a total of 238-5 in their rain-reduced, 44-over innings. Steve Smith (59) and Peter Faulkner (37) were the only others to feature. We topped that figure for the loss of four men, to win by 6 wickets, Ken McEwan and Graeme Pollock getting into the 60s, with my contribution being 45. This was a good start for South Africa and we were determined to remain on top for the remainder of the series. Learning from the previous year, we realised that they were formidable opponents if at any time they were allowed to gain the initiative.

The second match at the Wanderers was ruined by rain. Australia scored 147 in 40 overs, and we had lost one wicket for 3 when play was washed out. A distressing factor for South Africa was the injury to Henry Fotheringham, who had by now firmly established his place in succession to Barry Richards as my opening partner. Looking for his first run, he hit the ball and called. The Achilles tendon in his left leg snapped. He could barely crawl to the other end, was carried off and retired from the match and the remainder of the series.

The third fixture was the first to be played under the new lights at Newlands. It was a perfect batting wicket, but no one told the Australians. With Garth le Roux again relishing a chance to get to work on his beloved home wicket, and with the young Free Stater Corrie van Zyl also in a belligerent mood, the tourists collapsed like a house of cards. Van Zyl removed the openers and, needing only 30 deliveries, Le Roux sent five men back to the pavilion and finished with 6 for 21. This was without doubt one of the most incisive spells of bowling in his career. At one stage they were 15 for 7 and ended with a lamentable 85, which we easily topped in 15 overs for the loss of 2 wickets. The game was over well inside four hours, before the Western Province authorities even had time to switch on their new lights.

The crowd of 16 000 was flabbergasted. How the Australians felt can be left to the imagination. The question then arose: what to do next? There were hours in hand and the public had paid good money to see some entertainment. They had seen quite a bit, but should they now be told that the evening's proceedings were over? It was a unique situation. As far as the players were concerned that was that and we were changing into our plain clothes. But then Ali Bacher rushed into our dressing-   49 room and said we had to play another game. We declined, reasoning that we had done our job. Then the sponsors came along and offered us more money if we would play a scratch 25-over-a-side game. Reluctantly, we did, and we won this too.

The demoralised tourists hived off to Port Elizabeth to lick their wounds and recover their equilibrium, which they did to a certain degree by beating Eastern Province by an innings and 84 runs, and then they flew on to Durban for the fourth match. We mustered 183 and they won with 153 for 4, having the better run-rate after rain had reduced playing time. So, we went into the four-day Tests 2-1 up and feeling confident that we had the measure of them.

It was to be a series notable for high scoring, with numerous sparkling centuries on both sides. Natal's Brian Whitfield was my opening partner for the first Test, and I was in a hurry when we batted first on a firm wicket, slamming five fours before Rod McCurdy scattered my stumps with 28 to my name. The beefy McCurdy really came into his own in this innings, claiming 6 for 67, with only Rice (61), Le Roux (42) and Jefferies (27) – the last pair adding 44 for the tenth wicket – putting up much resistance. We managed only 254. Australia did worse, tumbling out for 142, with Rice breaking the back of their batting with 4 for 19. With honours fairly evenly distributed in our second innings, we totalled 182, giving us a good lead, to which they could reply with only 245, Kim Hughes making the top score with an undefeated 54, giving us a comfortable enough 49-run victory.

Controversy surrounded Kim Hughes' innings. He had scored about 20-odd when he played at a ball from Rice, which nicked the top of his pad and went through to wicket-keeper Dave Richardson, who dived and caught it on the bounce. Much to his surprise, Kim was given out caught-behind. Understandably furious and slamming his bat into the ground, he began walking off. Meanwhile, having rolled over when collecting the ball, Richardson did not at first notice Kim walking. Eventually, seeing him 15 or so metres on his way to the pavilion, Dave called out: 'No, no, I never caught it'. Rice drew the umpire's attention to this call. The latter then signalled Kim to return, and when he did he made it known that he had not touched the ball in the first place. But that was not the end of the drama of Kim's innings. Immediately afterwards he did nick the ball to Richardson, was adjudged not out, and did not walk. We were now upset, making it clear to him that he should have walked, especially as we had been sporting enough to ask for his recall when he had been given out unfairly. As it was, while he was still batting, an Australian victory was not impossible.

Anyhow, despite this incident, with victory under our belts, we were now certain we had our visitors by the throat and looked forward to underlining our mastery in the second encounter at Newlands. Unfortunately a dead wicket and rain defeated our prospects in what turned out to be a high-scoring game. It was not my day with the bat when the Springboks again had first knock, but Brian Whitfield (77) and Peter Kirsten thoroughly enjoyed themselves in their second-wicket stand, the latter rattling up a superb 173 in this his second Test century. After Whitfield had gone, he and Graeme Pollock piled on the runs, with Pollock needing only 102 deliveries to collect his 66. Clive Rice decided to join in the entertainment and helped himself to 72, and even though we lost the final 5 wickets for only 56 runs, our 493 left us comfortably placed. Anything you can do we can do better, said the Australians and, sure enough, they topped our score by 3 runs, with John Dyson (198) and Mike Haysman (153) having a glorious fifth-wicket stand of 225. It was a great performance, but a draw was inevitable, as South Africa replied in their second innings with 257 for 3, notable for Peter Kirsten's undefeated 103, his second century of the match. Only two South Africans, Bruce Mitchell and Alan Melville, had previously achieved two hundreds in a Test match.

In the third Test in Durban Steve Smith headed the Australian innings with 137 when they batted first and totalled 264. With 101 Ken McEwan was our top scorer, with Whitfield (59), myself (44) and Richardson (44) being the other main contributors in our first innings of 350. Leg-spinner Trevor Hohns was their best bowler with 6 for 96. Matching our strokemaking, that reliable pair John Dyson (101) and Mike Haysman (he of the flowing blond locks) again starred in Australia's second innings, as they had in the previous Test, hitting centuries and in the process denying the Springboks victory. They totalled 339, leaving us chasing 254 for victory in only 160 minutes. We did our best for a while, then gave up the chase, managing 143 for the loss of 7 wickets at the close of this drawn game.

The final International at Port Elizabeth was a veritable run feast, with five centuries and five half-centuries being recorded on this featherbed wicket. Kepler Wessels emulated Peter Kirsten's effort in the Cape Town game by registering centuries in each innings. First he rattled up 135 in their first knock of 449, Smith weighing in with 77, Steve Rixon 61 and Greg Shipperd 53, to which we replied with a mammoth 533, in which Graeme Pollock, playing in his last Test, gave his legions of fans around the world something to remember.

After our net practice prior to the start of the game, our team went off for our customary drink but Graeme, normally among the first to order, said that he was abstaining. And true to his word, despite the heat and the energy he burned up, he confined himself to soft drinks until after that first innings. My 84 was most satisfactory, but it was completely over-shadowed by the emotion of a Pollock determined to end his career on his home ground in the most fitting manner – with a century – and with the Australians equally determined to deny him this satisfaction.

The atmosphere was electric as Rodney Hogg who, until then, had been bowling at little more than medium pace, slipped into top gear and raced in from his long run at the start of Graeme's innings, desperate to tame the master. Fat chance. Graeme steered one delivery between the wicket-keeper and first slip to the boundary, edged another between third slip and gully for another boundary, and after a few more overs of thunderbolts Hogg gave up, exhausted, and repaired to the deep.

From then on it was sheer slaughter, with Pollock dominating the proceedings as he had done for so many years, his heavy bat carving the ball almost at will to all points of the ground. Only when his hundred went up did he appear to relax, but he carried on for another 44 runs before Hogg finally bowled him. By then it did not matter. One of cricket's giants had written his farewell in story-book style. Everyone – Springboks, Australians, and his adoring fans alike – applauded long and loud as he departed to the dressing-room. It was one of the game's great moments, and what a great pity it was that it had been accomplished under the guise of an 'unofficial' Test. Even Ken McEwan will admit that his undefeated 138 was something of an anti-climax.

With a draw a certainty, the Australians merely got in some useful batting practice in their final innings, going to 333 by the close, with Wessels getting an undefeated 105 and Steve Smith 113. So, we won the series 1-0 and looked forward to making a clean sweep of things in the four one-day games. This we did, with the first game, almost immediately after the last Test, turning out to be one of the most exciting, if not the best, that players on both sides had participated in.

I hooked the first ball of the match, a bouncer from Hogg, to the boundary, and this set the tempo for the day – the runs rattled along at a tremendous pace. After I was run out for my fast 70, Roy Pienaar hit 74, Peter Kirsten 87 and Graeme Pollock 43 in our total of 316 for 6 in 50 overs. With Steve Smith run out early on, the Australians started badly and fell behind the clock. But they rallied, John Dyson (69) and Kepler Wessels (122) pulling them round in grand style. What a week it had been for Kepler: three hundreds off the Springboks in only a few days. Kim
52 Hughes joined in the fun – so much so that the Australians were poised to

Early days: captain of the Hyde Park High School under-13 team, 1966.

Army duty in the State President's Guard, 1971. (The Argus).

Teaching days at Fairways Primary School in Johannesburg.

Backyard cricket in Taunton with the boys.

Football days with Wits University: playing against Hellenic at Milner Park.

With Henry Fotheringham, my friend and long-time opening partner for Transvaal.

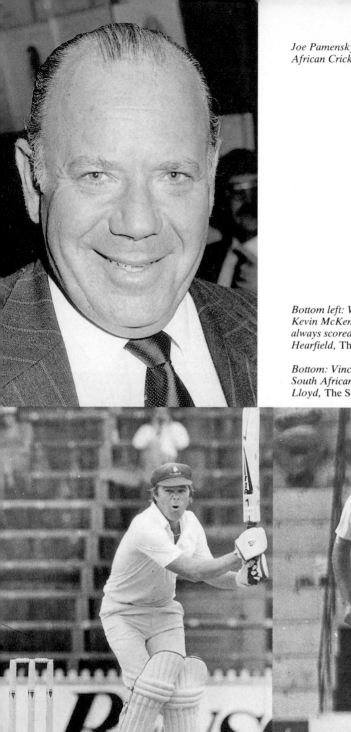

Joe Pamensky, former president of the South African Cricket Union.

Bottom left: Vastly underrated as a batsman, Kevin McKenzie was a positive player who always scored at a blistering rate. (Rebecca Hearfield, The Star)

Bottom: Vince van der Bijl, one of the finest South African bowlers I ever faced. (Clive Lloyd, The Star)

Top: Former England captain Mike Gatting. There can be few better leaders of men in the game today.

Top right: Sylvester Clarke: a fearsome fast bowler who thrilled the South African crowds.

Right: Opening partner Barry Richards – the most technically correct batsman one could wish to see. (Reproduced by permission of The Star).

Bottom: Clive Rice: a fine aggressive batsman, cunning bowler, excellent fielder and captain. I will always be grateful that I played my career with and not against him.

The model backward defensive! (*Jean du Plessis,* Die Burger)

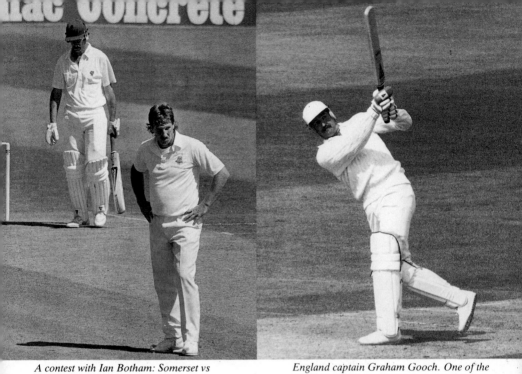

A contest with Ian Botham: Somerset vs Worcestershire, 1990. (Reproduced by permission of Alain Lockyer, Somerset News).

England captain Graham Gooch. One of the dominant batsmen of his era, he has an insatiable appetite for runs. (London Pictures Service)

Cheer up lads! Vince van der Bijl, Rupert Hanley and Mike Procter share a light moment at a reunion at the Wanderers in 1989. (Herbert Mabuza, The Star)

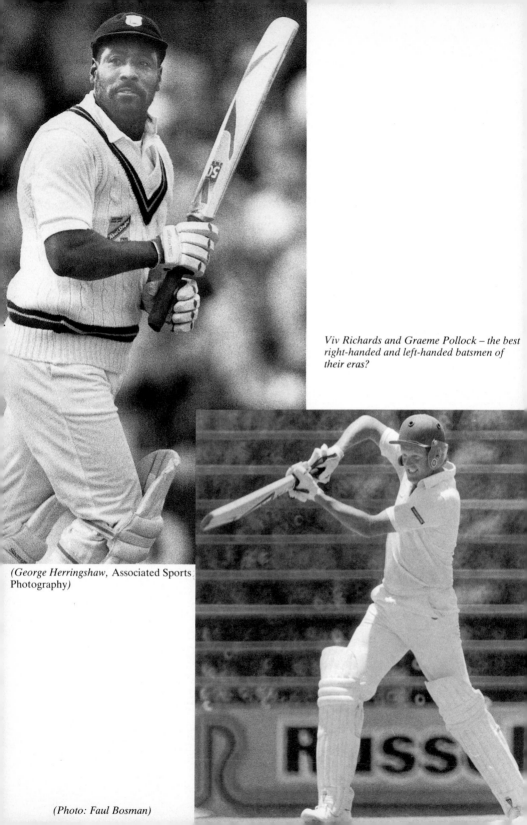

Viv Richards and Graeme Pollock – the best right-handed and left-handed batsmen of their eras?

(George Herringshaw, Associated Sports Photography)

(Photo: Faul Bosman)

Driving through the covers against Western Province at the Wanderers in 1992. (Joao Silva, The Star)

Meeting Somerset captain Vic Marks on my first day at Taunton. He was a shrewd off-spin bowler who was capped many times for England. (Somerset News)

The Somerset staff assemble for the 1989 season. (Reproduced by permission of Alan Casse, Avon Press)

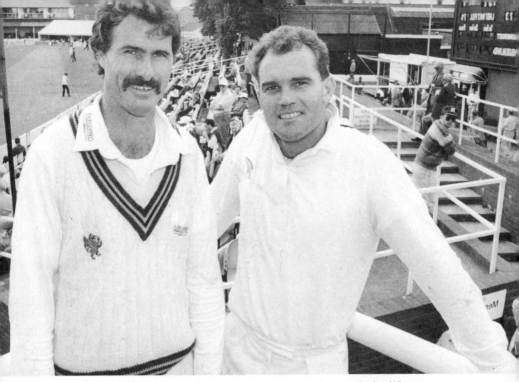

Chatting to ex-Somerset professional Martin Crowe during the New Zealand/Somerset match in 1990.

Relaxing with Somerset captain Chris Tavare, a fine man both on and off the field. (Reproduced by permission of Alain Lockyer)

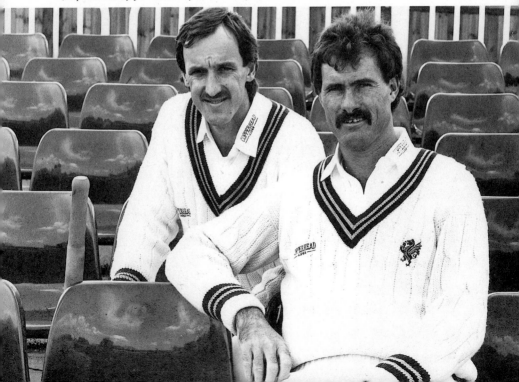

My farewell to Somerset in 1991 was an emotional moment. Happily, I was able to sign off with a 'thank you' century in my first innings.

beat the Springboks when only 2 wickets were down for 298. Only 19 needed with 8 wickets and 4 overs in hand. Yet they muffed it. They had not allowed for the fighting spirit of Clive Rice, known as the man who cannot spell the word 'surrender', and certainly he proved it on this occasion. Bowling his medium-paced deliveries with all the cunning he had garnered after almost two decades in the game, he proceeded to smash through the middle and the tail. Ball after ball was aimed right in the block hole, and the frustrated batsmen were unable to get him away. They panicked completely, and Clive took 4 wickets in 11 incredible deliveries. He finished with 5 for 50 – by his own admission, his greatest bowling performance. We won by 6 runs a game we realistically should have lost. Overall, a total of 626 runs was scored in 100 overs, an average of 6,26 runs per over. What more could one ask for?

The rest of the series was an anti-climax. South Africa won again in Cape Town by 8 wickets, and in Johannesburg by 4 wickets, losing by 5 wickets at Verwoerdburg. So we had mastered the Australians in successive series. The fact that this was not Australia's front-line combination should not detract from South Africa's performance. It was a good squad, and although they did not bowl as well as on the first trip – particularly Carl Rackemann and Terry Alderman, who subsequently did well for the official team – the inclusion of Kepler Wessels certainly gave them depth in batting.

Kim Hughes returned to captain Natal for a couple of seasons, but could not find the form that had made him such an impressive batsman only a few seasons before. He was dropped from the provincial squad and returned home a somewhat disappointed man.

Of the Australian batsmen, John Dyson was technically very efficient, had a positive outlook matched with plenty of courage, and was a most enjoyable person to talk to off the field. Steve Smith was perhaps their best batsman, particularly when in full flight. Always great company, we were later pleased to have him back with us in the Transvaal for a couple of seasons. We respected their bowlers but, whereas the batsmen mixed freely with us between matches, they kept very much to themselves. Whether this was done on purpose I do not know.

5

TRANSVAAL
REBUILD

Any cricket team that could boast Graeme Pollock in its ranks invariably went into matches with an air of confidence. In the same way as Australian Test and State sides in the Bradman era must have felt when the little man walked purposefully to the wicket, so did South Africa and Eastern Province for many years, and subsequently Transvaal when this greatest of all Springboks moved to the Reef to further his business career. He came on the scene when this mighty and proud province was in the process of rebuilding and re-establishing itself after some years which had not produced the results to which it was normally accustomed. It had a number of able men, but Lee Irvine, that fine wicket-keeper/batsman, was still missed at number four, and there was a compelling need to create a squad of real star quality to entice paying customers back to the Wanderers in any large numbers.

The genesis of such a squad began in the 1978/79 season. Henry Fotheringham had moved up from Durban to blossom eventually into an outstanding opener and partner for me, while Pollock slotted in second wicket down. Clive Rice was absent that season playing in the Packer series in Australia, but Kevin McKenzie was about to command a regular place in the lower middle order, which he ultimately held with distinction until his retirement. With David Dyer as captain and Rupert Hanley and Doug Neilson leading the bowling department, we won both the Currie Cup and the Datsun Shield. Needless to say our star was Pollock, for in that first year he scored 961 runs in only 11 innings – and by way of five centuries – still a Transvaal record. He was so consistent that he looked good for a three-figure score every time he was at the crease.

One of Transvaal's most thoughtful captains in recent years, David Dyer had a simple yet effective format when it came to batting tactics. As no bonus points were awarded in the Currie Cup after 85 overs, his game-plan was to go all out for that number of overs and then declare. His reasoning was that there was no purpose in continuing an innings if no points were at stake. We adhered to that formula as often as we could, and consequently we were often in the happy position of having enough time to win matches and gain maximum points.

Although he was going through a sticky batting patch himself, David never let this personal disappointment interfere with his leadership. He was both a shrewd tactician and a cheerful morale booster.

One of the most remarkable games that season was at home against Natal. We were shot out for 159. In turn, they could only scramble 71 (courtesy of a Doug Neilson hat trick), and we were 20 for no wicket at the close on that first day. Even for the renowned Wanderers greentop, 20 wickets falling in one day was somewhat unusual. Were things to be all over just as quickly on the second day? On the contrary, Transvaal came good and scored 400 for 3. This was particularly satisfying for me as I scored an undefeated 179 and finally secured my place as an opening batsman. Henry Fotheringham also hit 100 and it was perhaps this game above all others which began to signal to other provinces that a cricketing power of some magnitude was about to be born. This was underlined the following year when, further strengthened by the return of Clive Rice, Transvaal scored a full house, taking the Currie Cup, the Datsun Shield, the Protea Assurance and the Computer Science tournaments. The cry rang round the provinces – Transvaal was the team to beat, and each side did its darndest, but for the most part in vain.

Eastern Province was one side which had hopes of taming us when they came up to the Wanderers. They found themselves facing a particularly aggressive Clive Rice on a greentop after David Dyer had won the toss and without hesitation put them in to bat.

When Ivor Foulkes came in Clive walked up to him and said, 'I think you have forgotten something.'

'What?' asked a puzzled Foulkes.

'Your helmet. You should have worn one.'

Clive walked back to his mark, ran in and promptly hit Foulkes straight on the side of the head with a bumper. He fell as if pole-axed and was carried off. Three or four overs later Russell Fensham came in and immediately had his arm broken by another Rice special. Province were all out for 94.

They complained bitterly about the wicket, and Transvaal's answer was to go out and score 330, another Pollock 100 going into the record books and Kevin McKenzie getting into the 90s. In their second innings the wicket became faster and they fared even worse, crumbling for a miserable 46, to go down by an innings and 190 runs.

On a personal note, while the side was going great guns that year, I was otherwise occupied doing army duty on the border in November, December and January. The week I returned I found myself in the side for a Currie Cup game against Western Province, even though I could barely remember what a cricket bat felt like. However, I got 60-odd and a week or two later got 100 in a Datsun Shield final in which we beat Western Province.

Thus was the pattern for Transvaal: victory after victory. And a phrase began to do the rounds: 'Transvaal is beginning to play like a machine . . .'

6

THE
MEAN MACHINE

6

THE MEAN MACHINE

Every once in a while a sports team combines those elements that enable it to evolve into greatness. A mixture of talent, leadership, opportunity and the right chemistry takes this eleven, fifteen, or whatever, squad to the very top with a series of outstanding performances which rewrite the record books and leave indelible impressions on all who see them.

Most devotees of rugby, soccer and similar team sports cherish golden memories of the great occasions in which they have participated or which they have witnessed from the stand, touchline or boundary, read about or watched on television. Cricket conjures up memories of such gifted teams as Bradman's 1948 Australians, who swept all before them in England, earning them the title of 'the greatest ever'. Then there were the hugely endowed West Indies sides during the past two decades, true world champions, with their apparently endless stream of awesome fast bowlers and brutally destructive batsmen who crushed all whom they encountered on three continents.

South Africa has had its share of outstanding Springbok teams, such as those which Peter van der Merwe and Ali Bacher led in 1966 and 1970 to handsome victories over successive touring Australian sides. At provincial level, Transvaal has always been a power in the land, particularly during the decade which began in the summer of 1978 when for most of the time we were fortunate enough to have the services of legendary batsman Graeme Pollock, who had moved from Port Elizabeth, and the gifted Natalian Henry Fotheringham. During the period from the summer of 1978 to March 1989 the province played 93 Currie Cup matches, won 56, drew 34, and lost only 3.

As the seventies gave way to the new decade the team became even stronger. Clive Rice, a superb allrounder who had worn the blue and gold for several years and who had blossomed into a first-class leader of Nottinghamshire during the English county season, took over when David Dyer retired and welded a combination that became so successful that it was dubbed 'The Mean Machine'.

Mean it was when it came to dealing with opponents who stood between it and victory. Like a well-tuned machine, Transvaal went from 18 January 1982 to March 1989 without losing a first-class match. During the period 1982/83 to 1986/87 we played 44 games, won 27, drew 17 and never once tasted defeat. The Currie Cup came our way four times.

During the period 1978/79 to 1986/87 we won the Datsun/Nissan Shield seven times (losing in one final when bad light stopped play), and in the seasons 1981/82 to 1986/87 we won 24 out of 31 Benson and Hedges matches.

The majority of the players gained national colours in unofficial Inter-   61 nationals played in that era and it was without doubt the finest side I ever had the privilege of belonging to. Every department was rich in talent – batting, seam and slow bowling. We had the best wicket-keeper in the country, no one fielded better, and our team spirit was wonderful. We were feared, admired and respected, and our supporters were legion.

I was already a long-standing Transvaal player when the 'Machine' evolved. Good health, good fortune and consistent form had seen me play in virtually every match since 1977. We won the Currie Cup and other tournaments a few times in those early years, and for me the runs (and centuries) came regularly enough, and so did a series of opening partners. I respected them all, but none more so than my good friend and partner, Henry Fotheringham.

Henry came to us from Durban in the late 1970s and for a while played in the middle order. He did well, but it was not until it was suggested that he partner me at the beginning of the 1981/82 season after our captain and regular opener David Dyer had retired that he developed into one of the best batsmen in the land. He was reluctant to move up and face the new ball, but in our first match as opening partners – a one-day match against Natal – we put on 108 for the first wicket. The experiment had succeeded.

It was manifestly apparent that so good and reliable was his technique that 'Fothers' was the best man in the side to help me take the shine off the ball and build the foundation to the innings. He developed into a wonderful destroyer of any kind of bowling. Blessed with an ice-cool temperament, marvellous eyesight and sound reflexes, he treated pace and cunning seamers with equanimity and was ruthless with spinners. Well built though he was, he was quick on his feet, never hesitating to go down the pitch and thrash anything loose on both sides of the wicket or over the top. He had courage, verve, all the time in the world to play his shots, and I drew much inspiration and confidence from watching him in action.

Over the years we developed a kind of mental telepathy, instinctively knowing when to run and rarely needing to call to each other. In scores of partnerships only on three occasions did one run the other out. In addition, each felt comforted that he did not have to 'carry' the other, even when the going at times got rough. And the record shows that usually we scored at approximately the same rate, thus relieving the pressure on each other's batting.

We were able to give the side many good starts with high-figure first-wicket stands although, as it happens, of the two record partnerships that are attributed to us, the first was for the second wicket – 225 against Natal at the Wanderers in the 1978/79 season. Ten years later we set a first-wicket stand of 290 against Orange Free State in Bloemfontein.

For a four-year spell during that golden era the side hardly changed, and so the players became the best of friends. Henry and I socialised much together and I missed him when he eventually returned to Natal for a couple of seasons before calling it a day.

Before the start of the 1981/82 season the Transvaal cricket authorities took what was then a most bold step. They signed up a foreign batsman – and he was black. Remember, this was when the apartheid code was a rigid fixture in South African society. Non-whites did not play in white cricket teams, certainly not at provincial level. The great crusade initiated by Ali Bacher, Joe Pamensky and other national figures to liberalise the game and dismantle all racial barriers was still being conducted off the field. But those who ran the sport in the most populous province decided that it was about time they took the bit between their teeth and got a batsman of quality in their bid to rebuild and develop a really great side. If he were non-Caucasian, so be it.

So they signed up Alvin Kallicharran, the highly respected West Indies and Warwickshire batsman with impressive credentials at all levels, including more than 60 Test appearances, nine of them as captain. It was a stroke of genius. He did not come cheaply, but the cricket board and local businessman Arnie Witkin found the money and ensured that he would enjoy his years in the province.

Kallie was perfectly suited to slot in at number three, and he lived up to his reputation as a brilliant and consistent accumulator of runs. He was also one of the nicest and most popular players ever to wear Transvaal colours. He had a happy disposition, reflected in a non-stop infectious laugh which rang round the dressing-rooms of the country.

However, there was what one might call a slight quirk in his attitude towards the spirit of the game which took a little time to resolve. He often felt he was dismissed unfairly and did not hesitate to indicate the fact. Frequently, if he was caught or trapped leg before wicket, he would complain about it on his return to the dressing-room, hinting that perhaps there was a bias against him by the umpires and the other side. We decided to resolve this problem by agreeing among ourselves that whenever a decision went against him, whoever was partnering him at the crease at the time would say he was out, even if privately that partner believed otherwise. Our aim was to prevent him from getting upset, so that he would go into the next innings in a happier frame of mind. In this way we hoped the runs would continue to flow from his rapier-like bat and everyone would be satisfied. This policy worked well with the Transvaal side, 63 but when he played for the 'rebel' West Indies team during its two-year tour he resorted to his old habit, and on at least two occasions that I know of he complained bitterly about decisions which went against him.

Whenever a promising left-handed batsman got into the Transvaal side during the years Graeme Pollock played for us, the luckless fellow was invariably compared with the master. But no one was foolish enough to do this with Kallicharran. He was his own man, with his own individual approach to the job at hand. For a start, their respective builds ruled out comparison. Whereas Pollock was tall, with long, powerful arms which in the later years in particular were used to bludgeon the ball brutally with his extra-heavy bat, Kallie was the short, flamboyant stylist with a typically Caribbean flair for finding the most unexpected gaps in even the best set fields. Each man had enormous respect for the other.

Kallie had a simple yet effective approach to his batting: the ball was there to be hit as hard and as often as possible. When coaching at schools around the province he would study his charges, and whenever he saw a lad in the nets playing perfectly correct but ineffectual defensive strokes, he would call out: 'Hit the ball! Hit it!' How it was hit did not matter. He even introduced a new dimension of thinking among the established provincial players. He played the ball on length rather than our customary approach of line. We had honed our game in that if the ball was pitched just outside the off-stump, we would hit it to mid-off. If it was wide outside the off-stump we hit it to cover. Kallie often slammed those deliveries to mid-wicket. If the ball was short he would look to dispatch it square of the wicket. He never hesitated to break the cardinal rule and hit across the line of delivery.

In one of the first games in which I partnered him he was facing Vince van der Bijl, one of the finest fast-medium bowlers the country has produced. Vince sent down two deliveries outside the off-stump and Kallie flicked them behind square on the leg side for successive boundaries. I went up to him and asked why he wanted to hit the ball there. He replied simply, 'Because there are no fielders there.' I had no answer, especially as he had just collected 8 runs. But I would never have dreamed of doing that myself.

Although overall he scored a packet of runs for us, he made a most inauspicious start. In his first game, a sponsored triangular one-day match at the start of the season against Natal and Western Province in Durban, he opened with me. The first delivery he received was from the Western Province left-arm seamer Stephen Jefferies. The ball pitched on leg-stump, Kallie moved to hit it to leg, but the ball swung and clipped the top of his off-stump.

He looked down at what had happened with horror written all over his face. He could not believe it. Here he was, hailed in the media as a batsman of whom great things were expected, and he was out to the first delivery he had faced in Africa. It was a perfect delivery, the sort that would beat anybody, and one that Jefferies was able to spring so often during his long career. But that was no consolation to the diminutive West Indian. Back in the dressing-room he was both speechless and embarrassed. On my return to the dressing-room I made a point of going up to him and saying that it was no disgrace to be beaten in this manner. It was one of those nightmare deliveries which every batsman faces sooner or later. I like to think that this little gesture helped him to realise that he was among genuine team-mates who would always support him. Needless to say, he settled in very quickly and took a heavy toll of all the bowlers in South Africa.

A year later Western Province came to Johannesburg, again for an early-season Protea Assurance challenge match. Kevin McKenzie, a fine batsman and a great thinker about the game, said at a team talk that we top-order men were forgetting the value of taking quick singles. All of us – myself, Fotheringham, Kallicharran, Pollock and Rice – were too often looking for boundaries. The ones and twos were important and the fours would come in due course. This led to a long discussion and, as usual, Kevin's sharp, rational thinking won the day. I was out in the third over and in walked Kallie. He promptly scored 122 off about 90 deliveries. The majority of his runs came from sixes and fours in one of the most devastating exhibitions of concerted hitting I have ever seen. So much for batting theory. Transvaal scored 315 for 4, to which the Cape team replied with 311, leaving us victors by 4 runs. It was a superb game all round, but particularly memorable for me for the way Alvin Kallicharran went out and did it his way.

Regrettably, Kallie stayed only three seasons with Transvaal before going for a while to join Orange Free State, a province then embarking on a concerted effort to shake off its Cinderella status and become a cricketing power in the land. It took time, but strangely Kallie did not shape with them as consistently as he had done with us. The spark was missing. Maybe it was because, unlike the Transvaal side where he was free to play his natural, free flowing game, knowing that if he failed there was still plenty of batting to come, in the Free State side he was conscious of the fact that he was the mainstay and sheet-anchor. If he failed the side could be in serious trouble, and perhaps he became too defensive and paid the price. Whatever the reason, it was a pity that he graced our shores for only a few short years.

I should record that, despite the uniqueness of being the only non-white in the team, to my knowledge Kallie never experienced any embarrassment because of his colour wherever he played, coached or attended social or public engagements. He was respected and treated just like any other member of the side. He and his wife Nazli and son Rohan seemed very happy, and I am sure that the good reports he must have passed on in the English county circuit led to Sylvester Clarke and other West Indians joining our provincial ranks in later seasons.

These days, of course, men from the Caribbean are a permanent feature of South African provincial cricket. They have enriched the game enormously by their personal performances and by encouraging many youngsters from our black communities to take up the sport. With our township development programmes now very much to the fore, I am in agreement with the view that in the not too distant future the majority of a South African Test squad may well be non-white – if anyone notices the fact.

A team may be packed full of talent, but that in itself is no guarantee of success. All those skills have to be welded into a cohesive unit by a recognised leader – a man who commands respect for his own skills, his tactical brain, and his ability to handle people. We were fortunate to have such a man in Clive Rice, both as captain and as allrounder. He was good enough to be in the team as a middle-order batsman, and there was no better first change seamer. He was a stylish run-maker, with tremendous powers of concentration, hitting the ball extremely hard and enjoying nothing better than to make a mockery of carefully worked out field placings.

His bowling was of a consistently high standard. He was accurate, knew how to extract life from the deadest of pitches, and used length and direction with telling effect. Many was the time he would bring himself on to stem a run-flow by sending down a series of wicked yorkers or balls just tantalisingly short of a length.

As for his leadership – all members of the 'Mean Machine' will not hesitate to say that they thoroughly enjoyed playing under Clive Rice. Highly experienced when he assumed the captaincy, he had been a member of the side for 12 years. At the same time he captained Nottinghamshire with much success, having just led them to a county championship title.

Naturally, captaining a side as gifted as Transvaal was easier than struggling with a bunch of no-hopers. More often than not we were on top of a match, but there were occasions when the pressure was on and firm captaincy was called for. Not that Clive ever reflected the tension that might be building up inside him. He was coolness personified and the greatest compliment I can pay him is to say that in all the years I played with him I never saw him panic or buckle in indecision. Faced with a problem, he would slow the game down, talk to his bowler or bowlers, and work out the next tactic. We were a highly experienced bunch who needed little or no direction on the field. We knew our places to Vince van der Bijl, Rupert Hanley and the other seamers and when, for instance, Clive brought Alan Kourie in to the attack, he would merely say 'Alan's bowling', and off we would trot. If Sylvester Clarke was on duty, Alan would go to his customary spot at first slip, Henry Fotheringham next to him, Graeme Pollock at third slip, Kevin McKenzie to gully, myself in the covers, and so on.

In appearance Clive can at times look somewhat sour. Smiling in public does not come easily to him. Indeed, when concentrating on his game or in media interviews he can look a real misery. But this perception is a misleading one of the good-humoured man I know off duty. We had our team talks, but Clive was never one for long lectures or harangues at individual players. He set high standards and expected everyone to try to realise his own potential. But there were never any after-match bullying sessions when a man had failed. Rather, Clive was only too happy to help analyse what went wrong with the individual, or perhaps give him a quiet and encouraging pep talk.

He was a good listener, always ready to hear what others had to say before making up his own mind. He worked on the basis that he did not necessarily have all the answers. If someone made a worthwhile suggestion he would make a mental note of it, mull it over, and when he arrived at a decision his view prevailed.

Clive could be economical with words to the point of muteness. Once, on the eve of a Currie Cup final, he walked into the dressing-room and we waited expectantly for his game-plan. All he said was: 'I've seen the names of the opposition on the scoreboard, and I've seen our names. There's no way we can lose.' End of speech. And we won.

One enduring quality of Clive Rice is his acceptance of the quirks and quiddities of the game. When a bad decision was given against the side, or against him personally whether batting or bowling, he never complained. He would immediately forget the incident and get on with the job at hand. Never one for intimidating an opposing player by swearing or with body language, he epitomised all the qualities expected of a man who for so long was successfully at the helm of his provincial, county and national teams. His playing days at the highest level may be almost over, but Clive 67

Rice should not be lost to South African cricket. He still has much to give to the game on the other side of the boundary ropes.

Few people appreciated how important Kevin McKenzie was in the 'Mean Machine' squad. He was the genuine middle man, not only as a number six batsman, but off the field as the conciliator and arbitrator. If, for example, Clive said I had been scoring too slowly, or it was felt that another was not running well between the wickets, Kevin would raise the point at our next team discussion and it would be aired rationally. As in all teams, tension, pressure, disappointment and bruised egos would occasionally create a fractious situation. Kevin never hesitated to step in and resolve the matter with his customary tact and common sense. His honesty and reputation for speaking his mind without any ulterior motive were valued by all of us. We shared many a hotel room on tours over the years and I always welcomed his sage comments about my own game. Younger players also respected him, even if what he had to say was not always complimentary.

Louis Vorster, our promising début-making left-hander, came in flushed with pride after scoring an enterprising 48. He beamed in delight, but Kevin pounced on him, asking what reason he had to smile. Louis was puzzled. Had he not just hit a fine 48?

'So what,' came the reply. 'Anyone can hit 48. A class batsman would have gone on to make a hundred.'

The smile vanished from Louis' face. He said not a word, and we all knew that Kevin was right.

Kevin was vastly underrated as a batsman. Outside the Transvaal he could have commanded any spot he wanted, but he happened to reach his peak at the same time as Graeme Pollock moved to the Transvaal and when Clive Rice decided his place in the order was at number five. Therefore, Kevin had to follow him and, inevitably, coming that low in the order in such a powerful batting squad he was often overshadowed and denied the opportunity to show his true capabilities. He was good enough to play at four for South Africa and, to be honest, I think he should have gone in before Clive.

Thanks to the unwitting assistance of an English umpire, Kevin got his highest score in first-class cricket in the 1986/87 season. We were playing Eastern Province at the Wanderers and were in serious trouble at 70 for 4. David Capel of Northamptonshire was bowling and Barry Meyer umpiring. As he bowled Capel's back foot clipped one of the stumps and a bail dropped to the ground. Barry was momentarily distracted by the dislodged woodwork and looked down to see what had happened. As he did so there was a tremendous appeal from the Province players for a catch behind the wicket by wicket-keeper David Richardson. Barry said later that so confident was the appeal that Kevin must have nicked the ball and his instinct was to raise his finger. But he had not seen it and had no option but to turn down the appeal. Kevin had only scored half a dozen runs at the time, and given this unexpected 'life' he went on to register 188. This was hard on the other team, but it was also a demonstration of the high calibre of umpiring we know we can expect of English officials.

Kevin never complained of being in the shadow of others. There was not a selfish bone in his body. He was a member of seven Nissan Shield final sides, but only got a chance to bat in three of them. And so often it was his duty to go in and hit a quick 30 or 40 to clinch a game when the playing conditions were perfect for him to play himself in and build up a good personal score. His batting was always very positive and the many thousands of runs he made were always scored at a blistering rate.

Kevin represented his country with distinction during the 'rebel' tour era, but more is the pity that he was not born at another time, before politics trampled all over our sport, or in the same age group as Andrew Hudson, Jonty Rhodes and the new generation who are now carrying the flag abroad as South Africa rejoins the comity of sporting nations.

Ray Jennings was a member of that exclusive club of brilliant wicket-keepers who also shone with the bat. Not quite perhaps in the John Waite class of former custodians who scored runs, he was nevertheless a very good man to call on when runs were needed. The finest wicket-keeper I have ever seen, superbly athletic and with an incredible eye, he brought off some remarkable stumpings and catches year after year. His arms were like elastic as, with little apparent effort, he threw his body around in goalkeeper fashion to pluck the ball out of the air. And how often did we see him turn with amazing agility and go racing behind or to the side to take a skyed ball half-way to the boundary. Ray's ability to take seemingly impossible catches allowed Alan Kourie to stand in the customary position of second slip, as the former took anything moving towards first slip, thus allowing us always to have an 'extra' man behind the wicket.

The 'Mean Machine' was blessed with talent, but its members took nothing for granted. We trained hard at the nets three nights a week during the season and kept in top physical shape year in and year out. And none worked more conscientiously at maintaining peak condition than Ray Jennings. It is indeed a pity that he, too, was not able to display his skills at Test arenas around the world.

Every well-balanced team should have two genuine allrounders, and to partner Clive Rice in this department we had Alan Kourie. A bulky, unathletic-looking man, he was nevertheless endowed with rich sporting 69 talent. A Springbok baseballer, he was also good enough to command a place in the Transvaal side as a batsman, was an outstanding slip fielder, and one of the wiliest slow left-arm bowlers in the business. He was not a prodigious spinner, relying more on flight and direction. When batting, he was temperamentally suited to all situations. If quick runs were needed, he would not hesitate to wade in, his beefy arms flaying the ball mercilessly round the field. If defence was required, he could apply deep concentration and a broad bat for as long as the occasion demanded. And this attribute of limitless patience often proved invaluable on the notorious greentop Wanderers wicket when the top order sometimes collapsed horribly.

A highly intelligent cricketer, Alan took his game seriously and enjoyed nothing more than pitting his wits against an ambitious batsman set to take his bowling apart. He would study his opponent, probe for weaknesses and adjust the flight, pace and direction accordingly. He had the customary and obvious arm ball, but also one with a disguised action which gained him a crop of victims.

Once, in a match at Newlands, the Western Province batsman Stephen Bruce climbed into Alan's bowling, slamming him to the boundary for numerous fours and lofting several sixes. As was his habit, the harder he was hit, the higher Alan flighted the ball. This day he was the loser and naturally this dented his pride. But the Kourie memory was a long one. Two months later Western Province came up to the Wanderers for a competition final, and Stephen walked in, confident and anxious to cut loose again at the man he had humiliated at the coast. Alan walked up to the wicket, looked hard at Stephen and said: 'Let's see how far you can hit it on a decent-sized boundary.' He bowled three arm balls and then lobbed one high. Having played the three quicker balls, Stephen accepted the bait, had a full-blooded go and sent the ball high in the air to be caught for nought.

A hard man who hated batsmen who blocked him, Alan had a knack of getting under their skin, drawing them out, and compelling them to chance their arm and go for runs. Often he lost, but many was the time he walked off with a crop of scalps to his credit.

When he was not bamboozling batsmen, Alan Kourie had his mind on horses. For a while he was a bookmaker and thanks to his inside information the Transvaal players occasionally made a 'killing' on the races. One such time was when we went to play a combined Griqualand West/ Free State side in Kimberley. Alan had one of his hot tips for that Saturday, a nag called Main Man. So, trusting as ever, several of us handed over R100 or R50 to Alan. The start of the match was delayed by rain until well after lunch. Eventually play got under way with us fielding. At about 4 p.m., and with the home side about 4 wickets down, Henry Fotheringham was fielding at third-man. A radio was on and our scout, eavesdropping, signalled from the boundary that the race in which we were interested was on.

With one eye on the play and the other on 'Fothers' as the race progressed, we 'endured' another couple of deliveries, and then Barry van der Vyver hit a skyer to mid-wicket. Kevin McKenzie was fielding on the long-on boundary and he raced furiously towards the dropping ball. Diving like a goalkeeper, he brought off a magnificent catch.

Just as Kevin caught the ball, 'Fothers' signalled that the race was over, jumping up and down with excitement as our four-to-one shot had won. Kevin got up from his endeavours, anticipating the customary plaudits from his team-mates. But not this time. Ignoring the game, we had all run to third-man to join 'Fothers' and to get confirmation of our racing victory.

Vince van der Bijl, that outstanding national and Natal fast-medium bowler, had only one season with Transvaal before retiring, and our two regular pacemen during this era were Neal Radford and Rupert Hanley.

Radford was ideally suited to the Wanderers pitch. He bowled a consistently good line just outside the off-stump, moved the ball away a bit, was never afraid to pitch it up, and had enough pace to keep the batsmen continually on the back foot. He was perhaps not quite so successful playing away, and he could be hit. At times he was punished severely, but he was a consistent wicket-taker, and that is what counted, especially in three- and four-day games.

'Spook' Hanley was little more than medium pace but he was also consistent with line and length and was one of those bowlers who tempted batsmen to have a go at him – and pay the price accordingly. When Sylvester Clarke joined us, most batsmen used to face him with great trepidation, and if they survived his fearsome onslaught, they would tend to relax slightly when the deceptive-looking Hanley moved in from the other end. What a mistake this was.

Playing together for the first time, against Eastern Province, Sylvester was frightening, tying them up and making them duck and dive. But he only took 2 wickets. Hanley ended with 12. A talented artist with an infectious sense of humour, and a lion-hearted competitor, he was an invaluable colleague.

Having won all the five trophies that we contested in the 1982/83 season, Transvaal stood tall above the other provinces. Then the Natal-born Vince van der Bijl, one of the finest fast-medium bowlers of his era, hung up his boots. The Board sought out a replacement and was fortunate enough to sign up an equally gifted seamer in big Sylvester Clarke, the hero of Barbados and Surrey. He was in the closing period of his distinguished career, but during the three summers he spent with us he terrified the daylights out of all who faced him. A large man who carried much weight, he left us for a couple of summers with Northern Transvaal and Free State, but by then the years were taking their toll. Constant knee trouble slowed him down and forced him to miss numerous games. With Clive Rice rejoining the bowling ranks in the late summer of 1983/84 after missing a couple of seasons with a bad neck, our bowling line-up was as good as ever, if not better. Some say the side was not as good as that of the previous year. We did not win all five tournaments again, but we still won the Currie Cup and the Nissan Shield. Not only did Transvaal play superbly against the home provinces, but we also beat Lawrence Rowe's West Indians, even though both our West Indian players, Clarke and Kallicharran, were in the opposition camp for that tour.

Having stormed through the Currie Cup rounds that summer we found ourselves in a semi-final date with Northern Transvaal at the Wanderers. Henry Fotheringham scored 99 in the first innings and 115 in the second. But for a stroke of bad luck he might in this tournament have joined that exclusive club of batsmen who have scored a century in each innings. During his innings of 99 in that first knock he drove the ball beautifully for what would have been a certain boundary. It flashed past the wicket at the other end, but unfortunately umpire Ossie Schoof could not get out of the way and the ball hit him on the shin, raising a huge and extremely painful lump. And Henry was denied his century in each innings.

Henry and I had one of our big first-wicket partnerships in that second innings, putting on 226 runs in 186 minutes for that first wicket (I hit 166) and laying the foundation for victory. We went to Newlands for the final against Western Province and, strangely, their captain Peter Kirsten put us in to bat on a pitch where traditionally whoever won the toss almost invariably took first knock. What an error that was, for, at the end of our compulsory 100 overs, we had 425 on the board, with only 7 wickets down. Bowling unchanged into the south-easter from the Kelvin Grove end, Alan Kourie was in one of his best baffling moods in their second innings, taking 6 for 57. And so the trophy remained with Transvaal for yet another year.

Although we obviously had a talented combination, people used to wonder how we managed to win so consistently. The simple answer was that we were determined to play positively – such as the time earlier in the season when we were in trouble against Northern Transvaal. Not even for once being prepared to settle for a draw, we had a first innings lead of only 55 runs and lost 4 for 60 in our second knock. Seven were down for 102 and, not surprisingly, the Pretoria boys sensed that the game was swinging their way. But Sylvester Clarke, batting at number eight, had other ideas. In he strode to join me. The first ball he faced he swung furiously, got a top edge, and it soared over the heads of the slips for four.

I went up to him and said, 'Clarky, what are you doing? You cannot play like that. Do you intend continuing like this?'

'Yes,' he said curtly. 'I'm going to have a full go.' And he proceeded to enjoy himself.

The gods smiled on his courage, and we put on 120 between us in 22 overs, Clarke hitting a superb unbeaten 78. The game was eventually drawn, but what a grand performance by that likeable West Indian.

Because of his accent it took us a little time to understand what he was saying, but Sylvester was always clear in his mind what he wanted, particularly when it came to field placing for his bowling. Typical of a player of his calibre who had been around for a long time, he would tell Clive Rice how many slips he wanted, whether he needed a short-leg or leg-gully, and so on. He knew exactly what he was going to do with the ball and was quick at probing and discovering a batsman's strengths and weaknesses. With his fearsome pace and movement, Sylvester had a particularly good run in the Nissan Shield that first season – which we won – bowling 32 overs, taking 12 for 47, a wicket every 4 runs. No wonder he was named the player of the series.

The 1984/85 season was without doubt our best. Again, we garnered all the trophies on offer but, more importantly, we played consistently good cricket in all 23 matches, winning 22 and drawing 1. This last match, a Currie Cup fixture, was at Port Elizabeth. We set Eastern Province a challenge of 317 to win, and they were 109 for 8 when we ran out of time. During this back-to-the-wall struggle, with only a few overs to go, Eastern's batsman Philip Amm was caught at silly point by Kevin McKenzie off Alan Kourie, but the umpire ruled that he was not out. We, and particularly Alan, did not dare query the ruling because an incident in a match earlier in the season at Newlands was still very much in our minds.

This was the game in which Ray Jennings and Alan Kourie were fined for ungentlemanly conduct by the Transvaal Board. In an interesting match, Western Province were set a target of 271 to win, and at tea they were 4 down for only 97. Our tails were up, with Peter Kirsten and Adrian Kuiper the only two recognised batsmen really standing between us and victory. Two very inexperienced umpires were standing in this game, 73 neither having previously officiated in a Currie Cup fixture, and six or seven bad decisions went against us. As we were the top two sides in the country at the time, in retrospect I believe it was unfortunate that these two officials were allocated what was obviously going to be a tense affair. And I believe it was this inexperience rather than favouritism which led to the unfortunate incident.

In the first over after tea, Clive Rice got a straightforward catch from Kuiper in the gully and, so unusual for him, dropped it. This 'life' seemed to inspire the two extremely able batsmen and they climbed into our attack, running up 116 runs in only 81 minutes for the fifth wicket. The game swung Western Province's way. Going into the compulsory last 20 overs they needed only about 60 to win. Wickets tumbled, and with 7 overs left, they had 4 wickets in hand and 25 runs were now required.

With Peter Kirsten still there, Alan Kourie, who had been bowling over the wicket into the rough patches outside the leg stump at the other end, pitched a delivery into this rough patch. Peter got a top edge and the ball spiralled high in the air over Ray Jennings' head towards slip. Jennings turned, dived, and brought off a remarkable one-handed catch.

The atmosphere was electric. The outcome of the match depended on Peter. Alan was delighted with what he was certain was another scalp. But Peter stood his ground and umpire Bernie Glass ruled him not out. Ray, who was still sorting himself out after his incredible effort, missed the umpire's ruling and rushed down the wicket to congratulate his colleague. When he realised what the decision was, he joined a furious Alan in expressing his displeasure. Alan said bluntly that the umpire was a cheat. The fact that Bernie Glass was a Cape Town man did not help. Ray swore and shouted, the rest of us joined in the shouting, and the uproar was such that the game was held up for several minutes.

It was the last delivery of the over and Alan went to collect his hat. But Mr Glass held on to it and said, 'Say please.'

Alan reached for his hat again. 'Give me that . . . hat,' he said, and grabbing it he stormed off.

When he returned for his next over, Alan handed his hat to Clive Rice. The umpire asked for the hat, whereupon Alan replied: 'No, you cannot see what's happening down the other end. I don't want you to hold my hat.'

The situation was at breaking point but, typically, Clive Rice handled it well. The umpire went to Clive and asked him to calm his bowler down so that the game could continue. Clive replied: 'I'll tell him to calm down, but I want you to calm down as well because you are obviously upset at Alan's action. There are a couple of vital overs to go.'

Peter Kirsten was so upset by it all that he lost his wicket in the next over and Transvaal won the game by 15 runs with 20 balls to spare. But our victory was soured. Both Alan and Ray were each fined one thousand rands.

Our long-serving Transvaal manager Ronnie Eriksen, one of the most experienced and respected officials in the game in those years, wrote later in his book *A View from the Dressing Room*:

> While I am in complete agreement with the action taken by the Transvaal Board in condemning their [Kourie and Jennings] unsporting behaviour, which under no circumstances can be tolerated, I was present and I was conscious of the problem and of the tension that had resulted from a succession of doubtful decisions, and I felt obliged to voice in their defence my understanding of the reason behind their spontaneous outburst.
>
> It was the only occasion in all my years with the Transvaal XI that the integrity of an umpire had been challenged, so the feeling of injustice must have been intense, which would explain the players' reaction, not condone it.

Sylvester Clarke had another great season, taking 58 Currie Cup wickets, only Mike Procter topping him by one for most wickets taken in a season in this competition. Alan Kourie also had a good run, claiming 50 victims, while the very promising seamer Hugh Page, who was to win his Springbok colours, took 41 wickets.

We played Northern Transvaal in the Currie Cup final on a specially prepared greentop at Berea Park, scored only 232 in the first innings, yet won by an innings. Sylvester Clarke was unplayable, sending five men back to the pavilion at the cost of only 8 runs, and Northerns were dismissed for a humiliating 61, their lowest total ever recorded against their neighbours.

My own game was satisfactory enough. Henry Fotheringham and I had several good opening stands, and I registered two centuries and several scores of 50 or more. Western Province won the Currie Cup the following season, but even today I am sure they must blush when recalling their poor sportsmanship and tactics against us in the final. Batting first, they scored 368-6 and then proceeded to bowl to us at the ridiculous rate of 12,29 overs an hour. A bowler would deliver, stroll out to mid-wicket or the covers for a chat with a colleague, and then take his time getting back to his mark for the next delivery. We were so incensed that at one stage we began sitting down on the pitch between deliveries. Clive rightly protested to the umpires, to captain Adrian Kuiper and manager Robin Jackman. We were so frustrated that we lost our rhythm, were bowled out for 212 and were asked to follow-on. I scored 102 and Alan Kourie weighed in with 82, and we ended with a more respectable total of 298. Province were left to score 143 in 112 minutes, plus the compulsory 20 overs. They collapsed like the proverbial house of cards against some hostile bowling, and going into the last hour they were 49 for 8. We could smell victory, but Richie Ryall joined his captain Adrian Kuiper, and to their credit they held out for a draw, and won the Currie Cup.

The era of the great Transvaal 'Mean Machine' ended in March 1987, with the retirement of Graeme Pollock and Alan Kourie, and Henry Fotheringham's return to Durban. I think I played my best cricket in South Africa in those years, not only accumulating runs regularly and freely, but also getting them in a manner which I like to think matched the high playing standard I had set myself. I got my highest score in South Africa (201 against Eastern Province), and in successive seasons I scored over 1 000 first-class runs against provincial and touring sides. In a ten-year stretch from 1978 I scored a total of 6 650 runs by way of 17 hundreds and 34 half-centuries.

The reason for my consistent technical correction was possibly the fact that, in our strenuous thrice-weekly training sessions, I was always facing outstanding bowlers . . . Sylvester Clarke, Vince van der Bijl, Clive Rice, Rupert Hanley, Neal Radford, Hugh Page, Alan Kourie, among others. We gave each other no quarter and had to be on top of our form to survive.

During this golden era I remember in particular our two Datsun Shield semi-final games against Eastern Province in the 1982/83 season. At the Wanderers we scored 332 for 5, Kallicharran hitting yet another marvellous century, and they scored 208. With Eastern Province needing well over a hundred to win in the last over, victory was a formality. Clive Rice asked me if I fancied my chances with the ball. Laughingly, I said it looked pretty safe. He tossed me the ball, and no one was more surprised than I when I promptly bowled David Brickett. Overall, in a first-class career spanning two decades, I have now taken a grand total of three wickets, which perhaps does not warrant my inclusion among the ranks of the game's great allrounders.

In Port Elizabeth for the second leg, the home side scored 290 for 5, with Wayne Larkins, the English international then playing for Eastern Province, scoring a century. So confident of victory were the home spectators after this impressive performance that several told me, as I fielded on the boundary, that they were off to get their tickets for the deciding leg the next day. How they underestimated us. We went out to do battle, and 49 overs later it was all over – Transvaal 291 for 2. Graeme Pollock and I each scored a hundred, adding 215 for the third wicket.

We went on to beat Western Province in the final. We cleaned up the Currie Cup too, winning six out of eight games. Such was the power and quality of the 'Mean Machine'.

7

SOMERSET, 1989

A feature of British cricket since World War Two has been the growing number of players from Commonwealth or former Commonwealth countries who have joined county sides to gain valuable experience and, of course, in many cases to earn a handsome living. Players from Australia, New Zealand, the West Indies, India and Pakistan are now very much part of the scene and have enriched the game immensely. During the apartheid era numerous gifted and ambitious players from South Africa were determined to circumvent political barriers and compete with and against the best sides of the time. One thinks of Tony Greig in particular, the gangling blond from Queenstown who not only did well for Sussex but also went on to captain England with success. Such are the apparently loose qualification requirements that this situation seemed to be perfectly acceptable to the game's controlling authorities. After Greig came Allan Lamb from Cape Town, who became England's vice-captain under Graham Gooch, and the two brothers from Durban, Chris and Robin Smith, also won English caps. There were others – Clive Rice, Allan Donald, Corrie van Zyl, Ken McEwan, Roy Pienaar, Kepler Wessels, Peter Kirsten, Omar Henry, Barry Richards, Eddie Barlow, Mike Procter, Rodney Ontong, Garth le Roux, and Brian McMillan are but some who come to mind – who have enjoyed variable seasons with the counties.

As my own playing career progressed I, too, was interested in playing there but perhaps not ardently enough to make any concerted effort. During the home winter I played professional soccer for the University of the Witwatersrand, and when I became a schoolteacher and then got married, domestic responsibilities rather put the matter to the back of my mind. But still . . .

Then, as is so often the case, the opportunity came. I had toured England in 1988 as coach to a South African schools side known as the Albatross XI, and during that tour I happened to mention to Sussex captain Paul Parker that I would like to get some county experience. There was no opening with his club at that time, but if one for a batsman did occur he said that he would put my name forward. I returned home and thought little more of it. Whilst away on a school trip to the Eastern Transvaal, my wife Linsey took a phone call from England, noted the message and gave it to me on my return. It was someone called Brian from Somerset. I said it must have been Paul from Sussex. She was emphatic about the name and county, although I said that no one from Somerset knew me.

That same day the mysterious Brian phoned, and it was Brian Rose, the former England and county batsman and now on the Somerset committee. He said the club was aware of my record and would like to sign me 81 for the 1989 season. A contract covering salary, housing and travel arrangements seemed attractive and was tentatively agreed to, but I asked for and was given a week in which to make a final decision.

I immediately phoned Clive Rice, whose judgement in business matters I respect, particularly in this case after his years with Nottinghamshire. After hearing the details, he advised me to phone Brian at once and accept the offer as he felt I could not play for a better county nor be offered a more generous contract.

Linsey was enthusiastic, as were my sons Stephen and Ryan, even though they were perhaps too young really to understand what was going on. Then there was the question of my career. I was teaching mathematics, geography, Afrikaans and physical education at Fairways Primary School in Johannesburg. I had had a long association of 17 years with the school, having coached sport there before I became a teacher. Headmaster Ronnie de Klerk was agreeable to my being away from April to September, but the Transvaal Education Department ruled against it, saying that like anyone else I was only entitled to 47 days' leave. If I resigned and then signed on again after the season in England, I would lose my post as head of department, which would mean a big drop in salary. I was in something of a dilemma – which was my priority: my teaching or my cricket career?

My cricket hopes looked bleak, but good fortune saved the day. After 19 years with the Pirates Club, I had only just left to play league cricket for the Rand Afrikaans University Club side. Hearing of my problem, the Rector of the University, Professor Cas Crouse, tried to persuade the education authorities to allow me the extra leave. He was unsuccessful, but he offered me a post with the RAU sports department with the freedom to play abroad during the home winter. I accepted. It was a wrench leaving Fairways School after so many happy and satisfying years, but on balance I felt I had to take advantage of the generous offer made by the university. So I saw out my resignation term and flew to England on 13 April 1989 to report to Somerset, with Linsey and the boys to join me at the end of May.

Peter Anderson, the new chief executive of Somerset who was to become a good friend during the next three years, met me at the airport and we drove straight to Taunton and the county ground where I met my new colleagues, who were hard at it going through their pre-season training. I knew only Jon Hardy, who coached and played in the Western Province in the English winter, but was soon put at ease. Clive Rice was right. I could not have joined a better county side. From Peter Anderson at the

top through to the youngest member of the ground staff, there was a genuine warmth and enthusiasm. Somerset had done well in limited-over competitions, but had never won the county championship. This was despite the fact that over the years many great players had worn their colours. These had included such legendary batsmen as Harold Gimblett, Bill Alley, Viv Richards and Ian Botham. The famous pair, Richards and Botham, along with fast bowler Joel Garner, had left the club after much controversy two years before and Somerset was now anxious to rebuild and develop a squad which could become a real power.

Vic Marks, a shrewd off-spin bowler with numerous English caps, was a fine captain, with Chris Tavare, a fine high-order batsman and once an English regular (and like me another newcomer to the side), his deputy. When playing for Kent and England, Chris had had a reputation as a stodgy opener, but it was an unfair tag. Roy Pienaar, who had played with him at Kent, had already told me this and said he was a wonderful stroke-maker. I was to find out soon enough. In the first game he played for Somerset, a Sunday League game against Hampshire at Southampton, we were 19 for 3 at the 10th over of this 40-over game when Chris proceeded to clobber the bowling and scored an undefeated 120. He was also one of the finest slip fielders I have ever seen. Kent's loss was certainly our gain.

An interesting personality in the Somerset side was Peter Roebuck. A somewhat reserved man by nature, and a university graduate who had played for the second side when only 13, he was a most consistent opening batsman who was unlucky not to get the nod for his country. His writing skills had earned him a dual career as a columnist for *The Sunday Times*, Britain's leading quality newspaper. We did not perhaps achieve the best understanding that first year regarding running between the wickets, but overall he was a great help and I was guided by him when judging the pace of the new wickets I was facing.

We had a battery of young and determined seam bowlers, and we were to be managed by Jack Birkenshaw, a seasoned campaigner with several counties who was also making his début with the club.

After lunch that first day I opted to do some training but had no kit, so I borrowed some from Jon Hardy and went to work, doing some laps and then batting at the nets. Apart from Jon, none of the players had even heard of me, let alone seen me play, and they took a curious interest in this 35-year-old stranger who had travelled so far to make his county début. The local media were there in force, with TV and still cameras, all ready to record my action. But after the first couple of balls it began to rain, and then to hail. I was ready to pack up, but those cameramen wanted their pictures and so I had to carry on – never mind the hailstones beating down on me. However, after a few minutes, with Cook now dutifully recorded on camera, we gave up and dashed for the dressing-room.

The comfortable double-storey house the club had allocated to me for the season was in Galmington, only a five-minute drive from the picturesque ground, and I was most anxious to settle in and get to work. I must confess that I was surprised on my arrival that first morning to learn that the players trained all day; at home we thought we were hard done by having to put in two hours in the evening. I realised this was the world of genuine professional sport, not the half-and-half world I lived in back in South Africa. How would I shape? Could I adjust to the different pitches, the tough competition, the grind of continuous travel round the British Isles and, of course, the weather? I was soon to find out.

I made my début in a four-day county championship match against Hampshire at Southampton and took time to adapt to the slow wicket. But once I had settled down I began to enjoy myself and the runs began to flow quite nicely. Peter Roebuck was in fine form and the home bowlers realised their work would be cut out breaking our opening partnership. In fact we had 143 runs on the board before I edged a ball into the slips and went for 85. During this innings I reached the 10 000-run mark in first-class cricket.

By now I was really enjoying myself and should have got a century, which would have been a nice start to my English career. At least Peter went on to score 149 and we totalled 413, a most satisfactory beginning to the season. My countrymen, the brothers Chris and Robin Smith, were in the Hampshire side and Robin, who went on to become a regular England player, made 127 out of Hampshire's first innings total of 318. I scored an unbeaten 44 in our second innings, but rain interfered and the match was drawn.

Such is the confusion of the modern English fixtures system that on the Sunday of this Hampshire match we took a break from our county championship tussle to square up in a 40-over Refuge Assurance game. These limited-overs affairs are played everywhere these days as they are assured money-spinners, bringing in far more people than the three- and four-day games. I enjoy them, but they are no real substitute for the longer events, which are the real essence of the game.

England discard Chris Tavare joined us this day and thoroughly enjoyed himself on his début with his unbeaten 120. I only scored 2, but with our 220 we felt fairly confident of victory. However, to their credit, the home players got off to a flying start and, playing in rapidly fading light, they edged home with only 4 balls remaining. How wrong could I have been?

We drove up to Derby for a Benson and Hedges one-day fixture, and I was to have another experience of the frustrations induced by the English weather. I was phoned the next morning by a team-mate, who asked me whether I had looked outside. I had not. When I did I could not believe my eyes. The ground was covered by an inch of snow – and this was after continuous rain the previous day had ruined our Hampshire match. I wondered what I had let myself in for. Back home I used to take the sun so much for granted. In retrospect, I think that perhaps these spells of bad weather are a necessary evil for county professionals. They play so much cricket that the enforced rest periods enable the body to recuperate. However, this was at the beginning of the season and I was thirsting to play as much as I could. My immediate reaction on this snowy morning was that the game would be called off, but I was wrong. The unfazed ground staff went to work to clear the snow and by four that afternoon we were playing. It was freezing but, wearing long-johns and wrapped up like a Michelin Man in several jerseys, I went out to field. I managed 27 in our innings the following day and we won comfortably by 7 wickets.

One of the reasons I had gone to Britain was to get experience against the best bowlers in the world outside my own country, which would not be difficult as most of them were either on tour there each year or, like myself, playing for county sides. One, Michael Holding, was with Derbyshire. While some of my colleagues groaned at the prospect of facing this West Indian paceman, I relished the challenge. It came soon enough. He only took one wicket in this particular game, but I was mesmerised by his superb run-in. It was so rhythmic, so effortless, and the delivery at times so explosive. I also found him a most enjoyable person to talk to after the game.

After Derby it was back to Taunton for our first home fixture. The day before the match Jon Hardy and I went to inspect the wicket and we noticed what looked like a white dust on the surface. Jon had assured me beforehand that Taunton was normally a good batting strip, but this dust set us thinking. Our opponents, Glamorgan, went in first and struggled, particularly against Vic Marks whose off-spinners gained him 5 wickets for only 38 runs. Chasing their 118, we were on about 80 for one and near the close of play when a strange thing happened. Their opening bowler Steve Barwick, who had been bowling reasonable seamers, suddenly sent down a fast off-cutter which pitched a foot outside the off-stump and whizzed past my left shoulder. He was as puzzled as I was.

The next morning the seam attack was renewed without much effect, and then Steve sent down another off-cutter. Again it shot past my left shoulder, and immediately he realised this was the answer. Mixing 85 seamers with his off-cutters, he proceeded to eat through the side, finishing with 7 for 47. We still ended with a 68-run lead and, with none of our bowlers being able to exploit this peculiar state of the wicket, their batsmen helped themselves to 260 runs, leaving us needing 193 for victory in about 60 overs. This was a reasonable enough challenge, but again we found scoring difficult. I decided to lash out at anything on the leg side, and although we ended 41 runs short of our target and the match was drawn, I was pleased with the 79 that went with my first knock of 42.

There was an interesting story about this game which may or may not be apocryphal. Ted Dexter, the outstanding former English batsman and captain and now chairman of the selection committee, was a spectator and I am told that afterwards he phoned fellow selector Micky Stewart and said he liked the look of this new Somerset man, Cook, and that he should be seriously considered for the English squad for the forthcoming series against Australia. Stewart laughed and informed Dexter of my background. As I said, despite my years of playing first-class cricket in South Africa, I was an unknown factor to most Englishmen. I appreciated the compliment paid by Dexter and, although I had yet to score my first century, favourable comments were beginning to surface in the press.

I came close to that elusive maiden 'ton' with an innings of 91 off Sussex in a home game which we won by 5 wickets. Then, after an enjoyable drawn match with the touring Australians, it came at Taunton against Lancashire. The wicket could not have been more inviting and Chris Tavare and I proceeded to make the best possible use of it against a side that was weary after having just fielded for two consecutive days in their previous fixture. After both Peter Roebuck and Richard Bartlett each went for 20, Chris and I put on 276 for the third wicket, which was the best stand by any Somerset pair against that county. Chris was in wonderful form, slamming the ball all round the wicket, including 4 towering sixes, and easily outscoring me. I was still finding it difficult to score quickly and took the whole day for my 156.

Playing against the same team in another Refuge Assurance match the next day, my batting rhythm continued as I scored 123 off only 97 deliveries. I even smacked a couple of sixes, which is most unusual for me. Two centuries on successive days was, naturally, a most satisfying performance. I realised that I was now fully acclimatised and felt confident to tackle whatever challenge lay ahead. The only disappointment was that we lost the one-day game by 4 wickets and the county match by 6 wickets. We had totalled 244 to our opponents' 245 on the Sunday, and after our declared innings of 399-4 in the county match, they got 303 and 302 for 4 after we had closed our second knock at 203-4.

It was in the Sunday game that I faced another of those outstanding fast bowlers against whom I wanted to test myself. This time it was Pakistan's Wasim Akram, whom I rate one of the top five in the world today. Even though he was still nursing a slight injury – which was why he was not in the county championship match – he bowled superbly, moving his left-arm deliveries in quite viciously and then whipping another in the other direction. Taking runs off such a class performer was good reason to feel pleased with myself.

Apart from the fact that I had now had several games to reach top form, another important factor at this stage was my improvement against spin bowling. Throughout my career I had faced seam bowling with equanimity but was never entirely happy against the slow men, never being able to take them apart as Graeme Pollock, Adrian Kuiper and Clive Rice did. Soon after I arrived at Somerset I confided this to Jack Birkenshaw and, typical of the man who tackled his job with such enthusiasm, he got to work on me in the nets. He would bowl his off-spinners and second team coach Peter Robinson his left-arm stuff for long sessions. They would get me to use my feet and come down the wicket, sweep or smack the ball high into the top of the netting as if going for a hit over the bowler's head. This extra work did wonders for my confidence in playing spin bowling.

I was now settling into the life of a county professional. We criss-crossed England so much that after a while there was not much of the country I had not seen. Towards the end of the season I did find it somewhat tiring, but in those initial weeks and months it was all so new and exciting. The usual mode of travel was by car, two or three to a car and driving our vehicles in turn. I was with a happy and ambitious team, we stayed at good hotels, the club paid all but personal expenses, I found the people hospitable and enthusiastic, and it was a pretty good life overall. Of course playing well, as I was now, made life even more enjoyable. Were I not making the grade it might have been a different story.

After my most enjoyable game against Lancashire it was straight across country to Chelmsford to tackle Essex, and my good form followed me with an undefeated 147, although the match fizzled out to a draw. My opening partner Peter Roebuck was kind enough to give readers of *The Sunday Times* the following early impressions of me:

Unhurried and untroubled, Jimmy Cook is an old-fashioned cricketer, one who can be pictured arriving in a pony and trap. Not for him the bellicose backlift or the booming drive. Some men bat as if they were melting baseballs. Cook bats as if he were slicing the top off   87 an egg. At the crease he is peaceful, durable and solid, gentle with bat and ball, certain of his own mind. Bad balls are hit to the boundary, good ones are blocked. He is a simple fellow. Cook is a humble man. But he is also as confident as he is hungry. He is consistent with his technique forged in fire and with a will to succeed. Lacking Viv Richards' menace and Martin Crowe's surgical skills, avoiding their charisma, he has scored as heavily as either.

Commenting specifically on my centuries against Lancashire, he went on:

> [They] proved that Cook has a range which includes dominance and obduracy. In neither did he appear to concentrate unduly hard, for, like Hutton and Boycott, concentration comes naturally to him.

He said, quite rightly, that I was surprised when Somerset had approached me to play for them 'because he thought no one in England had heard of him'. But, 'by September everyone will know about Cook'. This was typical of Peter. His deep love of the game and appreciation of anyone who plays it well overrides any possible natural temptation to show the slightest hint of jealousy towards others' successes. To Peter the game was, and is, the thing. It would be unnatural for me not to feel pleased with what he wrote.

My captain Vic Marks also found nice things to say about me in *The Observer*:

> Statistics will record Jimmy's tremendous batting achievements, but there is far more to tell. Off the field, he offers a great example to our less-experienced players which will benefit the county for years to come. We knew of Jimmy's great record before he arrived, but we could not be certain that he would fit in and prove popular in the dressing room. There are no problems on that score. His genial personality belies an intensely determined approach to cricket and there is no one more disciplined in terms of practice and playing with a straight bat.

I only hoped I could justify the high expectations that were now building around me.

After a half-century against Glamorgan and a lowly 34 against Yorkshire in two drawn matches, we found ourselves in the lovely city of Bath for the traditional festival week and our matches with Kent and Gloucestershire. I had visited Bath the year before with the South African schools team and we had seen this large and attractive park. But never for a moment did I think that it would be the venue for our county match. During the winter the famous Bath rugby club uses it as their home ground, but for this festival week it is turned into a superb and colourful cricket arena. Stands are transported from Taunton, marquees and numerous small tents erected, and overnight the atmosphere is set as only the English can do it for an event which has so much tradition and which means so much to them.

Naturally we wanted to do well before our loyal Somerset supporters, but our first opponents, Kent, showed no mercy when they won the toss and batted first. They amassed 459 runs for the loss of only 3 wickets on that first day, with centuries by Benson and Ward, and my Transvaal colleague Roy Pienaar hammering a sweet 87. They declared at 526 for 7, and we replied with 274 for 5 declared. In order to obtain a result on as fine a batting strip as one could hope for, Kent scored 108 without loss in their second innings before closing, setting us the difficult task of finding 361 runs in 63 overs. We had a go, with Peter Roebuck hitting 107 and myself 72, but as wickets tumbled and we fell behind the run-rate, hopes of victory evaporated. We ended with 276 for 6 in this drawn and most enjoyable game.

Then came Gloucestershire and, as we were playing on a strip adjoining that on which the Kent match had been played, we naturally expected, when we went in to bat first, that we would find an equally co-operative wicket. Some hope!

Clearly nobody could have told Courtney Walsh that this was meant to be a batsman's wicket for he proceeded to steamroller his way through us, taking 7 for 19 as we staggered to a miserable 73. This was the county's lowest total in seven years. Courtney was simply unplayable. One delivery would fly at a frightful pace past one's shoulder, and then another would snake in low and almost york one. This was intelligent pace bowling of the very highest quality, and while our home supporters must have been dumbfounded at what they saw, they also appreciated the quality of Walsh and roundly applauded him when he wrapped us up soon after lunch. Gloucestershire showed that the wicket was not to blame, as they rattled up 402 for 4 declared, with Bill Athey and Kevin Curran getting centuries.

Well, we had to do something to save face and we did this by scoring 364 in our second knock. I scored 147, which in itself was of course gratifying enough. But what particularly pleased me was that those runs were won on a wicket which turned a great deal and which the visiting slow specialists David Graveney and especially Jeremy Lloyds (7-134) 89 exploited to the full. My hard work at the nets to improve my technique against spin had paid dividends. This was my third first-class century and my initial target of 1 000 runs had been achieved. Despite our fight back, Gloucestershire only needed to score 36 to win, which they did for the loss of 2 wickets.

One thing that this match highlighted was the fact that you will always see good cricket on good pitches. On this wicket at Bath, even though it favoured the batsmen, a good fast bowler was rewarded and the spinners came into their own on day three. Altogether, a well-prepared pitch. No side likes losing, but our defeat was, for me at any rate, partly compensated for by the enjoyment I got out of that festival week. When we were not playing, the wonderful people of the city entertained us royally. Every evening they laid on something for us to do or see. There was a jazz night (when yours truly was not allowed to sing), a skittles evening when the locals took on the team, a trip up the Avon on a river boat, then an evening watching horse-racing films when everyone had a bet on their fancy.

And all the time, of course, we were meeting the people, sharing their company over meals and sundowners, and for me, a visitor from South Africa, it was a really good opportunity to get to know the folk of this lovely island nation. I am proud to be a citizen of South Africa, but I am equally proud to know my forebears came from England. In all of my three seasons with Somerset I cannot recall a single occasion when I did not encounter genuine friendliness. Even when I was going through the inevitable bleak patches with my batting I was encouraged with the comment 'Don't worry, it will come right'.

Linsey and the boys joined me at the beginning of June. They settled in quickly and were immediately welcomed into the Somerset county 'family'. Wives were always included in social functions, and Linsey made a number of firm friends. There is no doubt that the homely environment in which we found ourselves contributed a great deal to my successes. Never having to worry about the family's well-being enabled me to concentrate on my work on the field of play. Had there been problems, my whole game would undoubtedly have suffered somewhere along the line.

I have mentioned the cordial atmosphere and fine team spirit in the Somerset club. I should add that, albeit as an outsider, I saw the same cordiality in the other county sides. I have always made a habit of calling in at the opposing team's dressing-room after a day's play to socialise, discuss the match, the game generally, and whatever else might crop up. I found this sort of fraternising often clears up misunderstandings and grievances that might have occurred on the field and it was best to sort them out before we went our respective ways. I continued this practice in England and in that way I made a host of good friends and swapped ideas with great players from all over the world.

People ask how I found the playing standard compared with South Africa. Generally, I found it as high, if not higher in some cases. Perhaps in South Africa we have a greater bowling depth. Our provincial teams usually have at least five good bowlers, whereas the county teams more often than not comprise, say, three good bowlers and two or three others who are average. Otherwise the quality of play is very high, very professional. And it is not easy to maintain a high standard when playing seven days a week for five months at a time. Frankly, this is too much cricket. On average one plays 24 three- or four-day games, and two one-day competitions, as well as the Sunday League. I know the vast majority of players would like just one day off a week, as in the old days. It would give them time to rest up and get a second wind for the next six days of hectic activity. I appreciate that these one-day events are great money-spinners for the clubs, but must money be the overriding factor all the time? Could not some other method be devised to give the poor chap in the field a breather? County clubs are, as far as I can ascertain, well run and all the officials I got to know were fine men who have an abiding love for the game. But one cannot help thinking that financial considerations are given too high a priority. Of course, this criticism can also be applied to other sports in Britain, particularly soccer. But my concern and interest in this case is cricket and I would very much like to see the day when life is made a little more tolerable for my old county chums. I am told that in the days before one-day competitions were introduced there was a tendency among some players to let their fielding standards slip a little during a county three-day game. If that was the case before, it certainly does not apply today. The one-day game has changed all that. Fielding has to be of the highest calibre all the time. It is concentrated, pressure cricket and heaven help the man who fails to give of his very best. As a result, fielding standards are usually very good.

I am not a temperamental person, and I have also made a habit of not reacting badly in the dressing-room if given a bad umpiring decision, or if I was the victim of or in the centre of some other possibly unfair incident. During that first season in England I found it somewhat disturbing at first when a colleague having a rough time occasionally stormed into the change-room, threw a bat or pads across the room, and stamped around swearing and sounding off with some ripe language. Even some normally even-tempered men would act this way. I could not understand why.

Then the penny dropped. County players are professionals. Their livelihoods depend on performance, and whereas the stars, the established internationals, can afford to let off steam knowing their incomes are safe, the vast majority of players do not earn very much and a bad trot of batting or bowling could lead to a reduced contract – or not receiving one at all – come the end of the season. A batsman might have a target of 1 000 runs for the season, or a bowler 60 wickets. If he failed to meet that target his future could be bleak. So it is understandable that nerves can get frayed in the heat of the moment. True, I was also being paid and was on a contract. But if I did not come up to expectations at the end of the season and my contract was not renewed, I always had my job at the Rand Afrikaans University to fall back on. I had no income worries. And of course that applies generally in South Africa. Have a poor game for your province and you might be dropped or relegated to a lower team, but your pocket does not suffer. The vast majority of provincial players are paid, but they also have outside careers.

At the beginning of July we drove up to Derby again, this time for a county match, with the weather decidedly warmer than our snowy April cup encounter. Once again I came up against the awesome bowling of Michael Holding, and it was during our second innings when we were set a target of 301 for victory (which we did not achieve and had to settle for a draw) that we had a glorious tussle. He was in superlative form and finally got me, but I thoroughly enjoyed my contest with him. Afterwards umpire Chris Balderstone paid us the supreme compliment of saying it was the most enjoyable hour he had watched in cricket.

This was the start of a truly purple batting patch for me, a series of innings which one can only dream about. From Derby we went to the lovely little ground at Guildford to play Surrey, where I only had one innings but scored 105 even if it did take five hours on one of the slowest wickets we came across that season. This game was also drawn, but on we went to the famous Trent Bridge ground at Nottingham for what was to be for me one of the highlights.

We were led to expect that the wicket would be a greentop. It was not. In fact, as far as I was concerned it was a perfect strip. Naturally I can afford to say this for, out of our first innings total of 186, I carried my bat with 120. This was the first time I had done so – a small personal milestone. The Notts batsmen revelled on this wicket they knew so well against a Somerset attack which, to be honest, was below par. Robinson (128) and Pollard (91) headed a 471-7 declared run-spree, giving them a 285-run lead. We began our second innings towards the end of the second day's play and Peter Roebuck and I comfortably saw out time. As coincidence would have it, Clive Rice was in England on business and came to see me that evening. He told me that the last time he had played for Nottinghamshire against Somerset he had scored a century in each innings. Whether or not this inspired me I do not know, but the next day I went out and played an innings which the Somerset club yearbook described as 'one of the great ones'. Everything came together as if by design. I saw the ball with perfect clarity, my co-ordination could not have been better, my concentration was one hundred per cent, and my overall application as good as it had ever been. Result: I carried my bat yet again, this time for 131 out of a total of 218. Nottinghamshire had a couple of good spinners and the wicket was turning appreciably in that second innings. Clive Rice acknowledged that my batting against spin had improved considerably.

About half an hour after the match I received a call in the dressing-room from a journalist who informed me that no one in England had carried his bat with centuries in both innings since Cecil Wood of Leicestershire against Yorkshire at Bradford in 1911. We lost the match by an innings and 67 runs, but at least my conscience was clear. Of a total Somerset aggregate of 404, my contribution was 251 runs. This was 64,5 per cent and 60,1 per cent of the respective Somerset totals. Only Tom Graveney, that glorious shot-maker for England, Gloucestershire and Worcestershire, is believed to have scored 60 per cent of the total in each innings – 100 out of 153 and 67 out of 105 against Essex in 1956.

The bowling was not weak, especially as their attack included another of that long line of excellent West Indian fast bowlers in Franklyn Stephenson. In retrospect, I think that first century of 120 was technically the best I played in England that summer. Yet I should have been run out before scoring. I hit a ball to mid-on, called for a run, set off and was sent back. Derek Randall, the former England batsman, scooped up the ball and threw it at my end. I was still a metre or two away from the crease, but fortunately the ball missed the stumps. With the gods on my side, I went to work with zeal, giving no chances and, as far as I can recall, not playing at and missing a single delivery.

Graeme Pollock will always be remembered for the 125 he scored at Trent Bridge against England in 1965. Whether my performance that week will be remembered by anyone else only time will tell, but I certainly will not forget it. As we know so well in sport, form, that elusive, baffling mistress, rarely remains with us too long, and I was anxious to cash in while she smiled in my direction.

Down we drove to Taunton once more, this time to take on Leicester-   93 shire, and the cricketing media were full of my exploits. The obvious question was: 'Will he score another hundred?' Carrying on where I had left off the previous day, I slammed 148 by way of 21 fours before being caught, and it was recorded that this was the first time a bowler had beaten me after 14½ hours at the crease. I was the first Somerset batsman to score four consecutive centuries.

I was as delighted as the rest of the team when we won this match convincingly by an innings and 47 runs, and I feel it appropriate to record what local cricket scribe Neil Robinson wrote about me in the *Somerset County Gazette* after this fourth century:

> Munch! Bill Alley takes another bite out of the humble pie he's been eating since suggesting on these pages that Jimmy Cook probably wouldn't succeed at Somerset this season. As one of life's more unfortunate predictions, it's up there with Chamberlain's 'peace in our time' and Palmerston's 'don't worry, I'm not going to die yet' uttered seconds before pegging out.
>
> Not that being wrong worries Alley who's getting ready to wash away the taste with a few jars of the rough stuff at the end of the summer if the phenomenal Cook beats his 1961 Somerset record of 2,761 runs.
>
> Says Alley: 'If he does it I'll phone him up and invite him out for the biggest bloody drink he's ever had. I must admit I always look to see how many runs he's scored. I've got people coming to me and saying, "he's got another century, Bill, he's getting closer". I wouldn't say I was worried, but if you see him you can tell him I'm drinking more now than I've ever done in the past.'
>
> A quick check on the records shows why. In first-class innings this season Cook has amassed a little matter of 1,854 runs – 800 more than Somerset's next highest scorer, Peter Roebuck. He now has a maximum of 17 innings left in which to score the 908 runs needed to beat Alley's record. It's worth noting that he totalled 990 off his first 17 knocks this season.
>
> If he continues at his current rate – four centuries in his last four championship innings – he will not only reach the 2,000 mark roughly three weeks before Graeme Hick managed last year, but also put himself in striking range of that cricketing Everest: 3,000 first-class runs in a season.
>
> Perhaps this analogy is not quite correct. Everest has long since been conquered, yet no player in the modern game has got beyond the second base camp in the quest for 3,000. Hick scored 2,713 last

year, Gooch 2,559 in 1984 and Boycott 2,503 in 1971, but the 3,000 peak has always seemed unassailable since the County Championship was reduced in size in 1969.

Indeed, Alley – the last man to score 3,000 runs (2,761 for Somerset) in 1961 – took 64 innings to get there. If Cook completes the 17 more innings available to him, he will finish on 43.

Put that way, it's not just a case of scaling Everest, but of sprinting up the North face to get there. The odds – and possibly the weather – are against him, but that won't stop him trying. Along the way he will reach such minor staging posts as the Somerset record for the most Sunday League runs in a season – he needs 71 more to go past Viv Richards' 578 in 1975 – and the record for most championship centuries in a season. Four more will overhaul Alley's 10 in 1961.

Yet to Cook himself, records seem unimportant. Each time he passes a new milestone he smiles politely and mutters the odd pleasantry and just sets off down the road to the next one. No-one took him particularly seriously when, back in May, with 376 runs in his first six innings, he said he wasn't playing very well. The astonishing thing is that he was right.

At 35 he has matured into the county scene with the passing of each innings, adapting to one, three and four-day cricket with almost disdainful ease. There was clearly a vulnerability at first to spin, but practice has made him, if not perfect, certainly better equipped to deal with the turning balls.

Alley rightly pointed out that Cook often gets out LBW, which suggests a tendency to play across his legs. In another more typically English summer, with drizzly days and wet wickets, such a technique could prove costly. If Cook – and the rain – return next year it will be interesting to see how he fares.

Back to the championship programme, where our match immediately after trouncing Leicestershire was at Hove against Sussex. During lunch on the first day I was walking along the balcony between the dining-room and the players' pavilion when an elderly gentleman stopped me and asked me to autograph his book. He purposely turned to a page with only one other signature on it and asked me to sign under the name. When I questioned him as to why I must sign on that particular page, he replied that it was because the other signature was that of the famous Cecil Wood, who was the last batsman to have carried his bat in both innings of a match and scored two centuries. What a remarkable thing, I thought, 95 but in fact this was typical of the British people and the way they do things. We spent quite a while chatting before duty called.

As for the game: Sussex batted first, and when it was our turn to bat in the last half hour on that first day my century run ended when I was caught at leg-gully for 6. But I managed a second innings of 130, making it five centuries in six innings and only 10 short of 2 000 runs for the season thus far. This target was passed in the next match with scores of 25 and 50 off Middlesex, and they said I was one of the fastest 2 000-run men on record.

Now, as Neil Robinson's article indicated, everyone was asking if I could keep it up and top the incredible aggregate achieved by that remarkable Australian Bill Alley back in the 1960s. It was not to be. Truth was that by the end of July the physical strain of it all suddenly began to tell. I was exhausted from playing hard, competitive cricket virtually seven days a week and from the constant travelling. As an opening batsman, and particularly when scoring runs, one is involved in play for long stretches, either at the crease or fielding. In addition, I had followed my usual habit of working hard and assisting at net practices, not forgetting the times at the end of the day playing for some time with my sons Stephen and Ryan. My body screamed 'enough', and I was finding it harder to concentrate, which I suppose was understandable, as on 31 July my 36th birthday arrived. The necessity of pacing oneself had been overlooked. This tailing off in physical and mental condition is reflected in our remaining county matches where, after that century against Sussex, only a total of 251 runs accrued in 13 innings.

But I had no reason to feel downhearted. On the contrary, while it would have been great to finish my first year on a higher note, my overall performance was far better than any expectations I had had when I flew into London airport that grey day back in April. If someone had suggested then that I might score more runs than anyone else in conditions which were completely new to me I would have laughed.

My figures for the 1989 season were: 23 matches, 41 innings, 4 not outs, highest score 156, run aggregate 2 241, hundreds: eight, half-centuries: eight, for an average of 60,57. On 19 September D J Rutnagur summed up the season in the *Daily Telegraph* thus:

> In a dry summer of exceptional warmth, only ten batsmen from outside the Australian touring team averaged above 50, with Jimmy Cook, Somerset's South African signing, at the head of the class with 60.57. As the only batsman to pass the 2,000 mark, Cook, playing his first season in England, also topped the aggregates – by as much as

664 runs – and the list of century-makers. His consistency was remarkable in view of his 36 years and the fact that, as an opening batsman, he always faced the new ball.

Statistics, as often said, spout the most outrageous falsehoods, and while they are not the soundest basis for theories, they do substantiate them and also support the eye's evidence.

There has been some significance in three of the top four batting places being occupied by men who learnt the fundamentals of their craft in southern Africa: Cook, Graeme Hick and Robin Smith. Two other batsmen in the top ten share their antecedence, Roy Pienaar and Allan Lamb, whose season was truncated by injury.

The writer might also have noted that the bowler who topped the county averages that season was Bloemfontein's Allan Donald. Wearing the colours of Warwickshire, he took 86 wickets for an average of 16,26. I am happy to say that Allan's good season was not to be a flash in the pan. As his bowling matured in the following seasons he rightly earned himself the reputation of one of the best genuinely fast bowlers in the world.

My only regret was that Somerset did not finish as well as we had hoped. We had a happy, experienced combination, enjoyed ourselves immensely, but could only finish 14th in the county championship, which was three places lower than the previous year. We only managed to win 4 out of 22 matches, drew 12, and lost 6.

Somerset did slightly better in the one-day Refuge Assurance League, finishing 10th, where my contribution was three centuries for 556 runs in 16 innings at an average of 37. We bowed out of the NatWest Trophy competition in the second round to Northamptonshire, but we did reach the semi-finals of the Benson and Hedges tournament before losing to Essex in a really pulsating game at Taunton.

On reaching the 2 000-run mark in the first-class averages, in addition to the generous treatment I received from the media, many people took the trouble to seek me out and shake my hand. I also received many letters, telegrams and phone calls from people in Britain and South Africa. I was flattered – but you cannot satisfy everyone! A letter dated 4 August came from Johannesburg:

> The staff of the Transvaal Cricket Council wish to congratulate you on your tremendous achievement in the English county cricket season, and should you not reach 3 000 runs . . . take an extended vacation to China!

Then Henry Fotheringham sent the following telegram: 'Congratulations partner on all your achievements. Delighted for you. Not bad for someone who can't play spin.'

The inner warmth which success engenders and statistics apart, I was particularly pleased to have justified Somerset chief executive Peter Anderson's faith in signing this unknown 35-year-old. Also, despite tiring in those final weeks, I did fulfil my promise to Peter that, if fit, I would want to play in every match – county, cup or friendly. Bowler Adrian Jones was the only other member of our squad to have a one hundred per cent appearance record for the season.

8

SOMERSET, 1990

During our festival week at Weston-super-Mare in August 1989 our chief executive Peter Anderson came to me and said that as I had made such an auspicious début for Somerset, he wondered whether I would be prepared to return for another season since Steve Waugh, whom I had replaced, wanted to have a break from cricket.

I felt honoured, but said there were two main considerations to be taken into account: my moving between two countries each year should not in any way affect my elder boy Stephen's education, and I had to have the blessing of my new employers in Johannesburg, Rand Afrikaans University. Fortunately Stephen's school reports were good – both Linsey and I were teachers and were always on hand to help out with his studies – and the RAU authorities were only too pleased to give me six months' unpaid leave, as my being in the public eye was seen as good publicity for them. In October I notified Peter of my willingness to return and a new contract was drawn up and agreed to – a far more financially beneficial one than that for the first year when I was virtually an unknown factor.

After a reasonable 1989/90 season at home for Transvaal I reported for duty in the second week of April and met new team-mates: Ian Swallow, an off-spinner from Yorkshire; Roland Lefebvre, a seam bowler from Holland; and batsman Andy Hayhurst from Lancashire. With Vic Marks going into retirement to become a cricket correspondent for *The Observer*, Chris Tavare became captain and I was appointed vice-captain. I was delighted to be chosen and to work with Chris. I respected him enormously both as a player and as a leader, and I like to think we justified the faith the club had in us.

Somerset had had a reasonable season in 1989. Finishing 14th, three from the bottom, in the county championship, we had reached the semi-finals of the Benson and Hedges tournament, were knocked out quite early in the NatWest event, and finished 10th in the Sunday League. We believed that with several fast-scoring batsmen we would again do well in one-day matches, but again would not have the bowling depth to do much better in the three- and four-day county games, and that was how it turned out.

After my good initial season there was speculation as to how I would fare this second year. My 2 000-odd runs were noted and appreciated, but there was a strong view that I would battle to top that in 1990. The reasoning, not without justification, was that in the first year I was unknown and opposing captains and bowlers did not know my strengths and weaknesses. But they would know what to expect the next time around. It was now up to me to rise to the challenge, one I was eagerly looking forward to. Little did I realise what a glorious summer it would turn out to be, not only in terms of the weather but for most of the batsmen.

We went to The Parks to play Oxford in what was really a pipe-opener for the season proper. My strongest recollection of that drawn game was the terrible weather. It was freezing, and after I had been trapped leg-before for a modest 28 I spent as much time as I could in the dressing-room sitting next to the heater. It was certainly not cricket weather. Why they play so early in England I will never understand. Far better to start in May and end later in September when the weather is almost invariably fine. Most foreign players complain about the weather. After the South Africans' opening match against Worcestershire in 1955, captain Jack Cheetham said it was so cold that any batsman wearing a box was boasting.

After Oxford I made some reasonable, confidence-building, but not particularly high scores, and as we moved into May I told our team manager Jack Birkenshaw that I felt I was coming right and was due for a really good innings. He said that the previous season I had failed to capitalise when I was well set and that I should now look beyond just a century. I agreed, aiming mentally for at least a 200 figure as soon as possible.

That desired form came in a magnificent Benson and Hedges match against Derbyshire at Taunton on 1 May. I scored 66, with Jon Hardy our star that day with 109. This was undoubtedly one of the best one-day games I have ever played in. The 55-over-a-side game produced a record 613 runs, Somerset registering 310 for 3 and Derbyshire replying with 303 for 7. Poor Derbyshire: both Peter Bowler and John Morris got hundreds in a 210-run second-wicket stand, yet they went down. It was one of those thrill-a-minute tussles in which fortunes swung back and forth until at last, with the visitors needing 13 off the last over, they were stopped by medium pacer Andrew Hayhurst, who allowed them to score only 5. In terms of runs scored in a high-scoring match, only the 'humdinger' be-tween South Africa and Australia during the rebel tour could match it.

We went to Cardiff on 3 May for our four-day match against Glamor-gan. The sun shone from a cloudless sky and one look at a magnificent batting wicket told me that the day of opportunity had arrived. I told Chris Tavare it would be nice to win the toss and bat first and, thankfully, he called correctly. As usual, I opened with Peter Roebuck and from the first over I felt good, timing the ball nicely. Runs flowed freely, but I kept saying to myself, do not do anything stupid like reaching 25, getting over-confident, relaxing and getting out. Concentrate and be patient.

The Glamorgan bowling was sound, if not spectacular, and we gave the appreciative crowd their money's-worth. I reached my hundred just after lunch in a first-wicket partnership of 210 before Peter went with 69. Jon Hardy joined me and about 15 minutes before the tea break, with my score around 150, I told him I was feeling very tired and that my legs ached. He urged me to hold on as I was bound to feel better after a short rest. It was hard to account for my fatigue. It was a hot day, but I was used to that. The season was young and I was certainly fit enough. Fortunately, the fatigue passed after tea, but it was a reminder that the human body is not a machine and that one should always be fit enough to take advantage of a good day.

Jon was yorked in the last over before tea and Chris Tavare joined me. With my strength now returned and Chris immediately settling into his stride and reaching for the century which eventually came his way, I continued my run-gathering on the tiring home attack. At the close Somerset was handily placed with 361 for 2. I was still there on 236. This was my best first-class score, passing the undefeated 201 for Transvaal against Eastern Province in 1983.

The pleasure I felt was shared by my sister Susan who had come to spend a month's holiday in England with me. She saw me start in the morning, went to do some shopping, and was delighted to return and find me still flaying away at the crease.

The Sophia Gardens electronic scoreboard at times had difficulty keeping up with the run flow. At one stage the unit two in the hundreds column went missing and my total slumped to single figures. My double century was the first reached on that ground since the scoreboard had been installed five years before, so perhaps I caught the computer system by surprise. I was also the first Somerset player to score a double hundred since New Zealander Martin Crowe had done so against Warwickshire three years before. As was the custom at Somerset, any CB (Career Best) warranted a round of drinks, for which I was more than happy to pay.

Additional personal targets were at the back of my mind when we resumed the next day. Clive Rice was forever teasing me with the fact that he scored 246 for Nottinghamshire, and Australian Steve Smith, who had a couple of seasons for Transvaal, liked to remind me that his best was 268. I just had to beat these two pals and rivals. Scoring at an average rate of 80 runs per two-hour session, I reached 300 after 498 minutes from 417 deliveries.

At lunch we were 535 for 2, and I was on 313. Chris said we would bat on after the interval as I was only 10 runs short of the record. A little bewildered, I asked, 'What record?' He said he was talking about the

Somerset record of 322 held by the great West Indian Viv Richards who, coincidentally, was playing that year and in this match for Glamorgan. I disagreed with him, saying we should declare now, and that personal milestones should never be placed before a team decision. While, as I said, I enjoyed getting one up on private accounts with my friends Clive Rice and Steve Smith, official personal records as such do not really count that much with me. The possibility of our getting into a winning position in this game was paramount. Chris eventually agreed, and probably in his own mind was pleased with my decision. Winning the match was his job. So Viv kept his record, and rightly so. I did not want to deprive him of this footnote in cricket history, bearing in mind the many wonderful years he had given to Somerset. After the match Viv was kind enough to come up and congratulate me on what he called a 'fantastic innings'. Coming from such a master batsman it was a compliment I will long cherish. My innings had lasted eight and a half hours with no sixes and 43 fours.

One small postscript to that innings occurred at lunch on the first day. I told Jack Birkenshaw I wanted to use a heavier bat, as the bowling was not fast and the wicket was somewhat slow. He disagreed and said I should continue with the bat which was already serving me well. But I swapped the 2 pound, 13 ounce bat for a 3-pounder. This bat, autographed and with the details of my innings inscribed on a plaque, now has pride of place in the Anchor Inn in Taunton, where the owner has always treated county players so well.

I have to record that, having played ourselves into such a fine position, Somerset did not win the match. The Glamorgan batsmen also took advantage of this featherbed wicket and replied with 412 for 6 declared. I did not bat again, and the game was drawn. Points were shared, but with over 1 400 runs registered over the four days, spectators certainly had good value, although the bowlers may disagree.

I should mention that, along with the superb weather, the conditions in 1990 were weighted very much in favour of the batsmen. Bowlers were given balls with a narrow and flatter seam, lessening the swing potential, and groundsmen were ordered to prepare straw-colour wickets. Penalty points were to be handed to clubs which did not prepare wickets judged by the match umpires to be not up to standard. This ruling in favour of the batsmen was, in retrospect, a mistake. High scoring can be exciting at first, but runs the risk of degenerating into a tiresome race of statistics. Maintaining a balance between bat and ball is the very essence of the game.

After Cardiff, speculation began among cricket followers and in the media – could I reach the perennial target of 1 000 runs before the end of May? My aggregate was now over 400 and this was only the first week of the month. As usual, my attitude was that if the runs came in time, all good and well; if not, it did not matter to me personally. It was more important for Somerset to do well.

But I was not the only batsman enjoying himself at the expense of the poor bowlers. This was evident in Cardiff, and on that same weekend Ian Greig (brother of Tony, the South African-born former England captain) scored 291 for Surrey, and Neil Fairbrother, who was to bat so superbly for England in the World Cup in 1992, scored 366 for Lancashire. The run glut over the next few months was such that, whereas in 1989 I was the only batsman to top 2 000 runs, in the summer of 1990 ten men reached this figure.

Run-scoring apart, I was thoroughly enjoying this second year in England. I have already described how in my first year I soon felt completely at home with a wonderful club, fine colleagues and a friendly town like Taunton where the true wicket was not only appealing to a batsman, but where the atmosphere of the ground was more akin to that of the village green of which I had read so much. It is no wonder that, regardless of how her national side fares, England is indeed the home of the game. The people are both knowledgeable and appreciative and most of the cricket grounds have special characters of their own.

What also appealed was the way I was able to see the country so thoroughly. Constant travelling was at times a burden, but it was nevertheless all worth it. The county fixtures system is such that the venues for games are reversed from the previous year's, so it was not a case of travelling along the identical route of 1989. I was thus able to visit for the first time Oxford, Basingstoke, Lord's, Grace Road at Leicester, Scarborough, Neath, and so on.

I would like to be able to record that my first visit to Lord's, the hallowed headquarters of the game, produced a score from me worthy of the occasion, but this was not the case. We played Middlesex in a rain-interrupted Benson and Hedges match and I only scored 6. Even so, I savoured every minute on that ground. Afterwards I had the privilege of chatting in the dressing-room to that legendary English batsman, Sir Len Hutton. I did get a 58 there in a Sunday League game later in the season, but how I would love to score a Test century there some day!

After my favourite ground, Taunton, I especially liked playing at Southampton and Trent Bridge and other big grounds like Edgbaston and the Oval if there were enough spectators to create the right atmosphere. The Oval is a far from pretty ground, but I was always mindful of the great history of the place and the many marvellous games played there.

On 12 May we were at Hove for a Benson and Hedges match against Sussex which we had to win to ensure a place in the quarter-finals. My Cardiff form returned, and after adding 194 for the first wicket with Peter Roebuck, we broke the county record for this tournament by reaching 321 for 5. I took full advantage of this superb fast wicket to reach 177, the last 77 coming off only 45 deliveries. This was my highest score ever in a one-day match. We put Sussex out for 214 and ended top of our group.

That evening we climbed into our cars and drove home to Taunton for a Sunday League date with Hampshire where, on reflection, I played the best one-day innings of my career. They scored 246 for 3 in this 40-over game, with Paul Terry (113) and Robin Smith (57) heading a whirlwind onslaught against our poor bowlers.

At our turn at the crease everything turned to gold from the first over. Each time my bat hit the ball it seemed to find the gap and the runs flowed in an endless stream. At about 90 for one the Hampshire captain, Mark Nicholas, sensing that we were about to launch into a winning sally, brought Malcolm Marshall into the attack. So began an enthralling duel between myself and this West Indian bowling legend. I recall saying to my partner Andy Hayhurst that, although I had the greatest respect for Marshall, I had to have a go at him. If he in any way got on top we could be in serious trouble. Malcolm was determined to stem the tide of runs, and I was equally set on keeping the momentum going. It was the most electric and enjoyable two overs I could ever recall playing, generating 28 runs in a contest which is still talked about by Taunton folk to this day. Thank goodness the odds were stacked in my favour.

My 132 came from only 87 deliveries as I found gaps along the ground and even hit three sixes over the top, which is most unusual for me. Even when it was obvious that we were heading for certain victory I could not slow down. My system seemed to have a momentum of its own. I was finally caught by Robin Smith in the 28th over. How nice it would be to play like that every day!

After my innings I collapsed in the dressing-room from sheer exhaustion, but recovered in time to give an interview to Tony Greig for Sky Television. While I was doing this, Malcolm Marshall, great sportsman that he is, went seeking me out in the Somerset dressing-room, saying he wanted to congratulate me on what he said was a 'remarkable' performance. He repeated this comment when I in turn made my customary post-match handshakes in the opposing dressing-room. Again, coming from a player of his calibre, it was a comment I really appreciated, and we struck up a firm friendship – something I would never have believed possible just two short years before.

My opening batting partner Peter Roebuck, whose love for the game takes him beyond the playing field and into the press box, where he writes prolifically and skilfully for the London *Sunday Times* and other publications, was kind enough to comment in print:

> Jimmy Cook played an innings that was awesome in destruction. Chatting afterwards I said it was one of the best limited over innings I had ever seen, right up there with Viv Richards in Melbourne and Sunil Gavaskar in Somerset. But, on reflection, it stands alone.
>
> Violent innings are expected from Richards, Waugh, Lloyd, Crowe and Hick, but not from Cook. Wasn't he supposed to bat as if he were taking the top off an egg? For 20 productive years he has been batting that way, chugging along, hardly raising his bat, patting bad balls to the fence, defending good ones, playing so late we wondered if he'd fallen asleep.
>
> This season, at least in one day matches, it has been so different, so very much better. Determined to win matches, Cook has widened his range of shots and, dropping his bat onto the ball, summoned unsuspected power. By seeking command and finding it with new shots, a very good accumulator has turned himself into a batsman capable of wreaking havoc.

It was back now to a first-class match, and we took on the touring New Zealanders at Taunton. This fixture could not have come at a better time. I was in form and here for me personally was a 'Test' match. Chris Tavare (156) and Richard Harden (104) were the chief run-makers when we batted first on yet another superb batting strip, while I contributed a modest 31. Somerset declared at 343 for 6. Looking for a decision, the tourists declared on 278 with 3 wickets down, and even though their bowling that day was not particularly strong, I still enjoyed scoring an unbeaten 117 in my second innings of this personal 'Test'. After reaching 256 for 4 we declared again, setting them a generous target of 321 in 65 overs, which they reached in the last over with 5 wickets to spare.

Derbyshire was one county I had yet to score a hundred against, and this hoodoo persisted in our next county match when I scrambled a miserable single and a 5. But such is the nature of this game of cricket that one day later at Taunton I played probably my best first-class innings, this time against Sussex. Batting first, I was out 15 minutes before tea,   107 with my 197 coming in the same number of deliveries in 258 minutes. A lazy, hazy Wednesday at Taunton had certainly agreed with me.

The strange thing about my dismissal was that during the latter stages of my innings Ian Gould had been assigned to field in the covers when I was facing, but at slip for Andy Hayhurst. In this particular over, instead of repairing to cover, he momentarily forgot and remained at slip. Medium pace bowler Colin Wells delivered an unexpected bouncer, I got a top edge and gave a simple catch over the wicket-keeper's head to Ian, who should not have been there in the first place. Who says fielders should always stay in the same position? That day saw Somerset on 500 for 5 declared, to which Sussex replied with 313 and, following-on, made 256 for 4 in a match which frittered to a draw.

Those who envy the life of a county cricketer should know that there is another side to the thrill of achievement, the adulation and the publicity, the good money, and the dining in fancy hotels and restaurants. There is the sheer weariness, the enormous strain placed on mind and body when one has to field and bowl for several days in a row. True, there is some respite when rain abounds and we kick our heels in the dressing-room. But there was not much rain about that summer of 1990, and the following is an example of what I mean.

After labouring for two hard days in the field against Sussex, we drove to Leicester the next day and fielded all day against the home side. That was the Saturday. The following day we had a Sunday League date against them, lost the toss again, and fielded from 2 o'clock until 4 o'clock. Thus we had fielded for three days in a row, plus two hours on the fourth day. And here was I, along with my colleagues, not only getting increasingly weary but also frustrated at not being given the chance to bat while in good form. How our poor bowlers kept going I do not know. We had to field three days in a row on one other occasion that season and, believe me, in a crowded seven-days-a-week season such as they have now in England, this is not funny. The strain on players can distort the relative strengths of sides and bring about many injuries.

Dismissing such complaints by saying it is the same for everyone is not the answer. As I have already stated, too much cricket is crammed into the five and a half months of the season. Give the players enforced breaks and they will come back refreshed. There is much to be said for a return to the pattern of years ago when Sunday was a compulsory rest day. All right, in these modern times objections to organised sport on Sundays has largely fallen away, even in South Africa, and they are potentially big money-earning days. So a compulsory day off – any day in the week –

would be the apparent answer. But try telling this to Test and county administrators who never stop complaining about rising costs and dwindling revenues.

I have always liked to judge any of my performances against the strength of the opposition's bowling and for this reason in particular I enjoyed taking a second innings 81 off Gloucester at Bristol at the beginning of June, even though it did not win us the match. Courtney Walsh, who was so devastating for the West Indies against South Africa in that Test two years later in Bridgetown, spearheaded their attack, backed by David Lawrence, Kevin Curran, and David Graveney, whom I rated as one of the best spin bowlers in England. It is not always the centuries which we batsmen like to look back on with fondness. The great Len Hutton often recalled with pride carrying his bat until the very end of the innings for 30 when England collapsed for a mere 52 in humid conditions at the Oval in the 1948 Test when those magnificent Australian fast bowlers Ray Lindwall, Keith Miller and Bill Johnston were at their rampant best.

I should note here that I did not make my 1 000 runs in May. The Leicestershire match was my last chance to do so and my scores of 42 and 8 saw me about 100 runs short. My run of centuries in the county matches ended, but I thoroughly enjoyed playing at Basingstoke against Hampshire, and at Canterbury, with its beautiful trees and lovely setting.

In the mean time we had beaten Middlesex in the quarter-finals of the Benson and Hedges tournament by 22 runs in a thriller at Taunton, but had no answer to a superb Lancashire attack in the semi-final at Old Trafford, where they walked all over us to the tune of 6 wickets. Against the combination of Akram, Allott, DeFreitas, Watkinson and Austin, we were fortunate to muster 212, to which they replied with 214-4. It is worth recording that we had to play this semi-final after a six-hour coach trip from Canterbury to Old Trafford, and that we arrived at our hotel at 1 a.m. – not ideal preparation for such an important match.

In one of those rare weeks of continuous rain that summer, our annual county matches at lovely Bath – this time against Essex and Glamorgan – were ruined in that declarations and contrived finishes were to no avail and both games were drawn. Essex took us to the cleaners in their first innings by hitting 431 for 3 declared, Stephenson weighing in with 202 and Prichard with 115. However, off the field we thoroughly enjoyed the wonderful festivities laid on for us: the cruise up the Avon, musical evenings, parties, and numerous other well-organised social events.

What made it even more pleasurable for me was the fact that Linsey and the boys had by now joined me. They had fallen in love with England the previous year, when the club had placed us in a house in Taunton, conveniently only five minutes from the ground. But this second year we had been allocated a 15th-century farmhouse about 25 minutes' drive away. I confess that I did not take to this at first. It was a large house, with four bedrooms, a lounge, study, dining-room and kitchen, and in those initial weeks I rattled around it feeling rather lonely. I phoned Linsey in Johannesburg and suggested I find a smaller house. But she rather liked the sound of the place, so I stayed on.

And of course she was right. Once the family was installed this large house became a super home for the rest of the summer. Several friends from South Africa came to stay, including Northern Transvaal's Lee Barnard, and looking back I realise how much staying there contributed to the overall enjoyment of that summer. Exquisitely furnished, it was owned by the author Susan Barratt and her illustrator husband Peter, many of whose superb paintings were hung in the house and enhanced its warm atmosphere. They lease their home to the Somerset club each summer while they go to Greece, and we were fortunate enough to be allocated it again for the 1991 season, when more of our family joined us for part of the time.

I remember the SABC's Trevor Quirk coming to do an interview and asking me about playing in England. I told him how each day I would go off to cricket, concentrating on the task ahead. But once play was over, and after the customary drink or two with my colleagues, I was able to drive off, forget cricket for a while, enjoy the delightful countryside, and finally arrive at this lovely residence where rabbits, deer, sheep and cows were our neighbours. I am certain this facility, where I was able to relax completely when not on duty, contributed largely to my continued good form. With no cares on my mind I was able to give my complete attention to my playing obligations.

Another aspect of the life of a professional cricketer in England which is not always appreciated is the constant need for clean playing apparel. Each day we are expected to take the field in immaculate white trousers and shirts, with equally clean boots. All the red and green stains, mud and general dirt must be washed out. At home in South Africa many players are fortunate enough to have wives or servants who will see to this for them, but not in England, and certainly not for James Cook those weeks before Linsey arrived. I learned to wash and iron shirts and trousers and to sew on the occasional button quite adequately, although I was only too pleased to let Linsey take over and send me off to work looking really smart.

110   Then there were meals. While playing away games, naturally I ate with

the team in hotels and restaurants, but back in Taunton, apart from the odd meal out, I did much of my own cooking. I feel more comfortable with a cricket bat than a frying pan, but I managed well enough. That said, I was grateful for pub life, that great English tradition where each town has its fair sprinkling of pubs and other good eating places. Their well-cooked meals certainly saved me from trying to live up to my name. Each pub has a character of its own and many a wonderful evening was spent recounting stories and matches with my fellow players.

Back on the playing scene, I took a century off Northamptonshire at the beginning of July, but in the process suffered a rare injury and retired on 112 in our second innings. With my 65 in the first innings and feeling in good form, I passed the three-figure mark and was looking for a really high score when the blow came. Strangely, I was not facing the bowling. Their off-spinner Chippy Williams was bowling. Richard Harden went down the wicket to him and drove the ball hard – straight on to my left forearm. My arm went into a state of pins-and-needles and I was rushed to hospital for X-rays. With important matches coming up, the club management even phoned Martin Crowe, their regular guest player before me, to see if he could be released by his touring New Zealand team to fill in for me for a few matches. But the injury was not as serious as had originally been thought, merely a bad bruise.

We lost that Northamptonshire game by 7 wickets and the next day we were hosting Warwickshire. The club doctor advised me to take a week off and rest the arm. But after some physiotherapy the arm felt much better and I declared myself almost certainly fit to play. It so happened that rain delayed the start of play that first morning and our final eleven had not been chosen. With the umpires due to inspect the pitch after lunch, I asked Chris Tavare if I could have a tryout at the nets to see how the arm stood up. He agreed, and much to my relief it felt fine. Chris still had reservations – then. But he was delighted when I scored 35 and then 137 and possibly only the rain prevented our taking maximum points in a match that for the most part went very much our way.

This was not the only occasion on which I was hit at the non-striker's end, as Chris Tavare claimed me as a scalp later in the Middlesex match.

That century enabled me to stay in the race for a prize for any batsman who scored 2 500 runs for the season. The National Power company was offering £10 000 to anyone who attained that figure, as well as further prizes of £1 000 for the first man to reach that target, and £1 000 for the leading run-scorer of the year. Overall, there was £12 000 up for grabs, quite a tantalising challenge. As it turned out, England and Essex captain

Graham Gooch, who was also enjoying a spectacular year with the bat, beat me to the target and got the extra £2 000, but we shared the £10 000 prize.

I have mentioned how I had been dismissed cheaply in my first match at Lord's and how I would love to have scored a century on this most famous of all grounds. Ironically I did take a hundred off Middlesex, the team whose home ground it usually is, but this year, for a change, they were spreading their domestic fixtures around a bit and took us on at Uxbridge to the west of London. And so I had to be content with taking 152 off them there. It was a good weekend for me: after our first innings and my century that Saturday, we drove up to Neath for a Sunday League date with Glamorgan, and an undefeated 136 was registered, and then it was back for the completion of our Middlesex match, where I rounded off this good spell with 85. When I reached that figure I asked Chris Tavare when he would be declaring, and he said after another over or two. I decided to have a go at that second hundred . . . and was out next ball. Unfortunately we lost that enjoyable high-scoring game (which included three other century-makers) by 4 wickets, Mark Ramprakash, the promising new England player, steering his team home off the penultimate ball.

The Neath match against Glamorgan was quite spectacular. In this 40-over fixture Somerset accrued 360 for 3. That is astonishing scoring by any standard and not surprisingly broke the Sunday League record by 50 runs. My 93-ball century was not exactly snail's pace, but the star of the day was undoubtedly my colleague Graham Rose. He simply exploded with a remarkable array of shots round the wicket, racing to 148 in 69 deliveries. Even Adrian Kuiper would be proud of that. Poor Glamorgan was demoralised, tumbled out for 140, and lost by 220 runs.

Graham Rose is a powerfully built man and his penchant for fast scoring was nothing new to us. Only a few weeks before, in a 60-over NatWest match against Devon at Torquay, Somerset scored 413-4, another English one-day record. At 224-3, with only 71 deliveries remaining, Graham joined Chris Tavare and together they put on 189 runs. Rose, with ten fours and seven sixes, reached his century in only 36 balls and was dismissed with the last ball of the innings for 110 after treating the enthralled crowd to an exhibition of truly awesome power.

Tavare hit a typically stylish undefeated 162, but he was overshadowed by the flaming Rose. True, it was a small ground and we were playing a minor county side, but even so it was a remarkable performance. Devon went to pieces after this onslaught. Roland Lefebvre, our Holland seamer, rolled them over, yorking 5 while taking 7 for 15, and we strolled home by the wide margin of 346 runs. Chris Tavare got the man-of-the-match award, but Graham Rose must have come pretty close.

So we moved into August and the last weeks of that glorious summer season and I had yet another opportunity to test myself against one of the world's most talented bowlers. This time it was the young Pakistani Waqar Younis who popped up suddenly on the Surrey staff and overnight became a fast bowling sensation.

On this particular day he was not frighteningly quick with the new ball and for a while when I faced him in the first innings I wondered why everyone had raved so much about him. But when he came back later to use the worn ball he swung it unbelievably. He had me caught behind for 52 and took 2 other wickets, and it became clearly evident that here indeed was a bowler on the threshold of a great career. His pace, swing and destructive yorker were proving too difficult for the English batsmen to handle.

It was a good batting wicket and high scoring was again a feature of this match. Somerset declared at 441-8, with Graham Rose again having fun with 85 off only 55 balls. Surrey replied with 302-5 declared (South African Ian Greig hitting an undefeated 123), and then I found three figures once more with an undefeated 116. Younis only bowled a few overs in our second innings and again I found it pleasurable taking runs off a good spin attack, an aspect of my game I had worked hard on the previous summer. With Surrey coming back strongly with 327-8 the match was drawn and the points shared. Near the end of the match our fast bowler Adrian Jones cut himself badly on the boundary stake in attempting a catch and was taken to hospital. As a result he missed a few games.

By the third week of August I was right in line for that National Power prize for reaching the 2 500 runs aggregate, and my 114 and 77 in a four-day game against Hampshire at Taunton, which we won by 5 wickets, gave me a real boost. Came the last county game of the season, at home against Worcestershire. I then needed only 48 runs for that magic 2 500, but this was one of those sides against which I had never been able to get more than 30 or 40-odd.

As we were getting our kit out of our cars one of the visiting players, Richard Illingworth, commented on this bogy factor and said I would probably not score this time either. Our wicket-keeper Neil Burns happened to walk by just then and said to me: 'He should never have said that to you.' He knew only too well how I loved nothing better than responding to a challenge.

Graeme Hick, the astonishing batting wonder from Zimbabwe, gave 113 one of his marvellous displays in this match, milking our poor bowlers with his elegant and powerful strokeplay for 154 and 81. I made 143 in the first innings, but all our efforts were not good enough and we slid to a heavy 173-run defeat, a sad ending to what had been a remarkable season.

So, having totalled 2 608 runs in first-class matches for the season, I got my £5 000 and National Power gave a similar amount to the club, which made me feel comfortable as, in a way, it helped the club recover some of the money it had laid out to employ me for the summer. No wonder our chief executive Peter Anderson wore a broad smile as the cheques were handed out.

Another milestone came my way that summer. With two more Sunday League games to go, our scorer David Oldham told me that I only needed 60 or 70 runs to beat the record aggregate for a Sunday League season. I said I thought I had done this in the Glamorgan game. He replied that I had only passed the Somerset record then; now it was for the national record. I added that it would be nice to get, but reminded him that records for their own sake were never really uppermost in my mind. Sure, when a big money prize was in the offing it was different, but not just to chalk up yet another statistic.

'I know all about that,' he replied, 'but you will want to go for this one.'

'Why?'

'Because it's held by Clive Rice.'

I laughed. 'Then the game's on.'

And as it turned out, in our next Sunday game, against Warwickshire, I scored an unbeaten 112 and ended the season in that league with a record 902 runs, surpassing my old buddy by nearly 100 runs. But records are meant to be broken, and mine went the following year when Tom Moody of Australia edged me out of my little niche with 910.

I should add that in the crowded, multi-competition English season the scorer is an integral member of the team squad. David Oldham travelled everywhere with us, always on hand with charts and a mass of statistics and information to help the captain review the form of players, his own and the opposition's, in one-day and first-class matches, enabling him to plan strategy accordingly. After all, cricket has rightly been described as physical chess.

At the end of my second enjoyable season with Somerset I had played 41 first-class innings, scored 2 608 runs, hit nine centuries and eleven 50s (highest score 313 not out), for an average of 76,70.

The run glut that summer is reflected in the fact that ten county players scored over 2 000 runs, with Graham Gooch topping the aggregate list with more than 2 700 runs, yet he played ten innings fewer than I did. And I thought I had had a good year! In my view Graham is not only a great captain of Essex and England, but also one of the most dominant batsmen of his era, able to score quickly all round the wicket, and with an insatiable appetite for runs.

In the Sunday League I totalled 902 from 16 innings, with three centuries and six 50s (highest score 136 not out), for an average of 64. In six innings in the Benson and Hedges tournament I managed one century (177) and 329 runs, while I slipped in two scores of 40 in our brief showing in the NatWest Trophy event. Overall, it was my best and most satisfying year thus far and I cannot recall playing once on a bad wicket.

So high was the scoring that almost every side had difficulty bowling out the opposition, especially us. Half a dozen of Somerset's batsmen scored over 1 000 runs that summer, while around the country only the very best seam and spin bowlers were able to get wickets with any consistency.

Somerset did much the same in 1990 as in 1989. We slipped from 14th to 15th in the county championship, won and lost eight Sunday League games to finish eighth, reached the semi-final of the Benson and Hedges tournament, and went out in the second round of the NatWest event.

Our coach Jack Birkenshaw, was kind enough to pen the following about me in the county club yearbook:

> Our Taunton pitches were perfect for batting and the batsmen took full advantage of them, with Jimmy Cook leading the way. No one would have believed that he could improve his technique and determination to better his performances of 1989. He certainly proved myself and many cricket enthusiasts wrong, who believed he would do well, but not achieve the aggregate of his first year. He increased his range of shots, hit the ball further and harder, without ever losing his appetite to score heavily all through that hot summer. All our young batsmen are taking advantage of batting with him, watching him and talking to him about his batting style.

I had no plans for a further year in England, but Peter Anderson made me another tantalising contract offer. Again, all depended on Stephen's progress at school and my employers back in Johannesburg. Once more I was given the green light, and in 1991 I returned for what proved to be the best season of all.

9
SOMERSET, 1991

SOMERSET 1991

In 1991 the Somerset County Cricket Club celebrated its centenary. It is a great and proud club, and even though it has yet to win the championship, as Sir Donald Bradman wrote in a special article for the yearbook: '. . . winning is not all, and the game has been enriched by the splendid part Somerset has played in the overall scene'.

From the very first day I flew in from Africa and set eyes on Taunton I have been in love with the town, the ground, the environment and the people, and over the following three years I did my best to justify the faith the club had placed in me. Engaged as a specialist batsman I played, metaphorically speaking, under the shadow of so many great local and contract batsmen . . . Harold Gimblett, Arthur Wellard, Ian Botham, Brian Close, Viv Richards, Bill Alley, Steve Waugh, Greg Chappell and Martin Crowe, to name but a few. Could I measure up? Could I, in this my final year, help them win the elusive championship? Like every other member of that 1991 team that was so astutely led by Chris Tavare, I gave of my best. We did pretty well but, once again, the gods did not smile our way.

True, the record shows that we finished bottom of the table, but figures can be misleading. How, for instance, could we get so few points when we registered 26 first-class centuries, whereas Warwickshire, who finished in second place, could only produce four centuries all summer? Simply, we made runs and they bowled people out. As in previous years we had several good seamers and this year also had in David Graveney a first-class left-arm spinner who had seen excellent service with Gloucestershire. But we lacked quality fast bowlers, and even though the pitches that summer favoured the bowlers a little more than they did in 1990, time and again we could not winkle out stubborn tail-enders and consequently were often denied valuable points which were so tantalisingly close. All the top sides – Essex, Warwickshire, Derbyshire, Nottinghamshire, Surrey – had that world-class quickie or pair of quickies who could roll up an innings, and that is what so often made the difference between victory, a draw, and defeat.

We started the season without one of our hitherto best seamers, Adrian Jones, who had taken more than 50 wickets in each of the previous two years but had now returned to Sussex. Then one of our real stalwarts, Peter Roebuck, retired at the end of August. One of many excellent and consistent county men who somehow was always overlooked by the national selectors, Peter was my opening partner for most of my three years at Somerset, and both the club and I owe much to his highly intelligent approach to the game, his solid performances, experience and enthusiasm. A gifted journalist, he is now making yet another valuable contribution to cricket from the other side of the boundary. If all this were not enough, we lost our cricket manager Jack Birkenshaw, one of the nicest and shrewdest men on the county scene, who returned to Leicestershire where he is now manager. His departure was a particular blow to me for he had helped me a great deal in that first season, assisting in developing my technique against spin and constantly briefing me on opposing players and conditions.

Jack was not replaced, and with second team manager Peter Robinson's help, Chris Tavare took on his responsibilities along with the captaincy. We won only 2 first-class games out of 22, lost 5 and drew 15, and in all fairness there were not many games in which we were totally outplayed. In order to underline what I said about our batting, only the eventual championship winners, Essex, collected more batting points than we did. They got 69 to our 66. Twice when close to victory we failed to attain our run target by a whisker – 2 runs (against Kent), and 5 runs (against Warwickshire). A team gets 16 points for an outright victory, and had we got those 32 points we might well have been several places higher in the final table. Of course, other counties also had their tales of what might have been: such are the vagaries of championship competition.

With scores of 41, 58, 76 and 38, I made a reasonable start to the season in the Benson and Hedges one-day tournament before we bowed out to Essex, but after a 57 against Sussex in the first county match my game went adrift for a while. Talk began to circulate that the bubble had burst; that, after two good years, my consistent shot-making run was perhaps ending. Numerous newspaper articles examined my technique from every possible angle, probing for the source of this slump.

Then, after a Sunday League game against Hampshire at Bournemouth, one of the umpires, Ken Palmer, said to me: 'For what it is worth, looking at you down the pitch, I believe that this season you appear to have opened your stance a little. You have drawn your left foot back and are more chest-on to the bowler than in previous years. I always liked the way you played so side-on to the bowling. As a result, you are giving more nicks outside off-stump than previously.'

Ken Palmer is one of the most knowledgeable students of the game, and I took his advice and did some net practice to re-examine my technique. He was right, and once I had made the necessary correction my form returned almost immediately. Against a good Middlesex attack I hit 45 and 89 in a drawn game, and immediately afterwards we were at home to the West Indies. The timing could not have been better. My confidence had returned and now I had this opportunity to underwrite it by playing in this personal 'Test' against the side which has dominated the game for the best part of two decades. It was freezing cold, but the conditions did not daunt the great West Indian players as, with Carl Hooper slamming 123 and Brian Lara 93, they soon piled on 342 for 7 before declaring.

Peter Roebuck and I went out to face the legendary Malcolm Marshall, Curtly Ambrose, Ian Allen and Hamish Anthony. I had played against the so-called 'rebel' men from the Caribbean in South Africa, but now it was the official team and I was most anxious to prove to myself that I could match them. I thoroughly enjoyed the experience. Apart from being dropped at square-leg when in the 40s after flicking a ball off my toes, I did not give a chance. In order to keep the game alive, Chris Tavare declared at 270 for 7, 72 behind, with me on an unbeaten 162. I felt confident enough to have scored a double century, but, again, the exigencies of the game deemed otherwise. Still, I felt I had passed my 'Test' and their players were most complimentary about my innings, which made me feel good.

In their second knock the tourists carried on as in the first innings and rattled up 263 for the loss of only 2 wickets before setting us a near-impossible target of 336 for victory in 66 overs. Chris Tavare accumulated one of his typically polished centuries, but wickets tumbled and defeat loomed. But the day was saved by our Holland allrounder, Roland Lefebvre. Batting last because of an injured foot, he joined Chris for the last 3 overs.

Came the last over, and in for the kill raced Carl Hooper, turning the ball prodigiously. Roland played four immaculate defensive shots, then snicked the fifth delivery to slip. But the fielder dropped the ball. He blocked the last delivery, and the game was drawn. For that last over every single West Indian player was within a few metres of the batsman.

Ken Palmer, who had helped correct that small fault in my game a week or so before, officiated in the West Indies match and afterwards said how much he had enjoyed my duel with these great bowlers. I am sure he found it easier watching than trying to play them.

I always looked forward to playing in the principality of Wales. This was not only because of the friendliness of the people, but so often I seemed to have reached top form facing Glamorgan. This happened again immediately after the West Indies match when we went to Swansea and with Chris Tavare (162) and myself (152) enjoying ourselves on a good batting wicket, Somerset raced to 370 for 4 in only 100 overs. On a family note, Linsey's mother had come over for her first visit to England, and naturally I was pleased to be able to say: 'There, Mom, that's a hundred for you.'

In order to keep the match alive when rain constantly interrupts play, county captains often set up contrived finishes. This fixture was a perfect example of this. Somerset declared at 422-5. No play was possible on the second day and the home captain closed their first innings at 57 for no wicket. In turn, we forfeited our second knock, setting Glamorgan a challenge of 366 in 90 overs. They went for it with alacrity. With 36 overs to go and all wickets in hand, they needed only to score at a rate of 5 an over, not an impossible target. But they suddenly ran out of steam, losing three men in 4 overs. We could not grab those last wickets and a thrilling encounter ended in a frustrating draw.

On to Edgbaston, the famous Midlands Test venue, for our encounter with Warwickshire. Taking a look at what I considered to be the greenest wicket I had seen so far during my time in England, I estimated that 150 would be a good total for any side. Chris Tavare went off sick during the first session and I took over the captaincy. I believed even the moderate seam attack at my disposal as a result of injuries could do well here. Some hope. Time and again we would have their batsmen groping, but wickets would not come our way. Eventually they declared at 359-5. On a strip tailor-made for seamers, our best bowler was spinner David Graveney with 3 for 114. We, too, expected to struggle on this greentop but, with an unbeaten 94 by myself and a 60 by Peter Roebuck, we also got more runs (210-3 dec) before rain again ruled out any hope of a decision.

Our saga of frustrating drawn games continued at Bath against Hampshire. Although the runs continued to flow my way with an unbeaten 107, I would have been far happier if we could have picked up some badly needed winning points.

Many batsmen have what might be described as their 'bogy' bowlers – not necessarily men they feared facing, but those who somehow often got them out. For example, the great England and Surrey fast-medium seamer Alec Bedser had a knack of beating the immortal Don Bradman in the Test series in the years immediately after World War Two. My 'bogy' was David Lawrence of Gloucestershire. I never faced him with any trepidation, and often went into reasonable figures when playing his team. But it would be David who eventually nobbled me. He had just come into the England side when we played Gloucestershire in our second match at Bath, and he was probably as aware as I was of our private little challenge. Being in good form this time, I was determined to get the better of him once and for all. But, sure enough, he got me again, this time caught at slip in the first over without scoring. It was my only innings in yet another drawn fixture.

The sweet smell of success eventually came our way in the first week of

July at Taunton, when we chased a target set by Lancashire of 294 in 61 overs in the second innings. We made it in the last over. Although the brilliant Pakistani seamer Wasim Akram was in their attack, he injured a foot and only bowled 10 overs, so our task was much easier.

On the subject of Pakistani cricketers, it was at Southend in mid-July that I enjoyed watching Saleem Malik in action, even though he milked us for 102 when representing Essex. Graham Gooch was leading a superb combination which deservedly won the championship that year. And although the latter dominated his team's batting line-up, as he did for England, Saleem was an invaluable member of the squad. He has that enviable knack of accumulating runs without any apparent effort. He fears neither slow nor pace bowling, especially not the former against which he has so much experience on the turning wickets in his home country. Against spinners, for instance, it is not his style to go down the wicket and hit them over the top. Not a great exponent of footwork, he prefers to wait patiently for the ball that drifts slightly outside the off-stump, and he then plays a delicate late-cut. Or he looks for the ball to sweep or glide finely to leg. Move the fielders to cut off his line of attack and he promptly finds another open space in which to drive the ball firmly, more often than not to the boundary. He relishes the challenge of working the ball into spaces where he can get the fielders into the positions where he wants them and not necessarily where the fielding captain wants them. Overall, he is one of those gifted men who have really made an art of batsmanship, and it was a pleasure to watch him. Congratulating him after the game, he told me he was annoyed with himself as he really should have scored a double century – he is that run-hungry.

The Southend ground will always be remembered for the record 721 scored in six hours on one day by Bradman's 1948 Australian team. The 1991 county combination could not match that incredible total, but their 413 for 6 declared, with Hussain (88), Gooch (79), and Stephenson (70) giving Malik solid support, was enough to place them in a strong position against us.

I came close enough to a double century myself, hitting an unbeaten 193, but it was not good enough and Essex took maximum points, skating home by 136 runs.

We drove up to Northampton the next day. I was anxious to impress against this county side because their manager was Mike Procter. As he is an influencing force at home in South Africa I thought that if I could produce a good innings it would help my chances of winning a place in any national side that was likely to play in the near future as our country moved out of political and sporting isolation. I had the satisfaction of making an unbeaten 210, only the third time in my career that I had passed the double century mark. That figure looked nice in the scorebook, but what it did not record was that I should have been out twice in the first over, nicking two deliveries from Greg Thomas at chest height between third slip and gully. But after those escapes I never looked back. In sport as in life, such is the often narrow difference between success and failure. Some days the luck is with you; on others it certainly seems to desert you.

This was my sixth century of the season, and yet another went into the books back at Taunton in the next game, this time 126 against Kent. This was especially pleasing as Kent was one of the counties against which I had not previously reached three figures. (The only two counties which escaped my century list during my three years in England were Derbyshire and Yorkshire.) A feature of this drawn encounter was some superb slow left-arm bowling by our veteran David Graveney who took full advantage of a turning wicket to collect 7 for 105 in their first innings.

The 2 000-run tally was now well within my grasp, but I came down to earth with a bump against Leicestershire at Weston-super-Mare. After making only 10 in the first innings, I was out first ball in the second innings for the first time in my career. On each occasion I was caught behind, snicking the ball off the English pace bowler Chris Lewis.

We remained at Weston-super-Mare for a fixture against Worcestershire, and it was here that I saw a great batsman going through one of those horrible patches which everyone experiences. Graeme Hick, that gifted Zimbabwean who was being hailed for his remarkable performances in previous seasons while qualifying for England, had just emerged from failing against the West Indies in his first Test series. Having seen him in masterly form against us during the previous two years, I was astonished at this temporary decline. He appeared to lose all confidence, going back to balls that were pitched up and asking to be hit. The authority he had previously commanded was gone and he looked like a novice. He only made 10 and 24 against our moderate attack.

In contrast, Australian Tom Moody, who was later to take my one-day Sunday League aggregate record off me, was confidence personified. A tall, powerful man, he strode in purposefully, placed his front foot down the wicket, and in that first innings took a handsome and well-deserved 77 off us. Although he could hit the ball with venom, he was not a slogger. In one Sunday match against us he got into his 90s, yet his first boundary only came when he reached 70. Primarily a front-foot player, the English conditions suited him perfectly.

124   At the beginning of August I captained Somerset against Sri Lanka,

Chris Tavare standing down. This was an honour but, unfortunately, I was not a victorious captain. In a fascinating game they thumped us by 8 wickets. Going out to toss the coin, their captain Aravinda de Silva noted the little tinge of green on the wicket. Thinking that his modest bowling attack might be able to extract some life from the strip, when he won the toss he put us in. I was delighted, knowing full well that this would again be a batsman's paradise. And sure enough it was. With Richard Harden finding top form with an undefeated 100, I also had a merry time, driving and cutting the ball all round the wicket and, by way of 30 boundaries, finishing with an undefeated 209 when I closed the innings at 377 for 2. It was comforting to add this double century to the century I had scored against the West Indies, thus coming out on top in my private 'Tests'.

The Sri Lankans did not have to struggle too hard to take 255 off our attack before declaring with eight men gone, and after declaring our second knock at 126 for 3, I set them a target of 249 in 49 overs, which I thought would be pretty reasonable. To their credit, they responded with gusto and won with 43 balls to spare. De Silva was particularly adventurous, slamming an undefeated 57 in just over 30 deliveries, and ending with a flourish. He pulled our young seamer Caddick for six and then sent the next delivery soaring high over the bowler's head to the boundary for another six. To be fair to Somerset, we were blooding a number of youngsters. It is nevertheless always good to see a team taking its chances and going all out for victory. The large home crowd was delighted with the entertainment, which was the all-important thing. Allowing the match to fizzle out to a tamer draw would have been meaningless.

The strain of racing all over the country to slot in one-day matches in the middle of county games began to tell on me in our mid-August date with Nottinghamshire at Trent Bridge. After playing two days there we had to go to Worcester for our second-last Sunday League assignment. I was not out overnight on the Saturday. Then at Worcester I was on the field all day, carrying my bat for 129, and then was present all through their 40 overs. We won by 18 runs, but I was exhausted. Little wonder that on returning to Trent Bridge the next day I was out first ball for 2.

Playing against Yorkshire at Taunton I again failed to find an elusive century against this great club, having to settle for 79 and an unbeaten 85. The main feature of this match was that it marked Peter Roebuck's retirement. It would have been fitting if he had been able to leave the game in which he had made such a mark with a century. But, as Bradman discovered in his famous last Test innings at the Oval in 1948, the gods do not always co-operate. Peter could manage only 31 and 2, but all followers of the county game, and particularly those at Somerset, will for ever be grateful to this man they called the 'Professor'. In 757 innings he scored 31 centuries, a tally bettered only by Harold Gimblett and Viv Richards.

Very much involved in the controversial sacking in 1986 of Ian Botham, Viv Richards and Joel Garner, and always clever with words, Peter Roebuck mockingly described himself as a mixture of Adrian Mole, a lion-tamer, and Robespierre. A man of high principles whom Botham called a Judas, Peter was at times a somewhat aloof personality, away somewhere writing when others were socialising. I respected him enormously as an opening partner and authority on the game and always found him an amusing character.

Being only human, he admitted on his retirement that he would have liked to represent his country. But with typical modesty, he said: 'I ought to regret it, but I don't. I am not a jealous man. With luck, I might have played a couple of Tests, but when you see Richards, Gavaskar and Crowe bat, when you are judged beside them, then you are going to have a pretty poor view of the world.' In a farewell newspaper interview he concluded: 'I've tired of it and I wanted to say goodbye to cricket before it said goodbye to me.'

One final note on Peter Roebuck. About 15 minutes before the start of our last Sunday League game of the season – against Yorkshire – he went to Chris Tavare and said he did not want to play, especially as he had not been in the side for most of this particular tournament. He knew – although I did not – that, as this was also to be my last Sunday League match playing before our home crowd at Taunton, the club was to make a presentation to Linsey and me and he did not want to take any of the spotlight. Learning of this later, I thought his attitude was wrong, but it was typical of the man – firm in his views, but modest about his own standing.

That day, 25 August, was indeed an emotional one for me. At the tea interval all the players gathered in front of the main pavilion and the Somerset Supporters Club presented me with a handsome watch, Linsey with a fine crystal bowl, and the boys with Somerset jerseys. At the end of the match the players were summoned to the committee room, and before them I was presented with a superb framed picture of the ground which I had grown to love, not only for the runs I had scored there but also for the wonderful support and encouragement I had received over the years from our loyal supporters. The gentleman who made the presentation to me said he had watched every ball I had faced during those three years. One could not have a more devoted fan than that.

126

About this time our chief executive Peter Anderson came to me and reminded me that, with my aggregate near the 2 500 mark for the second year in a row, I should bear in mind the National Power money prize which I had won jointly the year before with Graham Gooch. I had seen nothing in the press about it this year and wondered if indeed it was being awarded. Peter believed it would be and felt that I should aim for the 2 500-run target just in case, as the club would also benefit financially.

I had four games to go, so my sights were set. We took a very young and inexperienced bowling attack to a match against Hampshire at Southampton, while they had a more than useful attack. I assumed they would have prepared a wicket to suit their bowlers, but it turned out to be one of the best a batsman could hope to encounter. David Graveney and I went out for a close inspection and could not find a blade of grass. It was a 22-yard strip of bleached earth. How we enjoyed ourselves that first day! I went to town and rattled up 197 and we declared at 480 for 7. I was then 114 runs short of 2 500 first-class runs for the season. After Hampshire had totalled 338 for 8 declared, and facing the last ball at the end of the third day, I was on 113. I managed to hit that final delivery for a couple and achieved my target.

That night David Graveney, Hampshire's Robin Smith and Mark Nicholas and I went out to celebrate. I felt on top of the world and we had a quiet party. I do not know whether it was the rich food, or perhaps too much red wine, but the next morning I felt really ill. We were only going to bat for another three or four overs before declaring, but I felt so awful that I had to retire without adding to my score. I did not field, but lay down in the dressing-room and only woke up at tea time. Chasing 370 in 95 overs for victory, Hampshire won the match by 2 wickets in the last over, Durban's Robin Smith adding another good score of 107 to his first knock of 81, the kind of performance that has made him such a stalwart of the England team. My effort to win the National Power aggregate run award was in vain. They were not giving it that year.

Going up to Worcestershire, our poor bowlers took the biggest hammering of the season. Graeme Hick went cheaply, but Tom Curtis, one of the most consistent batsmen on the county circuit, had a really good time. A shortish man with little back-lift, he is sound off his legs, through midwicket and a good cutter. He missed four of the first six deliveries he faced and our hopes rose. But to no avail. With Leatherdale weighing in with 157, he did virtually as he pleased, hitting 248 runs, and the home side declared just before tea on the second day at 575 for 8.

A batting paradise, and what did Somerset get in reply? A miserable and humiliating 83 in only 30 overs. True, we had just fielded for the best part of two days, but this was no excuse. Their star was the Johannesburg-born former England player, and my old Transvaal team-mate, Neal Radford. He scattered my stumps with his first delivery and proceeded to take 6 more wickets for a personal cost of only 43 runs. He managed to get the ball to skid through low and trapped four leg before wicket. Following-on, we saved face to a certain extent by totalling 350, but Worcestershire deservedly won by an innings.

Seeking at least a second championship victory before the season ended, we took maximum points off Gloucestershire at Bristol, winning by 9 wickets. Chris Tavare (186) and Graham Rose (106) were our stars.

Our last fixture was at home to Warwickshire, a rather special, emotional occasion for me. This was the last time I would do battle for the county which was now my second home. Understandably, I felt it would be nice to round off this wonderful English career with a century. Going into the game I was level with Bill Alley's record of ten centuries in a season for the county, this great Australian-born character, and now good friend of mine, having achieved this feat 30 years before. Speculation mounted round the country as to whether I would get that eleventh hundred, and I also needed 173 runs in this match to better his aggregate of 2 761 for a season.

Outside that memorable game years before, when Clive Rice bowled Drummond with the last ball of the match at Newlands to win the Currie Cup match for Transvaal, this was without doubt the best first-class game I have played in.

Warwickshire were all fired up because they still had a chance of winning the championship, which was being decided on this the last weekend of the season. Essex were playing Middlesex at Chelmsford, and if they lost and Warwickshire beat us, then the title would go to the Midlands club. In typically solid fashion, the visitors went about their task in a workman-like manner and amassed 376 on that first day, despite some heroic bowling by Neil Mallender who returned an impressive performance of 6 for 68.

All eyes were now on me. Would I get that coveted century, and would I be able to master the fiery bowling of my fellow countryman Allan Donald, who has developed enormously in recent seasons to become one of the fastest and most devastating bowlers in the game? The wicket had been prepared for spin but, like Mallender, Allan was able to extract some life, although it eased as the game progressed. After a shaky start we settled down in our long run-chase, and I kept Allan at bay enough to be around for 212 minutes and get 127.

Reaching three figures was an emotional moment. The crowd rose in prolonged applause, and apparently none clapped harder than Bill Alley, the man whose proud record I had now eclipsed. Afterwards we had a celebratory drink together. But the main task of winning was before us, and hard though we tried we could only muster 289. Another solid batting performance saw them on 321 for 9 declared. We were left to chase 409 in an hour and a quarter, plus the last day, not an impossible task timewise but a tall order for the batsmen.

I needed only 46 to beat Bill Alley's aggregate and was 27 not out overnight. So close now. The next morning the runs came steadily, but at 40 I went on the sweep, got a top edge from a Booth delivery, and was caught. I failed by 6 runs. Disappointed? I think the spectators were more disappointed than I was. Certainly it would have been nice; yet again, perhaps it was only fair that Bill Alley should still be able to walk proudly around his adopted county, secure in the knowledge that no one had yet scored more runs for the club in a season.

With 110 runs needed for victory, Somerset still had 5 wickets in hand. But wickets fell steadily. The last pair came together with 6 runs needed. Could we do it? Alas, no. David Graveney tried to sweep spinner Booth, was bowled round his legs, and Warwickshire won by 5 runs. It was a tremendous match and a great advertisement for four-day cricket.

But despite this fine victory, our opponents could not win the championship. Actually they knew their chances were slight as, during their first innings news had come from Chelmsford that Middlesex were 19 for 7. The poor Warwickshire players were understandably deflated, but all credit to them for forging on with all the tenacity and skill that had brought them so close to the championship. Middlesex were shuttled out for only half a century, and that same evening Essex captain Graham Gooch was still flaying away with an undefeated double century. So, overall, the final championship tussle had turned into a one-horse affair in favour of the eastern county club.

My batting duties might have ended early on that last day, but not my other obligations. During the lunch interval a table was set up for me on the field in front of the pavilion and I spent the whole time signing autographs. I will long treasure a photograph taken of the queue of spectators that stretched right across the field. Such was the emotion of the occasion that some of the women were actually in tears. This process was repeated during the tea break. In addition, I shook the hands of so many well-wishers that in the end my right hand was more sore than it had ever been from batting.

On the night before that final game the Somerset Supporters Club organised a memorable farewell dinner for me, during which presentations were made and some kind things said about me in a number of speeches. A highlight was a witty presentation from Jack Bannister, former Warwickshire player and now contributing to the game as a radio and television commentator. The speech, printed in the club yearbook, is reproduced at the end of this book (page 211).

The evening the final game ended I left the ground with a real lump in my throat. No one could have had a happier three years playing county cricket, and happily I had fulfilled the faith this great club had placed in me. I had proved to myself that I could make runs outside my native country, and I was pleased to think that, in my small way, I had given pleasure to so many people who loved the game of cricket as much as I do.

The English media, writers and broadcasters, were kind to me during those years. Even though I hailed from a country which had been a political pariah for so long, I was treated the same as any other player, assessed and written or talked about purely on my performances as a professional sportsman. For this I am grateful. At the end of the 1991 season Jon Hancock, editor of the *Somerset County Gazette*, kindly wrote the following overview of my three years:

> Another season ends. The cricketing press is in a reflective mood. Its members reach for the bookshelf and trawl the thesaurus for new superlatives to shower upon one Jimmy Cook.
>
> Cook, the very model of modesty, would eschew such indulgence, of course. Chances are that he would far rather strap on his pads for a couple more hours in the middle and help himself to another 80 not out.
>
> Like most other Somerset followers, I knew next to nothing about him before the 1989 season, save his name was Jimmy Somebody and that he might score a few runs, given the odd flat wicket and a bit of sun on his South African back. Then I saw him play.
>
> It was bewildering – the clinical disarming demolition of a highly-rated county attack. Nothing Bothamesque about it, no smouldering ambition to belt the cover off the ball . . . nothing flashy at all, really. In fact, for all the world, S.J.C. looked like a kindly father facing an enthusiastic son's bowling on the beach; quite capable of dispatching into the pier amusements, yet anxious not to demoralise the little lad.
>
> But then, that's Jimmy Cook. A man who can take 29 off two overs off Malcolm Marshall, yet still graciously acknowledge the

ball that beats him. Ruthlessness tempered with generosity and respect for his fellow professionals. It's an engaging and rare combination.

To compare and contrast the Somerset achievements of Cook with, say, those of Vivian Richards is a tempting but flawless exercise; both men are touched with greatness, yet they are vastly different players. Richards will be remembered for his astonishing powers of improvisation, his extravagant strokeplay and healthy disrespect for bowlers which found its level somewhere between savagery and arrogance.

Cook is an altogether closer relation of the coaching manual, building each innings around a bat of plumbline straightness, caressing the ball to all points of the compass and working on the theory that, provided it reaches the boundary one tenth of a second before the fielder, that is good enough.

Where Richards and Cook have been entirely comparable is in the amount of time both seem to have to play even the most hostile attack. What wouldn't we have given to see them in partnership in the same Somerset side?

Taking into account all competitions, Cook has fed around 3 500 runs per summer into Somerset cricket – a colossal achievement, devalued only by the county's inability to field a bowling attack with the necessary penetration to extract victories from that rich seam of high scores. He has earned the undying admiration of every English cricket follower with half an eye for genuine class. And, one trusts, he has derived immense personal satisfaction from a job well done.

Statisticians are inevitably drawn to a man of Cook's run-getting ability. Interestingly, Cook himself betrays no such Boycottian obsession with records and averages. Last season, he'd sailed past 300 against Glamorgan and was within striking range of Richards' Somerset record when the declaration came. Cook's reaction was typically magnanimous – team interest must come first, and he thought Viv the better player anyway.

Well, you can argue that one until the cows come home. All I know is that it has been a privilege and pleasure to watch a master batsman going about his business with pride, dignity, charm and consummate skill. Best wishes, S.J.C. – and thank you.

Before that final end-of-season game with Warwickshire, *Somerset County Gazette* cricket writer Eric Coombes had penned:

After two run-filled Somerset summers, Jimmy Cook found the British climate a little less clement when he arrived for his third and final season with the county in April. There were those who questioned the Cook ability to rattle off another 2 000-plus runs this time round.

But as we approach the final game of the season that man Cook has again served up more runs than any other batsman in county cricket and has a few more records bubbling on the stove. The man who quests for runs as eagerly as a schoolboy hunts for autographs went into the penultimate four-day championship match against Gloucestershire at Bristol with over 2 500 first-class runs already in the bank this season and over 3 000 from all cricket for the third year running.

He slipped quietly past the 5 000-run mark in championship cricket during his 152 against Glamorgan at Swansea on June 4 this year, and in so doing became the fastest man in cricket history to achieve this target – both in the number of innings and period of time. For the record, Cook's 5 000 came from 85 innings (eight fewer than the previous best from Graeme Hick) and two years and 45 days – which is 64 days quicker than Bill Edrich of Middlesex managed in the late 1930s. In fact, Cook and Edrich are the only batsmen ever to achieve this target in under three years.

Cook also went into this week's match against Gloucestershire needing just one more century to beat the legendary Bill Alley's 30-year-old record of ten first-class hundreds for Somerset in a season. He could also pass Alley's Somerset record of 2 761 championship runs, set in the same summer of 1961. Whether he does or not will not bother Mr Cook one little bit. His staple diet is runs, not records, and he prefers to let others sort out the statistics. But he would like to finish with one big score for the Somerset fans at Taunton at the expense of championship-chasing Warwickshire – 'just as a way of saying "thank you" for accepting me and making me so welcome'.

Happily, I was able to sign off with a 'thank you' century. Despite the fact that this was my last match for Somerset, I know it will certainly not be the last time I see the place. Having enjoyed three magnificent years there I know that, given the slightest opportunity, I will again be heading for Taunton and a drink with the cider men.

10

THE GATTING TOUR

10

THE GATTING TOUR

The ill-fated tour of South Africa in early 1990 by the English team under the captaincy of Mike Gatting will be remembered not only as a controversial sporting event but also as one of the turning-points in recent South African political history. It was the catalyst which exposed and subsequently buried so many of the social ills bred by apartheid.

For years the South African Cricket Union had striven hard to eliminate racism from the sport. And when a vociferous element of the non-white community used the presence of the English players to take a clear and unequivocal stand on the inequality of resources, the lack of opportunity for coaching and the absence of genuine representation, the SACU set in motion a turbo-charged programme to speed up its equality policy. It was so successful that within two years barriers in all sports were virtually eliminated. It is true that the release from prison of African National Congress leader Nelson Mandela in February 1990, and the subsequent dramatic liberal political policies initiated by President F W de Klerk, created the climate for this sporting metamorphosis, but credit must nevertheless be given to the SACU and the leadership of president Geoff Dakin, managing director Ali Bacher, former president Joe Pamensky, and their board for having the courage to embark on their pathfinder role.

When the Gatting team flew home with the sounds and sights of the demonstrators still fresh in their minds, few would have guessed that within a comparatively short time cricket in South Africa would be run by one new controlling body representing people of all races, and an official South African team would be playing in India, the West Indies, and the World Cup in Australasia. It was an incredible, breathtaking transformation, and if any individuals are to be singled out for special praise they are Dr Bacher, brilliant administrator and former national captain; SACU president Geoff Dakin; and the ANC's 'representative' for sport, Steve Tshwete. They were on opposite sides at the beginning of 1990, but subsequently came together to form a dynamic team whose labours were richly rewarded when South Africa was readmitted to the comity of cricketing nations in 1991.

Racism is anathema to me and, like the majority of my fellow cricketers, I was pleased to see the day when the barriers were withdrawn and we moved into the last decade of this century once more respected, and judged by our cricket and nothing else.

While welcoming the news when the Gatting tour was announced, with hindsight I agree with the majority feeling that it was unfortunate and ill-timed. But from a cricketing point of view it created a new dimension in my career. I was appointed captain of my country. It was as much a 135 surprise as an honour for my only previous experience as captain had been at club level, in my schooldays, and as a stand-in when my Transvaal captain was not playing. But some time before this, before the Gatting team had even assembled, there had been a thorough debate on the question of who would be eligible to play for the Springboks. The provincial captains were asked to conduct a survey among their players as to what possible guidelines should be laid down. We live in an age when qualifications are relaxed or adapted to suit circumstances, where players born in one country are scattered all over the world wearing the colours of other nations, and the SACU wanted to pin down as far as it could how players viewed the issue.

There was no easy solution, and the case of Kepler Wessels was an example. Here was a brilliant cricketer who, frustrated at seeing his own country frozen out of international cricket because of politics, emigrated to Australia, qualifying and then gaining Test colours for that country with much success – one of the few men to score a century on his début. After some years he returned home to settle in Port Elizabeth, but was selected and played for Kim Hughes' unofficial Australian side which had made a two-season tour of the Republic only two years before.

The question arose: was it fair to consider him for South Africa – now, later, or never? There was nothing personal in this, Kepler being a most respected man and player. It was a case of some parameters having to be laid down. Again, could Allan Lamb and Robin Smith, two South Africans who had done so well in Britain, now fly home and be considered? Or what about Peter Rawson, the former Zimbabwe captain now playing for Natal? Then there were Mike Haysman and Rod McCurdy, Australian batsman and bowler respectively, who returned after the Hughes tours to settle in South Africa and play for Northern Transvaal and Eastern Province. Would they be eligible?

As requested, players debated the matter at length throughout the country. I attended one meeting during a match between Transvaal and Natal at the Wanderers, and the general consensus was that, to a certain degree, preference had to be given to players who had been loyal to the country, those who had remained at home. For example, if Robin Smith had flown home and declared his availability to play against Gatting's side, should he perhaps be considered ahead of Peter Kirsten? Our view was that Peter's loyalty should gain him preference. The overall conclusion was that a stringent time period should be laid down – seven years was mentioned – and in the specific case of Kepler, he should have to wait another two years before coming into the reckoning. Our recommendations were forwarded, but the SACU decided that Kepler would be eligible for South Africa immediately as he had been playing for Eastern Province for some years. This annoyed the players, who pointed out that they had been asked to submit their views, had complied, and were then ignored on this important issue of the time factor even though, on a personal level, everyone would have liked to see Kepler in the side.

Then there was the matter of the captaincy. General speculation was that it lay between Kepler and Clive Rice. As Clive had been asked by Ali Bacher to conduct the players' survey, there had been a general assumption that Clive was trying to promote his captaincy prospects at Kepler's expense, particularly as the players had ruled against Kepler's eligibility. Nothing was further from the truth. Again, with hindsight, it was unfortunate that Clive had been asked to handle this task.

A few days after the matter had been resolved Peter van der Merwe, the convener of the national selection committee, phoned me and asked me to have dinner with him when next he was in Johannesburg. He gave no reason, but I believed he wanted to obtain my views on the Kepler Wessels eligibility question. We did talk about it at length and then, towards the end of the meal, he said: 'We have decided to make you captain'. As I had thought the job lay between Clive and Kepler, and as my experience was very limited, I was astonished. My initial reaction was to refuse, saying that Clive Rice should be captain, but I did not want to do the selectors' job for them.

To my further astonishment, he then said bluntly that Clive would probably not be playing. While conceding my delight at the honour, I said that Clive was an experienced captain with a proven track record, and repeated my view that he was the obvious choice. But Peter said it had been noticed that I was the one who was always talking to and encouraging the bowlers and the other fielders generally.

I made it quite clear that Clive was firmly in charge of the Transvaal side. Usually I was merely passing on his instructions – with maybe a word or two of my own – particularly to the bowlers as Clive fielded in the slips and if I was, say, at mid-on, mid-off or in the covers I was nearer to the bowler. He reminded me that Transvaal had only won one match that summer, and it was when I had been captain. I did not see it that way. We won because we were the better team on the day. Peter said the selectors had already appointed me, so I was really left with no option but to accept. My one stipulation was that I captain the side for the planned two five-day Tests and the six one-day Internationals. This was accepted.

Our dinner was on the Tuesday and Peter said my appointment as captain would be announced on the Saturday, and for the next few days I

had to ride out the speculation among my own circle of friends, colleagues and the media. It so happened that on the Saturday night Linsey and
I were to attend a party at Clive's house, and before we left the captaincy
was announced on the 6 p.m. radio news bulletin. When we arrived at
Clive's house he expressed his delight and, typical of him, he opened a
bottle of champagne and toasted my appointment before hosting what
turned out to be a great party. His only regret was that no one had had the
courtesy to contact him in advance with the news.

The SACU had instigated the visit by the Gatting side because, with the
prospects of our returning to international cricket at that stage still very
bleak, it had been decided to continue the policy of inviting unofficial or
'rebel' teams in order to maintain public interest, keep up our standards,
and also give the players something to aim for. In addition, support was
gathering in the rest of the cricketing world for South Africa to be readmitted to the International Cricket Council, as the sport was seen as an
additional weapon for breaking down apartheid. Regular contact, they
maintained, was healthy, even on the playing field itself. Shortly before
the team left for South Africa, twelve former England cricketers, including Peter May and Mike Smith who had both led MCC sides to South
Africa some years before, wrote to *The Times* of London spelling out this
view most strongly:

> We share the SACU's distaste for the apartheid system and applaud
> their efforts to break down the constitutional barriers between races'
> sporting contact. We believe this enterprise should now be encour-
> aged by further international support. The South African tour by
> Mike Gatting and his team could help promote the long-term inter-
> ests of young black enthusiasts.
>
> We recognise the real changes that have been brought about by
> boycotts, but accept the view that now is the time for inspiration, as
> within South Africa itself cricket is now known and accepted as a
> force for change.

Of course there were others with opposing views, none more strongly
expressed than those of Peter Hain, the South African-born political acti-
vist (and now Labour MP) who made a secret return visit to the country
and wrote:

> I came away convinced that the sports boycott was as necessary now
> as it has ever been. Rebel tours are simply a diversion and will post-

138

pone the day when South Africa can be readmitted. White sports officials like Ali Bacher should abandon rebel tours and stop making extravagant and dishonest claims on behalf of their welcome but meagre township coaching schemes.

Ali Bacher took issue with Hain and wrote:

So this English tour is going against ANC strategy. It is breaking sanctions. But is it not unfair that cricket is being targeted while scores of South African companies are constantly improving their bottom-line profits by trading internationally, and therefore breaking sanctions?

If people want to demonstrate against the tour, that is their right, provided it is peaceful. If people want to watch cricket, that too is their right.

Into this highly publicised and politically charged atmosphere flew the Englishmen. On paper it was a good side, comprising Mike Gatting (Middlesex), captain; David Graveney (Gloucestershire), player/manager; Bill Athey (Gloucestershire), Kim Barnett (Derbyshire), Chris Broad (Nottinghamshire), Chris Cowdrey (Kent), Graham Dilley (Worcestershire), Richard Ellison (Kent), John Emburey (Middlesex), Neil Foster (Essex), Bruce French (Nottinghamshire), Paul Jarvis (Yorkshire), Matthew Maynard (Glamorgan), Greg Thomas (Northamptonshire), Tim Robinson (Nottinghamshire), and Allan Wells (Sussex). Fourteen were seasoned internationals, nine having played in a recent Ashes series against Australia.

Having seen and played against Mike Gatting the previous year in my initial season with Somerset, and knowing his impressive record, I had gained an enormous respect for him both as a player and a man. This respect was fully justified during this tour which put enormous strain on him and manager David Graveney in particular, as they had to deal with tricky political issues and circumstances for which their background as professional sportsmen from a foreign country had not prepared them. But such are their respective characters that, in my view, they were to go home with their consciences clear and reputations enhanced.

When the demonstrators – for or against the tour – were around, both men handled the situation with real aplomb, never getting rattled, always dignified, and using common sense to help defuse matters.

Gatting has a puckish sense of humour. On numerous occasions the staff at hotels and restaurants refused to serve the South African and 139

English players. While they were in Kimberley for the game against the Combined Bowl Eleven the staff of a local restaurant walked out when Gatting and some of the players came in for a meal. Undaunted, he took off his jacket, went into the kitchen area and called out to the customers that he would play cook for the evening. It would be a great meal, with a choice of steak or steak. To me, Mike Gatting is the archetypal English bulldog – tenacious, scrupulously fair, and a great fighter. He played cricket one way only: hard, but always within the rules and spirit of the game. As his record indicates, he is a superb batsman – one of the best it has been my fortune to see. While very sound against pace bowling, apart from Graeme Pollock I do not know a batsman who plays spin better. When he was in the mood it was impossible to control him. He was the spinner's nightmare. He would relish dancing down the wicket, sweeping, cutting, driving, doing what he liked as he sought and found gaps in the field.

I recall one Benson and Hedges match in England when David Graveney, for Somerset, was bowling to him. Now David is one of the best exponents of slow bowling in Britain, yet Mike was in such a ruthless mood that he scored off him for 17 consecutive deliveries. In the end poor David did not know where to bowl to him. He was in such devastating form that he scored a hundred in that match, scored another century in a Sunday League game, and then proceeded to hammer our Somerset bowlers for 180 in a county game. And this gifted batsman, along with the other 'rebels', was to be denied an opportunity to play Test cricket for some years because he had the audacity to make a tour of South Africa.

The tourists played some warm-up games in January and February against combined sides and then prepared for the first Test at the Wanderers. At the time the Currie Cup final was being played in Port Elizabeth between Eastern Province and Western Province, and I was invited to fly down for the day to have a say and a vote in the selection of the 12-man Springbok squad for both the first and second Tests. I did so, outlining who I thought should be chosen. All my nominations were discussed except one – Clive Rice. Peter van der Merwe said he was out of consideration, and the silence from the other members of the panel indicated that they did not support me. I was disappointed, not only out of loyalty to my friend and provincial captain, but because I believed we needed his all-round bowling and batting skills, especially on a Wanderers wicket that was going to help the bowlers, and particularly as we were not as strong in

the bowling department as I would have liked. I did say that when the teams were chosen for the one-day games Clive should be given serious consideration as, once again, his batting, bowling, and all-round experience would be essential. This was accepted.

The South African squad comprised: myself (Transvaal), Henry Fotheringham (Natal), Kepler Wessels (Eastern Province), Peter Kirsten (Western Province), Roy Pienaar (Transvaal), Adrian Kuiper (Western Province), Brian McMillan (Western Province), Ray Jennings (Transvaal), Dave Rundle (Western Province), Richard McGlashan (Natal), Richard Snell (Transvaal), and Allan Donald (Orange Free State).

Among cricket aficionados at least there was much interest in the Wanderers game, but it was to be ruined by the condition of the wicket. There was far too much grass and it was not at all conducive to producing an even tussle. Indeed, on the afternoon before the match as some of us were going to net practice, John Emburey, who with David Graveney had been looking at the pitch, said to me in all seriousness: 'Where are we playing?' From the players' changing rooms it was not possible to see the designated strip. I said flippantly, 'It must be out there somewhere', but he had a point. With the weather overcast I knew the grass would remain green, and that preparations for the pitch had been hampered. I told my parents, who had planned to attend the game, not to buy tickets for the last two days: the game would be over inside three.

I hoped that I would win the toss the next morning and be able to turn our seamers loose on that inviting track. It turned out that way, and our up-and-coming fast bowlers Allan Donald and Richard Snell went to work. Because of their lack of experience they did not take full advantage of the conditions on that rain-affected first day, but they settled down the next morning and the Englishmen were shot out for only 156, Donald taking 4 for 30 and Snell 4 for 38. South Africa made a poor start, and then in marched Adrian Kuiper, one of those unpredictable batsmen who can turn the course of a match with some sustained explosive strokeplay. Fortunately for us, Adrian was in one of his most positive moods that day. He was dropped before reaching double figures, but then, taking advantage of this good fortune, he proceeded to tear the bowling apart, racing to 84 off 143 deliveries by way of 1 six and 15 fours.

We totalled 203 and the visitors went in a second time against a home pace attack just itching to get at them again. Overnight I had told the groundsman Chris Scott not to roll the wicket as I wanted to retain as much life in it as possible. There was sun on the second day, so the pitch had hardened up and the ball flew off it much faster. Having only just come out of winter hibernation with not enough match practice, they had no chance and were shuffled out for 122, with Donald (4-29) again spearheading the attack. We knocked off the required deficit easily enough by 5 o'clock on the third day to get home by 7 wickets. It was a disappointingly one-sided game, made so by the devil of a pitch.

Towards the end of the game, as we were coasting to victory, Kepler Wessels called me aside and said he did not want to play in the second Test. I was puzzled and said so. He explained that there had been so much written and said about whether or not he should be playing that the pressure had got to him and he felt emotionally drained. He could not guarantee to give of his best in the second Test in Cape Town. I admired his honesty. While wanting a batsman of his calibre in the team, I certainly did not want a man who could not be sure of pulling his weight. I asked him to sleep on it – maybe he would feel better in a day or so. But he said that his decision was final: he would not be available. Peter van der Merwe also had a word with him, but Kepler would not budge.

So Clive Rice was pencilled in as his replacement in the squad. There was media speculation that the players did not want Kepler in the team, but this was not the case. The rest of the team and I would have been delighted if he had travelled to the Cape with us. But of course it was all rather academic as the second International was cancelled, as were two of the planned six one-day games. One of the reasons was that a small bomb had gone off in one of the booking cubicles at Newlands, with an accompanying warning of further trouble if the game proceeded. Naturally the authorities could not risk lives and took the only course of action open to them.

Several younger players were drafted into the squad for the one-day games, and South Africa won what turned out to be a tight series by three games to one. Without doubt one of the most memorable highlights was an incredible 117 by that man Adrian Kuiper in Bloemfontein. His century came off just 49 balls by way of 8 sixes and 7 fours. The English attack just fell apart, Greg Thomas conceding 19 in one over, and then Richard Ellison 20 in another over. South Africa's total of 301 for 7 was a match-winning target as the visitors collapsed to be hustled out for 94 and to lose by 207 runs. In mitigation, it must be said that they were batting under lights, an unfamiliar situation for most of them. In addition, one bank of floodlights failed, adding further to their misery, particularly when Allan Donald was in full flight on his home pitch. But they never made this an excuse for their defeat.

This victory put us 3-0 up in the four-match series. As captain, I would have liked to finish the series at the Wanderers with a whitewash, but Gatting and his men were determined to deny us that. Kim Barnett, their elegant opening batsman, found his best form and, on a wicket that this time was tailor-made for good strokeplay, he hit a wonderful 136, simply toying with the Springbok bowlers.

Chasing a target of 297, our batsmen felt that anything they could do we could match but, of all people, Mike Gatting turned the tables on us. Never recognised as a frontline bowler, we decided that we could enjoy ourselves at his expense and began hitting out and taking chances. But, trundling his stocky frame up to the wicket for six and a bit overs, he made the ball nip around just enough to break through the cream of our batting and take 6 wickets for only 26 runs. It really was an astonishing performance and Mike will probably never again return such impressive figures. But all credit to him for rising to the challenge.

So they won by 134 runs and finally proved to the South African public that they were indeed capable of better things than they had hitherto shown. Regrettably, because the tour had blown up into a political storm, the return tour was cancelled.

The Gatting tour was a personal nightmare for Ali Bacher. He had done so much to organise these unofficial tours over the years. He believed they were good for South African cricket and staked his considerable reputation as one of the game's most able and far-sighted administrators on making a success of them. But as the demonstrations grew, the animosity heightened abroad and among large sections of the non-white sporting public. The African National Congress, in the person of their articulate spokesman on sport, Steve Tshwete, stepped up the political pressure. So all the intended goodwill vanished, to be replaced by an anger which could not be ignored.

Ali, who accompanied the Gatting team for most of the tour, stepped in personally whenever things became rough and tried to ease the situation. He was scrupulously fair to both sides and pleaded for reasonableness. In Pietermaritzburg he even requested that the police allow a crowd to demonstrate peacefully against the very tour he had organised, saying it was their democratic right. He won his point.

Even his detractors respected his personal courage in facing what at times were angry mobs. As he admitted later: 'It was the first time in my life I lost confidence in myself. When the tour was called off, it was seen as a capitulation . . . I took flak from both sides. A friend I asked for advice simply said: "Disappear for months."' Former England captain Mike Brearley was later to write in *The Observer* about Bacher's request for the police to allow that demonstration in Pietermaritzburg while he and Gatting walked through the crowd to accept a petition:

To avoid further turmoil, his board called off the tour. Sport in such abnormal conditions was not worth the candle. As Bacher says now, the lesson was that sport cannot be sport if it is totally against the will of the people.

This débâcle was a watershed. The futility of cricket in such a setting proved to be Bacher's road to Damascus. The white cricketing authorities determined on a radically different strategy; virtue was born of pain, if not necessity. Seeing that both the justice of the complaints and the level of dissent overrode short-term cricketing factors, they made it their dual goal to unify cricket administration and to develop the game vigorously throughout the country.

Thus, the township programme, begun in 1986, became the main thrust of policy rather than an element of it, an element that to many had up to then smacked of window dressing.

11
THE INDIA TOUR

II

THE INDIA TOUR

The year 1991 was a most important one in South Africa's history. It was the year all racial legislation was removed from our statute books, which in turn led to the country's being allowed to rejoin the international community in virtually all spheres after decades of ostracism. Of course apartheid did not, and will not, disappear overnight. Apart from the myriad of petty laws that must be rewritten, human nature being what it is, it will take years for everyone to adjust to the fact that no longer will the law discriminate on the basis of a person's skin colour.

In my world of sport, 1991 meant that at last those of us who aspired to compete internationally at the highest level could do so after years of frustration. True, many of us had been able to test our skills unofficially – in the case of cricket, in so-called 'rebel' tours – and as individuals quite a number of us had also been fortunate enough to play abroad, in my case for the English county Somerset for three wonderful years. But for the vast majority it was a situation of being on the outside looking in, and not getting an opportunity to represent their country, the highest accolade to which a sportsman can aspire.

For us cricketers the crucial date was 10 July when, at the game's headquarters at Lord's in London, the International Cricket Council (ICC) voted South Africa back into the fold after many years of hard lobbying by our top officials, headed by the president of the United Cricket Board of South Africa (UCBSA) Geoff Dakin, his predecessor Joe Pamensky, and managing director Dr Ali Bacher. This trio and their predecessors had long been in the forefront of removing all racial regulations from associations under their control, and had also embarked on a concentrated and determined programme of taking the game to aspiring players throughout the nation, irrespective of their race.

Cricketers had always been pretty liberal in their thinking, but it must be said that not a great deal of effort was made to right the situation until South African-born Peter Hain showed us the error of our ways with his organised demonstrations in England, and until former prime minister John Vorster barred the Cape Town Coloured allrounder Basil D'Oliveira from touring the country in 1968 with an MCC side – a decision which created an international furore. To be fair, once we were driven out of international competition, once we had been put firmly in our place, our officials did a marvellous recovery job. We did make what, in retrospect, many considered to have been the mistake of bringing out unofficial sides from England, Sri Lanka, the West Indies and Australia to slake the thirst of the players and the public who were bored stiff with domestic competitions. But no one can fault the way the sins were expiated, and there was understandable joy when, at the July meeting at Lord's,   147 the Indian delegation proposed South Africa's readmission. And herein lies the basis for what was to become one of the most dramatic, historic tours any cricket side had ever undertaken. And I was very proud and privileged to have been a member of the team selected for that tour.

Although South Africa was back as a legitimate member of the ICC, there were reservations about whether it was too soon to allow us to be slotted into the international fixture lists, beginning with the World Cup tournament being played in Australasia in February and March 1992. Former England captain and president of the ICC, Colin Cowdrey was particularly worried on this point and unilaterally, and on shaky legal grounds, decided to reserve his position until the game's legislators met at Sharjah in the United Arab Emirates in October for the Champions Cup tournament when he could again canvass opinion.

I have never understood Cowdrey's thinking. Either we were back in the ICC, or we were not. However, at Sharjah we were warmly voted in as the ninth country in the World Cup tournament, and the UCBSA delegation which attended the meeting flew home delighted and with the news that India had invited South Africa to make its first foreign tour in 26 years by replacing Pakistan which had withdrawn at short notice from a short tour of that country.

It really was too soon for us to think of tours of any description. Our season had barely begun, but the UCBSA delegation had no sooner stepped off the plane at Johannesburg's Jan Smuts airport than a hasty executive meeting was called at a nearby hotel and India's invitation was gratefully and officially accepted. There were many, including our greatest batsman Graeme Pollock, who said that we should not go; we were on a hiding to nothing; but general consensus was that the outcome did not matter. Playing the game was the thing – and we wanted to play, to show the flag once more for our country.

Abiding by World Cup rules, only a party of 14 could go, but who? Those eligible had at most only played a few matches that season. On a personal level, I was still partly resting from my last and strenuous season with Somerset, and had played only in one day/night game and a few club games for my league side, Rand Afrikaans University. So it was a case of relying mainly on the previous season's form.

The squad selected was: Clive Rice (Transvaal, aged 42), captain; Jimmy Cook (Transvaal, 38), Allan Donald (Orange Free State, 25), Clive Eksteen (Transvaal, 25), Andrew Hudson (Natal, 25), Peter Kirsten (Border, 36), Adrian Kuiper (Western Province, 32), Craig Matthews (Western Province, 25), Brian McMillan (Western Province, 28), David Richardson (Eastern Province, 32), Tim Shaw (Eastern Province, 32),

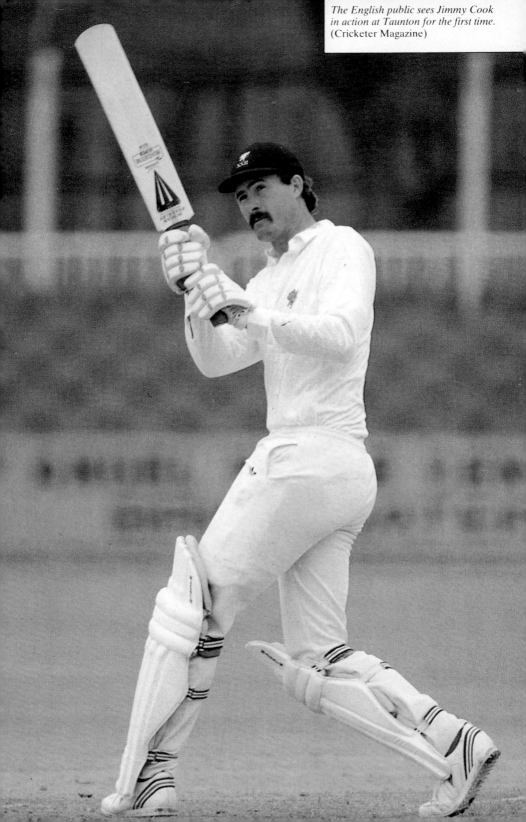

The English public sees Jimmy Cook in action at Taunton for the first time. (Cricketer Magazine)

The South African side for the only test against Mike Gatting's 'rebels'.

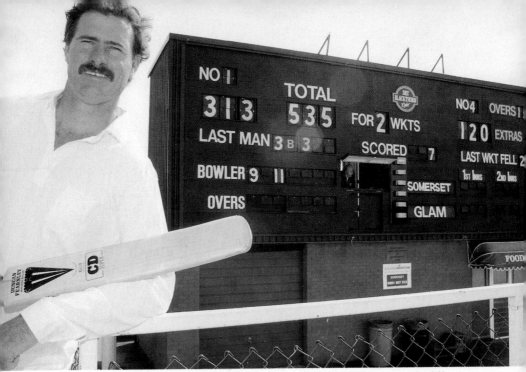

The scoreboard reflects my highest first-class score: Somerset vs Glamorgan, Cardiff, 1990. (Reproduced by permission of Alain Lockyer, PR Industrial and Commercial Photography)

With Somerset manager Jack Birkenshaw and chief executive Peter Anderson at Old Trafford for the Benson and Hedges semi-final in June 1990. (Reproduced by permission of Alain Lockyer, Somerset Photo News)

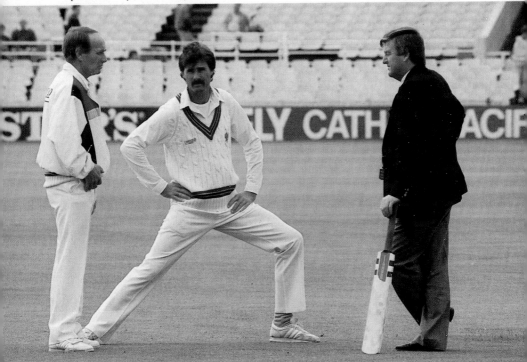

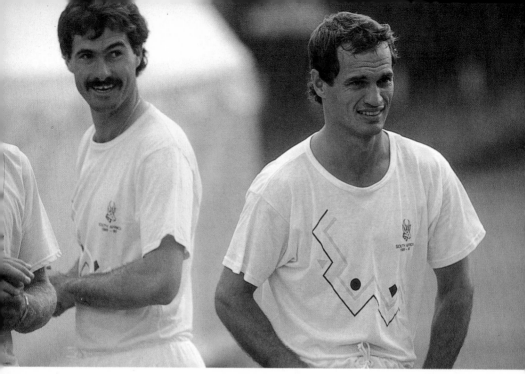

Practising with Kepler Wessels, a world-class batsman whose temperament is ideal, especially for the big occasion.

Leaving the field with Graeme Pollock, arguably the most gifted and talked-about South African cricketer ever.

Sweeping Omar Henry in Transvaal's Currie Cup match against Free State in January 1992. (Joao Silva, The Star*)*

The Mean Machine: Transvaal side 1983/84, winners of the Currie Cup and the Nissan Shield.

Garlands and flowers greeted us wherever we went in India. Left to right: myself, Richard Snell and Clive Eksteen.

The 'rogues' at Taunton: Stephen batting and Ryan preparing to bowl.

Training time: grinding out the kilometres before the start of the new season. (Sunday Star)

Historic moment: Krish Mackerdhuj, Geoff Dakin, Ali Bacher and Steve Tshwete at Lord's after South Africa's readmission as a full member of the ICC in July 1991.

On duty at my second home, the Wanderers Stadium in Johannesburg.

Richard Snell (Transvaal, 23), Kepler Wessels (Eastern Province, 34), and Mandy Yachad (Northern Transvaal, 30); manager, Dr Ali Bacher; coach, Mike Procter.

There was some discussion as to whether or not I should have been elected captain. As I had led the team in the one Test against Mike Gatting's 'rebel' side and as Clive, at 42, was getting a bit long in the tooth for top-class cricket, it was felt that perhaps I should have taken up where I had left off. This was not how I saw it at all. As far as I was concerned, there was no question about the captaincy. True, Clive was of an age when most men had long turned to less strenuous activities than professional cricket, but he was a superb competitor and one of the shrewdest and most experienced leaders in the game. His bowling may have lacked the fire of old, but what he lacked in pace he made up for in guile, while his batting was tenacious and had proved to be most reliable when any side he played for was in trouble. I have never held any strong feelings about the captaincy. After more than two decades playing at a senior level, I obviously like to think I have learned a great deal and when it was handed to me I accepted this additional responsibility. But actually I preferred to be left to get on with my batting and make my contribution to the best of my ability when in the field. Some men yearn for and thrive on the leadership role. Clive Rice is obviously in that mould. But not me.

Questions were raised about taking four opening batsmen in myself, Hudson, Yachad and Wessels, and two spinners in Shaw and Eksteen. Unlucky not to be chosen were wicket-keeper Ray Jennings of Northern Transvaal, Transvaal middle-order batsman Daryll Cullinan, and Transvaal fast bowler Steven Jack. That said, however, it was a good combination, maybe a little on the old side but in itself that was probably a good thing as we knew we were heading for a journey into the comparative unknown, a cricketing *Star Trek*.

After being named captain, Clive Rice, in typically positive manner and scrambling his metaphors somewhat, told the media: 'We are entering the lion's den. I feel like Christopher Columbus leading my team into the unknown.'

The acceptance of the tour and the team selection took place so quickly that those of us involved were caught up in a whirlwind. Coincidentally, on that Sunday Clive and I were playing against each other in a league match at the RAU ground. He was batting when his wife Sue came to the ground and called across to say that the tour was on. After his innings he met up with Lee Irvine, one of the national selectors, and they asked me to join them. As we had both captained South Africa and were among the more experienced candidates for the likely squad, Lee, who was on his way to the executive meeting, valued our opinion on the likely party. We gave our views; Lee said the team would be announced on the Monday, and then left. But when I arrived home at about 8.30 p.m. one of my sons rushed out and told me that the team had been announced on the TV news bulletin. I had scored a century in a club game, but mentally and physically was not really prepared for what lay ahead. My original plan was to ease myself into the season and reach peak performance in February when the World Cup team for Australasia was chosen. But naturally I was thrilled to have been selected.

Predictably and understandably, the news that South Africa had finally broken out of cricket isolation became a major event in Britain and most Commonwealth countries. Our golfers had been the first to come in from the cold a short while before, when Gary Player captained a side that narrowly lost to Sweden in the final of the Dunhill Cup event at St Andrews, but as race featured prominently in cricket, the impact of our going to India was much stronger. It dominated the British media for 24 hours and several leading cricket writers, sensing a good story and no doubt anxious for an excuse to escape the winter for sunnier climes, packed their bags for the first venue, Calcutta.

Much emotional nonsense and hype was written by some of the more extreme Fleet Street papers, but the following extract from *The Independent*, one of the more sober and influential papers, pretty well put the situation and the background leading to the tour in the right perspective:

> The true international pioneer of the South African cricket establishment, the man most deserving of the Columbus tag is Ali Bacher, manager of the present team and captain of the last one to play international cricket, against Australia in 1970. After the fiasco of Mike Gatting's 'rebel' tour 18 months ago, Dr Bacher was in despair, convinced that South Africa was condemned to the cricketing wilderness for years to come. Yet he did not give up and, shrewd enough to realise that the way back to world competition lay through Nelson Mandela's African National Congress (unlike his more bull-headed counterparts in the rugby fraternity), he assiduously wooed that organisation and surprised all by clinching South Africa's cricket place back on the world stage before even such convincingly multi-racial sports as football and athletics.
>
> The key was the merging of the 'black' and 'white' cricket unions into the United Cricket Board of South Africa, and the energy and enthusiasm with which Bacher set about developing a hugely impressive coaching programme in the disadvantaged black communi-

ties. On the strength of that he established a warm rapport with the man the ANC have appointed to the sports portfolio, the former political prisoner, Steve Tshwete. It was Tshwete who convinced Mandela to come out and state last month [October 1991], in what proved to be a watershed, that the time had come for South African cricket to come in from the cold. The floodgates opened and South Africa was duly included in next year's World Cup in Australasia and as a full member of the International Cricket Council. The UCBSA now enjoys a far better relationship with the ANC than any other sporting body, let alone the government of F W de Klerk. The measure was the response of the ANC to the news that the 14 members of the squad for India would be white. Tshwete said this bothered him less than any bogus tokenism would have done. The crucial point was that black youngsters now had a chance to play in a future national team.

Indeed, as Bacher pointed out: 'If we had a South African Under-15 or Under-17 team, there is no question it would be composed of players from all the population groups'. Such was the potential among young players, he said, that he was convinced South Africa would dominate world cricket by the end of the decade. 'We were a force when the teams were all white. Can you imagine what the potential will be when we utilise all our people, all our resources?' Which is not to say he underestimates the capacity of the present team to give India a difficult time in the first of the three one-day internationals at Calcutta's Eden Gardens stadium. 'That will be one of the most dramatic moments in the history of cricket,' he said.

How prophetic were Ali's words. It was indeed a dramatic moment, but before we left there was the question of what we would be called. A strong controversy had been running in the country as to whether or not we should be called by the traditional unofficial tag given to all national sides, the Springboks. Most whites seemed to want the tradition to be continued, but there were strong objections from many non-white organisations and interested individuals who felt that the Springbok should go as it represented the old, whites-only South Africa. It was decided we would not wear the Springbok emblem on our blazers, and in the end we wore on our shirts for the day/night game in New Delhi the name of the company which sponsored us. I was proud to have worn the Springbok badge during those 'rebel' tours, but it was not an issue which occupied too much of my time. As I packed my gear for the adventure that lay ahead my main thoughts were about what it would be like tackling Kapil

Dev and his colleagues in a country where cricket is a near-religion and where vast crowds are the norm. We would soon find out.

Most of us assembled at our Johannesburg hotel on the Wednesday prior to departure, but even then some had day/night provincial commitments and it was only the next day, barely hours before we took off, that we had our first full squad net practice. Had an international side ever before been gathered and dispatched in such haste? I doubt it. I must salute the organisers who made it possible – the workload must have been daunting. It reminded me of the incredible challenge which faced the British defence forces when, a decade before, they had been ordered to prepare a task force to sail and relieve the Falkland Islands, and they accomplished this feat in the course of a weekend. Dispatching our 'task force' was an infinitely smaller and less complicated affair, but it was done in the same spirit of dedication to the job at hand. The adrenalin was pumping, and the deed was done.

The jet plane used by President de Klerk for overseas trips was hired and our party, plus about 50 media personnel and 120 supporters, flew off late on the Thursday afternoon. We were too excited to sleep much and 12 hours later, after refuelling at the Seychelles, we landed in Calcutta to what was an unimaginable reception. We knew that, because of the controversial nature of our tour, there would be some interest in our arrival, but we were not prepared for what happened as we stepped off the plane, the first from South Africa ever to land in that country. People of all ages had turned out in their hundreds, waving flags, shouting greetings – a reception which few cricket sides must have experienced before. We were all garlanded with floral bouquets and had our foreheads smeared with vermilion, a traditional Hindu greeting, and then we began our 20-kilometre drive to our headquarters, the Grand Hotel. It took us about two and a half hours. With an escort of over 100 motorcycle outriders we made our way slowly through vast crowds which lined the streets and called out to us 'Welcome, South Africa', 'Good to see you', and the like, while we waved like royalty from our team bus. We were all choked with emotion.

Twice our convoy had to stop to allow Ali Bacher, UCBSA president Geoff Dakin, Clive Rice, and coach Mike Procter to clamber up on to stages which had been specially erected for them to make brief speeches. Reported the correspondent for *The Independent*:

Calcutta, described by its ruling communist government as the last bastion of Marxism in India, seemed to have forgotten its traditional anti-apartheid stance. Grandparents waved from balconies while children beat on drums and blew trumpets at crossroads with such enthusiasm that the South African captain, Clive Rice, described the experience as 'the happiest day of my cricketing life, truly incredible'. He went on: 'From South Africa's point of view, this is a fantastic moment for our cricket – and for the country for that matter' . . .

However, there were discordant notes among the celebrations. Subhas Chakravorty, the Minister of Sport who cut through red tape to make the historic visit possible, did not appear as promised at the roadside, because of strong criticism in the leftist press, which is describing the South African visit as the second defeat at the battle of Plassey inflicted by another Clive, a reference to Clive of India's victory over Siraj-ud-daula to gain control over Bengal in 1757. Mohammed Azharuddin, India's captain, and his squad did not stir from the Grand, and were not impressed by such ostentatious support for the South Africans. 'For the first time in India the home crowd seems to be on the side of the visitors,' said Azharuddin.

Former Somerset captain Vic Marks, who has a column in *The Observer*, was one of the London scribes who flew out for the tour, and he wrote in the following Sunday's issue:

The tour is a triumph of opportunism, not only for the South Africans, but also for Jagmohan Dalmiya, the former secretary of the Indian Board. Once the Indian government decided that they were unable to guarantee the safety of the Pakistan team, who were due to play a short series of one-day matches in India, Dalmiya found the most spectacular of replacements. It was he who, in a series of 50 phone calls, forged a telling link with Dr Ali Bacher before the ICC meeting at Lord's on July 10. There, he proposed, on behalf of the Indian Board, that South Africa should return to world cricket. Bacher confirmed that 'We are here because the Indians were determined to give us a place in the sun'. Such was Bacher's gratitude that he was prepared to organise a tour at helter-skelter pace . . .

Bacher is managing the South African team, and he was clearly elated upon arrival in Calcutta, though, as the day wore on, he became increasingly disorientated by the combination of emotion and fatigue. But whenever a microphone was thrust under his nose, articulacy soon returned. This was 'the happiest day of my cricketing life'; the reception that his team had received was 'overwhelming, spontaneous . . . incredible'. He also recalled that in 1948 India were the first country to withdraw their embassy from Pretoria and the first to institute sanctions, just in case the credentials of the hosts needed any confirmation. He added that today's [the first] match goes beyond cricket; it gives confidence to the South African people that they will be rewarded if they move in the right direction.

After lunch at our luxury hotel we attended the inevitable media conference, at which Ali and Clive spoke and introduced each member of the squad in turn. Still with little or no sleep, we went to the ground nearby for our first net practice, and found that the authorities, to their credit, had prepared the net wicket to be similar to that in the middle – that is, with little grass and cracked – it would play slow and low. That night we all collapsed in our beds, exhausted. But on the Saturday morning we assembled for a visit to meet the legendary Catholic nun, Mother Teresa, whose many years of devotion to the poor of India, and Calcutta specifically, had earned her a Nobel Peace Prize. Although she has been fêted extensively around the world over the years, she was totally flustered when we went to see her. Had it been just the team she might have coped, but we were accompanied by all our supporters and the attendant media people. It was a moving experience to talk to and shake the hand of such a marvellous woman, and we were pleased that our board donated about R10 000 to her organisation, which she said she would use to build another school. It was a surreal moment. Clive Rice put it succinctly: 'I have to pinch myself at regular intervals to convince myself that all this is really happening.'

We were free for the rest of the morning and went sightseeing, but were obliged to take escorts as massive crowds followed us, keen to greet and chat to us. After a good net practice there was quite a ceremonial media conference that evening to announce the respective teams for the next day's match. Unlike at home, when the side is usually announced by way of a phone call to a news agency for general circulation, this time, as the name of each player was called out, details of his career background were also given. It was useful for the South Africans to learn something about the opponents, as the majority were unknown to us.

I gather a few eyebrows were raised at home over the selection of Natal's Andrew Hudson, instead of Northern Transvaal's Mandy Yachad, to open the batting with me, especially when we lost the toss and were asked to bat in unfamiliar surroundings and on such an emotionally charged occasion. However, our selection panel took the view that Andrew was a proven provincial opening batsman with the right credentials and would, after all, have an experienced partner in myself. Also, it had been decided that, for the first game at least, no one should play out of his regular position. On seeing the enormous crowd of what was reported to have been a world record of 96 000 packed into the Eden Gardens stadium that Sunday morning, we would rather have fielded first to settle our nerves and get some idea as to how the pitch would play. But it was not to be. Rice lost the toss, and Andrew and I took a deep breath and went out to do battle.

We had been warned that the ball did move around quite a bit in the first hour at Calcutta and, starting at 9 a.m. the outfield was still soaking wet from dew, so boundaries would be at a premium. Andrew was a bundle of nerves and, seeing his condition, I asked him if he would like to take first strike and break the ice early, so to speak, but he declined. After the tour Vic Marks wrote that I suffered occasionally from nerves and showed a hesitancy which had been evident more than once when I was playing for Somerset. This was simply not true. As I mentioned earlier, after my initial games for Transvaal I never again experienced nervousness. It is not part of my makeup. The only emotion I felt as I went out to face India was one of excitement.

When Kapil Dev prepared to bowl there was, as can be expected, a tremendous buzz of excitement around the ground. But instead of subsiding, as is normally the case when the bowler runs in, it got louder and louder. I was determined not to yield to the temptation to pull away and declare that I could not play under such conditions. Uppermost in my mind, well attuned to the challenge after 20 years in first-class cricket, was the customary self-instruction of 'watch the ball and ignore all else'. I was also well aware of the fact that the eyes of my team-mates were riveted on me and that I had to set an example of temperament. Unfortunately for Andrew, he received a ball in his first over that moved away late, he got an edge, and was caught behind.

One wicket down for only 3 on the board was not an auspicious start, and Kepler Wessels and I quietly set about to do some repair work after this initial setback. The ball did move around a bit, but when the two opening bowlers had finished their first spells, and having hit a satisfying boundary, I was starting to feel good. I was moving towards my 20s, when I was trapped leg before wicket by Srinath for 17. There was not much of an appeal and I thought I was outside the line of the off-stump, but as our camp had agreed beforehand not to show any reaction at any time during the tour no matter what we felt about any controversial decision, I walked without hesitation.

When I reached the dressing-room, the players who had seen the delivery on television also thought it was outside the line of the off-stump. On seeing the replay on TV on my return to South Africa, I too am certain that this was the case. But I accepted the decision at the time and have no complaint.

When Peter Kirsten also fell for only 7, the momentum dropped and we never really recovered. Kepler and Adrian Kuiper did a fine repair job as far as they could. Kepler knew the country and the ground from his previous tour with Australia, and he settled into form almost immediately. His half-century was typical of the class of the man: solid defence, patience, and no hesitation in hammering the bad delivery. Adrian relished the challenge confronting him and thrilled everyone with his pugnacious hitting round the wicket.

But 177 was obviously not a winning total. India had bowled well. With no one particularly quick, they bowled intelligently, were on target most of the time, usually just short of a length on a pitch that did not allow the ball to come on to the bat and enable one to play shots. Azharuddin set his field well, and with their excellent fielding we had to work hard for every run. As expected, Kapil Dev, their veteran international, was their best bowler, moving the ball away appreciably and then, when he wanted to, bringing one back into the batsman. What was noticeable was the way they managed to swing a ball that was more than 30 overs old even more at the end of the innings than at the beginning, especially Prabhakar.

This led to the controversial business of the allegation of the 'scuffed' ball. At lunchtime, quite innocently, Mike Procter went to the umpires and asked to see the ball. His only intention was to see how it had worn on a type of pitch we had never seen before, a justifiable request. He had no suspicions whatsoever. The umpires handed it over without hesitation. When he looked at it he could see that one side was shiny, but the other side appeared to be cut and scratched. He asked permission to show the ball to Clive Rice because we were deliberating how early we could bring our left-arm spinner Tim Shaw into the attack. Having played in Britain, Clive and I immediately cottoned on to the situation and why the ball had swung so late in the innings. A deduction was that the marks had been made with a foreign object, but it was decided to live with the situation as nobody could completely pin down the reasons.

The next day Ali Bacher went to the Indian manager Madhavrao Scindia and said that as his team had come on a goodwill tour, it would be best to put the matter of the 'scuffed' ball aside. The manager agreed, said he would speak to his players, and promptly went off to see them. They denied doing anything of the sort, at which the manager reported that Ali had accused them of making the marks. No further word was said on either side, but by the end of the second match at Gwalior there was no improvement in the situation. If the ball had been damaged on both sides then one could easily accept that perhaps the pitch was doing the damage, but not if only one side was marked in such a way. At Gwalior, we were batting quite nicely when all of a sudden the ball began swinging again in a quite extraordinary manner. Our worst suspicions were confirmed, but again we kept mum, adopting the attitude that if that was what was allowed in India, we had to live with it. Certainly we were not going to emulate them.

I first came across this phenomenon of late swing playing in England in 1990 when some bowlers were unable to move the ball much when it was new, but did so appreciably when it was old. There is no doubt that the ball is affected if it is scuffed on one side, perhaps in its balance and weight. We tried it out by really scuffing old practice balls with bottle tops in the nets at Taunton, and there was no question about the difference it made. I had not noticed it in 1989, my first season with Somerset. In my final year, 1991, the umpires, being aware of the problem, decided that if they found it had been done they would give a warning, and if it continued they would swap the ball for one very much the worse for wear. Every four or five overs suspicious umpires would call for the ball and examine it. Nothing was said: the ball was just quietly checked. Those apparently guilty of the habit became nervous and soon stopped. It happened in one game I played in in 1991, but after all the publicity following our Indian tour and the firm steps now taken by the English umpires, I am certain that this practice will die out.

I might add that in our final game, the day/night match at New Delhi, we used a different kind of ball, a white Kookaburra which has a softer leather, and it did not swing at all. I am not saying that we were able to win because the ball did not play tricks as it had in the first two games. This would be grossly unfair to our team. I am merely recording the fact.

But to return to the Calcutta game. We lost, but only just and initially, thanks to some superb fast bowling by Allan Donald, it looked as if we might overcome that moderate 177 total. I should add that, in their allotted time, the Indians only bowled 47 out of the scheduled 50 overs. While it is true that they in turn were now obliged to reach the 178-run target also in 47 overs, had we been given a chance, our tail-end batsmen might well have thrown caution to the winds and pushed the total nearer the 200 mark, which might have made a closer finish and even have affected the outcome. But of course cricket is full of stories of what might have happened. After all, we too might have managed to send down only 47 overs.   157

When India batted we knew we would have a formidable task restricting their powerful batting combination on a familiar pitch, and our hearts rose when Allan Donald, the blond Free Stater who, playing for Warwickshire in the English county championship, had firmly established himself as one of the best fast bowlers in contemporary cricket, immediately began hurling the ball down with fiery pace and perfect line. He had Shastri caught behind in the first over, and then in his third over clean bowled Manjrekar. When he had got rid of Sidhu for only 6, Donald had India on the rack at 20 for 3 and the South African camp was elated. Although he had had a good rest after his fine season for the English Midlands team, Allan had not been out of action long enough to lose his form. This was evidenced by his good rhythm – so essential to a fast bowler – and his ability to make almost every ball count. The crowd, although naturally partisan, fully appreciated what they were witnessing and roared with approval at this great performance – Allan's ability to move the ball at such speed on such a slow wicket. I could only imagine what damage he could do in this form if let loose on a Wanderers greentop.

The much-heralded teenage wonder boy Sachin Tendulkar should have been run out before he had scored, Richard Snell having the misfortune to fumble a chance at the bowler's end. For us it was one of those unfortunate things, as this batsman, remarkably mature for one so young, went on to pull his side out of a crisis and lay the foundation of the winning Indian total of 178 with a fine 62. He was well supported by another young batsman, Amre, who was making his début. Showing no sign of nerves, he settled down to construct a most impressive 55 before Donald trapped him leg before wicket. Even when Prabhakar came in and India needed about 20 to win, we thought we were in with a chance, but it was not to be and they clinched the game by 3 wickets.

But although we lost we did not think we had been disgraced, playing as we were, so early in the season, in strange conditions and in an atmosphere the likes of which we had never before encountered. In particular we had to get used to the stream of fire-crackers thrown on to the field throughout play. We accepted this form of demonstration as part of the Indian scene, but fielding in my customary place in the deep, I can now record from experience that the continual explosions around one are not good for those of a nervous disposition. My ears rang for a long time after the match.

We were now getting the measure of the opposition. While Kapil Dev produced the quality of cunning seam bowling that underlined his reputation, and the other bowlers did a remarkably good job and were backed by excellent fielding, it was obvious that their main strength lay in their batting. We had yet to see the best of Manjrekar and Shastri but, as I have noted, we were much impressed by the gifted Tendulkar. He was particularly strong on the leg side – as were his colleagues – and initially our bowlers tended to change direction and deliver more down the off side. However, if any delivery was sent only a foot outside the off-stump the umpires would signal a wide, which was disconcerting. Our umpires at home never did this, so our bowlers were somewhat put off. Thus they aimed more to the middle, but any delivery which drifted slightly to leg was immediately pounced on by the home batsmen. Maybe it is because of this situation that the Indian batsmen have become so adept on the on side.

Because he had been studying hard before suddenly finding himself on tour, Richard Snell, my talented Transvaal colleague, had bowled little and was far from match-fit and inclined to over-pitch. So it was understandable that he was unable to reveal the qualities which had earned him the reputation of one of the most exciting fast bowlers the country has unearthed in years. As a result, the real hostility of our opening attack was from Allan Donald – his 5 for 29 reflected how brilliantly he bowled. The British cricket writers, who of course knew him well, went into ecstasies about their 'Warwickshire Lad' and enjoyed themselves writing purple prose about South Africa's dramatic return to international competition. 'Full speed ahead Donald blasts door wide open', screamed the London *Daily Mail*, typifying the line most of them took. Strangely for him, Vic Marks was slightly off-beam when he told his readers in *The Observer* that we 'embarked on the Indian tour not just to make history but to win'. He added: 'It is not enough for the South Africans to be back in the fold. Their cricketers, supporters, even their journalists, want to win immediately.' Sure, we wanted to win; no one goes into a match seeking defeat. But our primary aim was the playing thereof. We were thrilled to be 'legitimate' after so many years out in the cold. If we won, all good and well. This would be a bonus, but not the be-all and end-all of this pathfinder tour.

After this first, emotionally draining game we got together with our Indian opponents and had dinner right there on the ground, creating a friendly rapport which lasted throughout the week. At no time was there any animosity. We found the home captain Azharuddin and his colleagues to be most companionable and we knew then that the remaining two matches, at Gwalior and New Delhi, would be played in the right spirit, even allowing for the matter of the so-called 'scuffed' cricket ball.

As far as food was concerned, like all visitors to the subcontinent we

159

had been warned about the dangers of local water and to be careful what we ate. In the main, we sensibly adhered to this rule, eating chiefly fish, chicken and salads. We drank a great deal of mineral water and did a good job on the 200 cases of beer kindly donated for the trip by South African Breweries. But after the last match some of the lads did slacken off a bit and tried local curries and iced water. They paid the penalty with upset stomachs on their return home.

We flew from Calcutta to Gwalior for the second Test, taking a side trip on the way to visit the incredibly beautiful Taj Mahal, and arriving in what we hoped was enough time for a good workout at the nets. But mysteriously – or was it coincidental? – our kit was nowhere to be found and after hanging around for an hour and a half we had to call off the practice, which was somewhat disconcerting to say the least. Later, our kit was found at the hotel, but there was nothing more we could do about badly needed preparation. As part consolation we looked forward to an early night. But our hosts had other ideas and we were obliged to make an hour's drive for yet another welcoming dinner. The meal and hospitality were fine, but rest was what we needed most. As it was, we only got to bed about midnight, with the selection committee barely finding time to decide on the next day's side.

For the second match the three who had not yet played, Yachad (for opening bat Hudson), seam bowler Craig Matthews (for McMillan), and spinner Clive Eksteen (for Shaw) now had their chance. Because of the heavy dew we could only start at 10 a.m. and were restricted to 45 overs a side. The wicket looked much better than Calcutta, was much harder, and promised to bounce through. I would have loved to open the batting on that strip, but India batted first and the openers Sidhu and Srikkanth batted superbly and at a cracking pace, adding 130 before being separated. When Srikkanth fell to Snell, Manjrekar came in and after settling in proceeded to build a handsome half-century. The run-rate had slowed, and when their middle order failed to follow up their excellent start, succumbing to some good seam bowling by Donald, Rice and Matthews, and they were restricted to 223, we believed we were well in with a chance of squaring the series. We estimated they were 25 to 30 runs short of a winning total.

But we made a disastrous start. I went in the first over. A ball from Kapil Dev aimed at my off-stump which I had to play, swung late and I edged it behind to the grateful wicket-keeper More. I was furious with myself to go this way on such a beautiful batting wicket. I had been thinking that if I could stick around for the first ten overs or so I would be 160 on my way to a good score. My dismissal brought Kepler Wessels to join

Mandy Yachad, and what followed probably led to our undoing. In trying to repair the damage after my mistake, they fell way behind in the run-rate, only registering 15 runs in the first ten overs. As a result the Indians' 223 looked a reasonable score. Nevertheless we did get to 94 before the second wicket fell, Yachad falling leg-before to Raju for 31. But more vital overs had been used up and the pressure was on. Then Peter Kirsten was adjudged leg before wicket when he had only scored 2, even though he had touched the ball and it was running down the leg side. Adrian Kuiper and Kepler Wessels pulled us around and prospects improved for a while, but we were looking at a target of between 6 and 7 runs an over. With 15 overs to go, the ball suddenly began swinging like never before. Both batsmen now struggled to get the bat anywhere near the ball, let alone score from it. But when they went we lost our way and could only muster an unsatisfactory 185.

Even allowing for the mysterious way the ball swung more at the end of the day than when it was new, and for the long spells when we had fallen woefully behind in the run-rate, we were annoyed with ourselves for not pulling it off. Perhaps in the final stages we panicked somewhat, trying to slam our way out of trouble instead of playing it cool and taking singles and twos where we could find them.

To work off our frustration, when we left the ground we bought a box of the fire-crackers that had, inevitably, been going off all day. As our bus pulled away we tossed them out of the window, and the crowd who were streaming home laughed and enjoyed the fun. One poor fan was unlucky, however. During a stop shortly after leaving the stadium one of the team tossed a fire-cracker which landed behind two policemen on a motor-cycle. The pillion passenger spotted this innocent pedestrian, mistook him for the culprit, and promptly whacked him one with his bamboo cane. The man was not amused.

We had lost the Charimar Challenge series, but as is often the case in adversity, something positive was now emerging – team spirit: we were binding together into a cohesive, determined unit. We realised most of us were playing below our true capabilities. We had been too tentative and needed to come out of our shells and put some aggression into our performances. This is often the case with touring sides, and especially one like ours which had been thrown together in such haste. A side often needs two or three matches to sort itself out, for players to get to know and understand one another better on and off the field and not as the adversaries we had been in our domestic tournaments.

Both teams, officials and supporters of our respective camps – about 500 in all – were invited to dinner that night at an enormous and beautiful palace belonging to the old India of which one had read. It was set in immaculate gardens and had obviously once belonged to a maharajah, but was now occupied by a senior government office. The food was rich and plentiful, but the drinks were not served by the customary waiter. Instead, our host had fun with a miniature train set, the drink-laden carriages stopping in turn before each guest. There was also a mighty fireworks display, as if we had not had enough of fire-crackers! That night we flew to the capital city, New Delhi, for our final game on the Thursday. We were tired, a little downhearted because success still eluded us, but determined to wrap up this experience of a lifetime with a whacking good victory under our belts. We owed it to ourselves and to the public back home.

After a two-hour flight and a slight delay in getting to our hotel, we finally tumbled into bed around 2.30 a.m., but at least we had no early call and could catch up on badly needed sleep. Rising late, we had a good session at the nets, and although we were again invited out to dinner, we all managed to get to bed by 10 p.m. with our spirits up and ready for the final encounter. As this was a day/night game there was no customary early morning bustle. Once the team had been selected it was a case of trying on our locally made attire. The stadium was not really built for cricket and had been erected for the Asian Games some years before. The game had been allocated there because it was rightly anticipated that the normal cricket stadium would not be able to accommodate the expected crowd, which was good thinking because about 75 000 turned up to watch. It reminded one of the Green Point stadium in Cape Town, where we first played night matches with Western Province before lights were installed at Newlands. The lights were the finest we had ever experienced, hanging right over the playing area and hailed, probably justifiably, as the best in the world. Surrounding the playing area was a tartan track, then more grass and more tartan surface. But unlike Green Point, this was a full-sized field. The outfield conditions were obviously not easy, but we accepted the situation as it would be the same for both sides.

The wicket looked great, full of runs, and so it turned out to be. Batting first and taking full advantage of the conditions, the Indian batting machine went into top gear from the start, first with Shastri and Srikkanth and then Manjrekar giving a classic display of forceful hitting and underlining why India are so hard to beat at home. The openers put on 86 for the first wicket in double-quick time, with Shastri getting 109 before being run out. Manjrekar then proceeded to hit our bowlers all round the ground in a scintillating exhibition, racing to his century in only 80-odd deliveries. Our all-seam attack did not bowl badly – it was just one of those wickets on which any batsman worth his salt, certainly at international level, was fully expected to do well.

There had been criticism of our fielding in the first two matches, the critics saying that some of us were a little long in the tooth and that it showed. We were aware of this and it was noted as one area where we would have to sharpen up for the World Cup series. Without trying to make excuses, we were not match-fit and were playing together for the first time as a side. That essential unity on the field, that cohesiveness brought about by working together frequently was obviously missing. But that said, I do not think we did too badly, even on that field with its tartan areas and plastic covering over a jumping pit.

India lost only 4 wickets when totalling 287 runs, and although we South African batsmen knew that the wicket was still very much in our favour, such a target was a tall order. However, coach Mike Procter, that great allrounder of recent years on whose shoulders rests a very wise cricket head said without hesitation 'We can get those runs', and I agreed. Our slow start at Gwalior was uppermost in our minds and Clive Rice emphasised that it was essential for us not only to make a good start, but also to emulate our opponents and score at a much faster run-rate, at least 90 after 20 overs.

I welcomed the suggestion that Kepler Wessels open the batting with me, as a left- and a right-handed batting combination often has an unsettling effect on the bowlers. For example, every time a batsman takes a single the bowler has to change his line to the new man at the other end. If, say, he sends a delivery outside the off side to me – a right-hander – and I score a single, he will then have to change his line by about two feet to get the ball in the right line for the left-hander, in our case this time, Kepler. Then if *he* gets a single, the poor bowler has to start all over again, sometimes losing whatever rhythm he may have developed or was looking for. These are little tactical points which many spectators are inclined to overlook but they often count, especially at the highest level of the game when the individual skills of both sets of players are often even.

This target of 90 runs after 20 overs was uppermost in my mind as we faced up to Kapil Dev and his attack, and I was determined to honour this commitment, even if I lost my wicket along the way, and particularly as we had depth in our batting. It was no good being, say, 60 for no wicket. After only two or three overs I knew that winning target of 288 was attainable, especially after Adrian Kuiper had said to me before the game: 'You look a bit tentative when batting on this tour. We hated bowling to you in the Cape because you always came at us, knowing when we bowled a bad ball we were going to get hit. Try and play your usual   163 game.' So when, in those opening overs, I saw the ball was coming on to the bat nicely and it was not swinging, my optimism about winning this match increased.

Runs came at a satisfactory rate until I fell during the 16th over, with 35 to my name and 72 on the board. What was essential now was to keep the momentum going, to remain in contention. This was done, pleasing our skipper when we reached 89 in that 20th over, only one short of the target he had called for. How the crowd loved this. They had cheered their home side until they were hoarse, and now they saw we were making a game of it and that a thrilling finish was on the cards.

The fire-crackers began spewing on to the field at an even greater rate and the match was taking on a momentum of its own. It increased even more when Peter Kirsten joined Kepler and after a slightly shaky start began revealing the quality of educated batsmanship which for years had made him such a favourite all round South Africa and in England where he had such a distinguished career with Derbyshire. I had not seen much of him in recent seasons since his move to play for Border in the B Section of the Currie Cup, and when he was chosen for this trip I know there were some who were muttering that perhaps he had passed his peak and perhaps the selectors were being sentimental and picking him on his reputation. He had been most impressive in the nets, and after failing at Calcutta (7) and Gwalior (2), he confessed his disappointment to me, particularly after he had worked so hard. But I said bluntly: 'Class is permanent, form is temporary.' I was so pleased that Peter, one of the game's real gentlemen, came right this time when the occasion called for it.

Confidence now began to ooze through the South African camp, particularly when we reached 147 after 30 overs, only 3 short of our 150 target. Kepler was moving majestically towards his century when at 90 he got what I thought was a rough decision, trapped leg-before to the left-arm spinner Raju bowling round the wicket. Andrew Hudson was due to come in next, but it was decided that the situation was ideal for Adrian Kuiper. Having failed in the first match and with the pressure really on him, good player though he is, Andrew might have slowed the tempo down just that little bit while regaining his confidence. Whereas, apart from his particular style of whirlwind batting, Adrian was a form man with 43 and 21. Clive's decision was correct, and how Adrian rose to the occasion, tearing into the bowling as only he can and ripping it to shreds in scoring an unbeaten 63 in about 40 deliveries. And this was despite the fact that he had suffered a groin injury while fielding and was off the field for about half the Indian innings. I was padded up and ready to run for him, but he would not hear of it. He wanted to revel in every moment out there, despite the pain he was enduring. Of course the way he hits a ball needs a runner less than most other batsmen. His target is invariably that boundary board, and preferably sending the ball high and handsome over it as frequently as possible. On his day Adrian must rank as the hardest hitter in modern cricket.

At the end of what was one of the most exciting matches I had ever played in and will certainly never forget, we were not even rushed. We reached that 288 target with 3 overs to spare. The huge grin all over Peter Kirsten's face told its own story.

There was great excitement among our camp followers and, as we had anticipated, among all the people back home watching on television or listening on the radio. But we as a team did not go overboard in our celebrations – no racing round the field or wild shouting. We were delighted, naturally, but not demonstrative. I like to think we won humbly. The Indian team congratulated us, as did their officials and countless supporters, and so the series finished as it had started in the best possible spirit. The New Delhi match, and indeed the games at Calcutta and Gwalior, exemplified how international cricket should always be played. We who were privileged to be members of that first cricket team to represent what in political terms these days is called the 'new' South Africa returned home exhausted, but thrilled by the experience.

As players we would naturally have liked to come home the victors of the series, but as citizens of our country we were proud to have shown the flag and revealed ourselves to the international community, not as the racist ogres we are often made out to be but as ordinary and, we like to think, decent human beings. We had enjoyed competing against Mohammed Azharuddin and his team and the spirit with which they played, we had appreciated the hospitality of all those in India who entertained us so royally, and had garnered much experience which we hoped would serve us in good stead in the World Cup.

I reproduce here extracts from what Dr Ali Bacher, managing director of the United Cricket Board of South Africa and our team manager, and Clive Rice, our captain, wrote for the Johannesburg *Sunday Star* on their return:

Bacher: Before we left South Africa, I told a media conference that the results of our historic tour were not important. The occasion itself and the vast implications stemming from it were crucial issues. Now that the tour is over, I can say from the bottom of my heart that the mission succeeded beyond our wildest hopes. Our country is   165 undergoing a period of progressive change and people are looking for role models and reassurance of the innate good that lives with mankind. India, through this cricket tour, has helped to do just that and the result of the tour has been probably the most important of all. It was written in fate that it was to be India to achieve this because it was the father of this great nation, Mahatma Gandhi, who began his teachings in South Africa, and the message of goodwill he brought to South Africa and the world that has been resurrected on this tour. I believe that history will record this great moment, not for cricket alone, but as a moment when our two nations lit the torch of peace that will be carried into the hearts of all our people.

Rice: We learned a lot of lessons during our week in India, and maybe the biggest of all was to discover how much more we still needed to learn. South Africa has not toured anywhere for 26 years and that has been a big loss to our cricket. Everyone on this trip will have benefited from the experience. The reception we received all along the way was fantastic. We will never forget the friendliness and warmth of the Indian people. It was a special week for all of us and a special week for South African cricket. None of us will ever forget those wonderful seven days.

12
THE WORLD CUP, 1992

The role of a selector in sport can, by its very nature, be controversial. In most aspects of life, we all have subjective views on events, people and places, but there are not too many who are prepared to go out on a limb and commit themselves and make decisions which lend themselves to public scrutiny and possible ridicule. This is particularly the case when it comes to choosing a national sporting team, and even more so in countries where emotion tends to supersede logic.

The almost total boycott by home supporters of the historic first cricket Test between the West Indies and South Africa in Bridgetown, Barbados, in April 1992 because one of their local players had not been chosen, is a case in point. There were no riots, but a thrilling match was played before near-empty stands and the financially strapped West Indies cricket administration was deprived of much-needed revenue. Yet selectors there must be, and there are always those who are prepared to place their reputations on the line if in doing so it will be beneficial to the sport in which they are involved.

In some sports, such as soccer, the trend in recent decades has been to appoint a manager who also selects his team. If he cannot come up with the right combination his career could be short lived, but if he does consistently well he becomes a national hero. Alf Ramsay is one who comes to mind. He already had a reputation as a great England fullback and captain of Tottenham Hotspur and England, and then as manager of the Ipswich club. He could have retired gracefully, basking in the glory of his illustrious career, yet he was prepared to become manager/selector of the English team. Some of his selections were controversial, such as the omission of recognised wingers. But he won the World Cup for England in 1966 and was knighted for his efforts.

In South Africa the tendency is still to select teams by committee, the panel invariably comprising former national stars, occasionally including a person or persons who were not necessarily outstanding players in their day but are there for their perceptive qualities. And, to be honest, sometimes selectors get on the panel for what one might describe as 'internal political reasons'.

All of which leads me to focus on one of the most controversial periods in South African cricket history, with myself unwittingly very much involved.

With this country suddenly becoming 'fashionable' again and half the world wanting to play us in almost every sport, national fervour, patriotism, call it what you will, swept the Republic. And nowhere more so than in cricket, which had kept a high playing profile during the dark years of apartheid with controversial 'unofficial' tours. The game which once was 169 the preserve mainly of English-speaking South Africans has long been 'adopted' by Afrikaners – and what a rich seam of talent they have and are producing – and so, fuelled by this very much broader permanent school of cricket devotees, interest boomed in a hitherto unprecedented fashion. Far more women than ever before began going to matches, reading the sporting press, watching television, listening to radio commentaries, and entering heated discussions in homes, shops and offices.

Men who previously had dismissed cricket as a silly game had second thoughts (United States ambassador Bill Swing was a convert), while the massive, ambitious and successful programme devised by Ali Bacher and the United Cricket Board of South Africa to take the game to non-white schoolchildren began to pay dividends in that numerous homes in black suburbs around the country began tuning into radio and televised commentaries. Cricket was the 'in' sport in the 1991/92 season, so, when the World Cup team selection controversy broke out it was indeed of national proportions, at times pushing major political events off the front pages.

When the South African team returned in November 1991 from the hastily arranged and historic three-game tour of India, most of the players assumed that they would largely comprise the combination to play in the World Cup in Australasia in March 1992. After all, if we had been considered the best in November, most of us should be equally the best a couple of months later, particularly as there would be precious few domestic games from which to judge other contenders. I must confess that privately I was confident of continuing my role as my country's first choice as opening batsman, even though my scores of 17, 0 and 35 in my three innings on the Indian subcontinent were not exactly something to shout about. I worked on the assumption that the criteria would be my overall career record for Transvaal for more than two decades, for South Africa for a decade, and three highly successful seasons with Somerset. I was 38, fit, as keen as ever, and in no doubt that my technical ability was as sound as ever it had been. Without wishing to be big-headed about it, many commentators and my peers rated me as one of the leading opening batsmen in the current game, especially after my three high-scoring seasons with Somerset.

As always, and particularly this time after completing a heavy season in England, prior to the 1991/92 South African season I planned a careful training and playing programme, aiming to find peak form and fitness in January in the weeks immediately before the selection of the World Cup party of 14. From past experience I knew it would be foolish to throw everything into the opening provincial matches and burn myself out be-

170

fore what I knew would be a punishing travelling and playing schedule in Australia and New Zealand. The unexpected Indian tour upset my schedule somewhat, and although I did not put together any high scores in the few provincial games we did play in the interim, I was content, and in retrospect I suppose I was over-confident about being selected.

On the weekend that the shortlist of 20 was to be announced Transvaal was playing at home at the Wanderers against Eastern Province. We were told the names would be released on the Sunday night, and on that Sunday afternoon I felt really good and scored a most comforting 88. Everything was going according to plan – peak form with the tour selectors about to put pen to paper. It was now simply a question of waiting for confirmation of my name being read out that night. Had not every newspaper, television and radio commentator, numerous officials, players and many others pencilled me into their side?

Little did I know which way the selectorial wind was blowing. Clive Rice, who led us in India and who had been a brilliant captain of Springbok and Transvaal teams through his all-round ability and leadership for the previous decade, had been told on that Sunday morning by one of the selectors, Lee Irvine, that he was not being considered, but he had said not a word. Rightly, in my view, he felt he should at least have been considered, even if he did not make the final 20. I will have more to say later about Clive, but I do think this was an incredible mistake. Here was one of the game's most respected allrounders, whose form was not at all bad and whose experience would be invaluable against the best national sides in the world, being tossed aside like a worn-out shoe when he was needed most.

The Transvaal side was still in the dressing-room at the conclusion of the match against Kepler Wessels' team when our manager Alan Kourie came in and announced that fast bowler Richard Snell and batsman Daryll Cullinan were the only Transvalers among the 20. We were all flabbergasted, and inwardly I felt sick with disappointment. I congratulated Richard and Daryll while my own mind was buzzing. What on earth had happened? Where had I gone wrong? What was in the minds of the six selectors – convener Peter van der Merwe, Tony Pithey, Lee Irvine, Peter Pollock, S K Reddy and Rushdie Majiet? Apart from Clive and myself, I believed that several members of the Transvaal team would get into the squad along with Richard. Our young left-arm spin bowler Clive Eksteen had barely got a chance to turn his arm in India, bowling only two overs, but again, if he was rated good enough for that tour, on what grounds could he suddenly drop out of the top 20?

The more I contemplated my own omission, the more illogical it 171 seemed. Having played with and against some of the best bowlers in the world during the past three seasons and having done pretty well, was it really a fact that I was not good enough to be included among the country's top 20? I drove home from the Wanderers a very depressed man indeed. Then the phone calls came, and if there was any consolation at all it was the fact that many of them were from fellow cricketers, those who could assess me best and whose judgement I respected. For a while their words brought comfort of a sort. 'Don't worry, this is not the final side. You will get into the final 14', they nearly all said. Then, when the furore over the omission of Peter Kirsten, Clive Rice and myself erupted in the media all over the country, a glimmer of optimism began seeping into my mind.

As the days passed, logic crept back into my thinking and I resigned myself to the conclusion that only a couple of hundreds in the three or four innings available to me before the final list was announced could persuade the selectors to change their minds. Well, it did not happen, although I did register a satisfactory 63 in a friendly game against Western Province. Having ruled out the age factor (shortlisted spin bowler Omar Henry was 40, and anyhow the selectors later confirmed this), I went back over the years and examined my relations with my fellow players and with officials. There was conjecture that somewhere along the way I had crossed swords with Peter van der Merwe, or had made some injudicious remarks. This belief took hold round the country, but it simply was not true. As far as I knew Peter and I had always got on well. Indeed, had he not been instrumental in my being chosen to captain the Springbok team which played Mike Gatting's English 'rebels' only two years before? And after that tour he had taken the trouble to phone and thank me for the job I had done.

Another line of conjecture was that I had spoken out of turn to the press. I was quoted in one newspaper as saying that they had chosen an athletics team and not a cricket team. But I had not actually said that. The reporter put it to me that it seemed that they were picking an athletics and not a cricket team, and I had replied that it did appear so. Maybe I should have refrained from making any comment at all, but to this day I cannot believe that this report would in any way have influenced the attitude of the selectors. They could not be that touchy. At worst, it was only a gentle dig. Much stronger opprobrium was being heaped on them from other quarters.

I ran the rule back on my batting in all competitions. Although I had not been a prolific run-getter in South Africa for the past season or so, I had those three wonderful seasons with Somerset and scored 2 755 runs in

42 innings in the season only recently ended. This was a far better benchmark than an assessment of my performance over the few innings I had managed to play thus far in the South African season. All right, I said, it was not form, age or upsetting anyone. The World Cup is a limited-over affair, so how do I stand there? In Nissan Shield at home I was the leading run-scorer with an average of over 50, and at that time I shared with Henry Fotheringham the domestic record of scoring three centuries in Benson and Hedges day/night competitions. In England I averaged over 50 in Benson and Hedges games and around 60 in the Sunday League. Overall, I was fit, experienced, and over the years had been a consistent compiler of runs against the best bowlers of my era. For the life of me I could not put a finger on what the selectors had against me. I still cannot.

I was pleased that Peter Kirsten was eventually included in the final tour squad. Whether it was because of a sudden return to form or the intensity of the pressure from the media and the cricket public at large, only the selectors would know. But whatever the reason, I was thrilled for my old friend and colleague for, like most other people, I rated Peter one of the best batsmen South Africa has produced in the last four decades. His record at home and for Derbyshire has rightly earned him an international reputation and it only made sense that his wise batting head would be invaluable when the pressure was on in Australasia. And of course this proved to be the case. Peter was the foundation in almost every innings and had the second highest aggregate in the tournament. If he had not travelled I am sure that South Africa would not have made it to the semi-finals.

All credit must go to Kepler Wessels and his side for getting as far as they did, only to lose to England in that controversial rain-hit match. Like so many other South Africans, I was glued to my television set for every pulsating minute. I was itching to be out there fighting with the boys, sharing their elation – and dejection – as the match ebbed and flowed. Whether my presence would have made any difference to the outcome we will never know, but there is no doubt that Clive Rice was missed. Selection panel chairman Peter van der Merwe took a lot of personal flak over the selection of the tour squad and he and his colleagues must have felt very relieved when the side got as far as it did. And rightly so, for it was a tremendous effort for the country after being out of the international game for over two decades.

However, Clive's tenacious batting was sorely missed in the middle order, while he would have been the ideal fifth bowler with his cunning

173

medium pace deliveries. As it was, Peter Kirsten, Adrian Kuiper and Hansie Cronje, none of whom were considered front-rank bowlers, did their best, but sadly it was not good enough. The need for a top-rate fifth bowler in one-day cricket was one of the fundamental lessons learned from this tournament.

I am not saying that with Clive Rice South Africa would have won the World Cup. He could have flopped. But on the logic of analysis of his career record I do not think so. He loves the world stage. He is a cricketer who thrives on the pressure of the big occasion, and even if he had gone as an ordinary member of the team and not as captain, and even if he had been used only sparingly for the key matches, I am as positive as I can be that he would have performed superbly somewhere along the way. Clive has his detractors: outspoken personalities usually do. But even his sternest critics will concede that he is one of the truly great performers of his era, both as an allrounder and as a captain.

Because of its excellent showing, the same team was retained for the short tour of the West Indies, although Western Province allrounder Brian McMillan, who had such a good World Cup, dropped out through injury and was replaced by Free State's Corrie van Zyl. Dropping half the squad, as had been done after India, was not on. At least now the players felt some confidence and the selectors had been consistent.

The Caribbean trip was arranged at the last minute as a gesture by the United Cricket Board of South Africa to a region which, during the apartheid era, had been one of our severest critics but, with the political metamorphosis that was taking place, had swung around to become a firm friend.

From a cricketing aspect, the tour should not have taken place as the players were exhausted both physically and emotionally from the just-concluded two-month Cup series, and with half the squad having been in India only a few months earlier. But politically it was vital, and the fact that South Africa lost all three one-day games and a thrilling five-day Test was, in the long run, immaterial. Besides, many valuable lessons were undoubtedly learned and stored away by Kepler Wessels and his colleagues. Kepler himself underlined his reputation as an excellent captain and world-class batsman, while Natal's Andrew Hudson confirmed his emergence as a first-rate opening batsman with that polished 163 in the Bridgetown Test. As so often happens in sport, coincidence raised its head here. Andrew's century was the first by a South African on his Test début for his country, while the only other South African to have scored a century in his first International was his batting partner Kepler – but for

Australia during the years he lived there.

Returning to the question of team selection, I dismissed in passing the question of age when the shortlist of 20 and the final 14-man squad was chosen for the World Cup (and, subsequently, the West Indies). It was, however, a major talking point among critics and the public in South Africa. The fact that Clive Rice was 43 and I was 38 was raised time and again, with most people believing that performance and not age should have been the criterion. Ah, went out the cry from some quarters, what about the future? The selectors had to look ahead and invest in a new generation of players, particularly as South Africa had now regained its place in international competition.

My answer is that a selection panel must concentrate on one thing: winning the next match or competition. As I saw it, that was the simple instruction which should have been, and maybe was, given to Peter van der Merwe and his colleagues: 'Pick a side to win the 1992 World Cup, not build for the 1996 tournament'. All right, the final squad did include 'veterans' like Wessels, Kirsten, Kuiper and Allan Donald – although the last was a veteran from experience in county cricket rather than age. But there is no doubt that some were there because of their 'potential', because of what they were likely to do in the future. Well, apart from Andrew Hudson, it did not work out among the younger batsmen. On numerous occasions a crisis called for a more seasoned campaigner.

Long before the World Cup I felt confident that we could put together a squad that could win in Australasia. I had played against most of the world's best batsmen and bowlers in England for the previous three seasons. I knew their strengths and weaknesses. I had taken runs off the best of them and was most positive about our prospects, especially after the way we had played and won that last one-day Test in India. Apart from the omission of Clive Rice, I had no argument with the seam bowlers chosen. I knew they would do well and in general they lived up to expectations. Obviously the number of wides delivered under the competition rules was too high, but lessons were learned and this technicality should be ironed out easily enough.

I should make it clear that I am not against selecting young players. What I do say is that any young player chosen must be better than the older man he supplants. Cricket history is full of brilliant teenagers. India's gifted batsman Sachin Tendulkar was only 18 when he played us, and between them both the cricketing nations on the subcontinent, India and Pakistan, have a knack of unearthing many a mature player barely into puberty. South Africa's own Graeme Pollock was an established century-making international at only 19. In my own home province of Transvaal, whenever there was a move to bring in younger men I always 175 raised the stock question: are they better than those already in the side? There must be no other rule.

If the choice of a place lies between a man of, say, 40 and one of 22 and the former is the better player, then he should be picked. I like to think that whenever I was selected for Transvaal and South Africa it was because I was rated among the best 11 or 12 men in the province or country and for no other reason. The only possible exception to this rule is perhaps at a lower league club level when a young batsman with promise is slotted in at nine or ten for a few matches in order to 'blood' him. This happened to me and obviously it paid dividends, but the line must be drawn at the higher level.

I mentioned a little earlier that the tendency in soccer is to have a selector/manager. After the furore surrounding the picking of our 1992 World Cup squad, perhaps in the future the UCBSA will look in this direction and offer the job to one man who has the courage of his convictions and is willing to shoulder such a responsibility. Current national coach is Mike Procter who, I am sure, would relish the post. No one has better credentials than this highly respected man who was one of the game's truly great allrounders. He could, however, have a rival in Eddie Barlow, an equally gifted playing contemporary whose disciplined manner worked wonders with the Free State side in the 1991/92 season. If he can work the same magic in his new job and rejuvenate Transvaal, then 'Bunter' would have many supporters.

Taking an overall look at the World Cup, it was a superb tournament, with Pakistani rightly justifying its highly fancied ranking. Like many other aficionados who know something of the game, I had long held that the team that beat Graham Gooch's polished and well-balanced English combination would win the Cup, and so it proved to be.

The only disturbing factor, which I am sure will be recognised for the next World Cup (and South Africa must be a firm candidate to host it), is the rule which applied to interruptions by rain. Every competing captain and manager was aware that the complex formula favoured the side which batted first, so there appeared to be more dismay than anger when rain did indeed alter the outcome of some matches and, in particular, of course, South Africa's enthralling semi-final against England.

This rule needs to be changed before the next World Cup series, possibly allowing a match to finish the next day, or to continue for another half-hour or so, as we play it in Benson and Hedges matches in South Africa. After all, maintaining a balance between the mathematical and
the physical challenge must be paramount.

I understand and respect the requirements of commercial interests, which these days are an essential financial factor. They are very much part of modern cricket and do much to keep it alive. Television stations in particular like sporting events to start and finish within defined time slots, especially if a particular channel is underwriting some or all of the cost of an event. I know many purists shudder at what they consider to be too much of an intrusion by business into sport by way of sponsorship and advertising. But where would we be if business did not see sport as an ideal vehicle for promoting its image or wares?

Heavy commercialisation of sport began in the 1960s when a golf-loving American lawyer called Mark McCormack answered a request from the champion golfer Arnold Palmer to handle his business affairs. Out of this humble beginning sprang the massive sports sponsorship industry we know today. We cricketers are thrilled to be chosen for our provincial, county or national side, but we want to be paid for doing the job. And the escalating cost of organising competitions at all levels leaves the authorities with little option but to seek sponsorship, even though it goes against the grain for many of the more conservative of them. That said, however, control must remain in the hands of the sports administrators. I believe most fair-minded sponsors accept this.

As I write this chapter during the winter of 1992, I examine my own playing future. I turned 39 in July, so obviously time is not on my side. But I am blessed with a good physique and maintain peak condition all year round. My eyesight and co-ordination are still good, I believe my fielding is still up to scratch, and my enthusiasm for the game is as strong as ever. So, I hope to go on playing at the highest possible level open to me until such time as my mind and body tell me otherwise. In cricketing terms, I am not that old. Apart from Clive Rice, I could give numerous examples, but for the record, Geoffrey Chubb made his début for the Springboks as a seam bowler at 40, and Dudley Nourse captained the Springboks in England when he was 41.

With South Africa now back on the international tour scene I like to think that I may again be called upon to represent my country, provided my selection is based on form and ability and not on sentiment.

13

PLAYERS AND TEAMS

13

PLAYERS AND TEAMS

Apart from the actual playing and watching, what one might call the third dimension of sport is the appraisal and selection of one's favourite players and teams. Nearly all of us indulge in such a pastime, either at home, at dinner parties, in our clubs and pubs, and in the media. During my two decades as an active cricketer I, too, have compiled my portfolio of favourites, basing my selection on those who have either been team-mates or against whom I have had the pleasure of competing.

Choosing my Ten Best South African batsmen and bowlers was not easy. Despite our comparatively small cricket-playing population, this country has been able to produce a high percentage of gifted players. Only a few managed to attain international status, particularly as we were 'frozen out' of Test cricket for most of the period I am looking at. And again, there were those who did not get a look in for even the unofficial or 'rebel' Test series because the prevailing representatives were so good. For example, for 20 years who could dislodge Graeme Pollock at number four or, for a slightly shorter period, Barry Richards at number one?

I think of Dr Ali Bacher, one of the great personalities of South African cricket. An exemplary captain and brilliant administrator, he played in a number of official Tests and once scored a double century for Transvaal against the visiting Australians, yet he would be the first to admit that he could not claim a place among the Top Ten.

Then there are Robbie Muzzell, Adrian Kuiper, Brian Bath, Andre Bruyns, Daryll Bestall, Chris Wilkins, Hylton Ackerman, and a host of others. All were splendid, as their records show, but not quite up to the mark for my final list. The same applies to the many bowlers around the provinces who gave me such a hard time and whose skills I could appreciate and admire.

The batsmen I have chosen (in no particular order) are:

Barry Richards: As a fellow opener, he was the one I looked up to and tried so hard to emulate. He was the most technically correct batsman one could wish to see, doing everything straight out of the coaching manual. I would study him for hours, initially off the field and then later, towards the end of his career, as his privileged partner. I tried to model myself on him but was never able to attain his high standard. With his head rock-steady and his feet always in the correct position, the bat was held straight, with an equally straight back-lift. He played with incredible assurance through the line against anything that was short or well up. It was almost as if the bowler had told him what he was going to do and then placed the ball there for Barry to react accordingly with all the time in the world, the hallmark of a great player. His shot selection was magnificent 181 and he always scored at a good rate, invariably finding the gaps against even the best-set fields. Because of the intervention of politics his Test career was limited but was none the less outstanding. How he made up for it in provincial, county and state competitions in South Africa, England and Australia! Bowlers of his day still shudder at the mention of his name.

Graeme Pollock: There is only one word to sum up the most talked-about South African cricketer of this or any other era – genius. The son of a Port Elizabeth newspaper editor, he made headlines for years with his superb left-handed batsmanship. He did not have Barry Richards' technical perfection: he did not need to. His footwork was limited yet, with his left foot invariably anchored to the crease, he would hit where and when he wanted, across the line if he deemed it necessary. His eye and his judgement were so good that he did not believe it vital to get his front foot to the ball, being content to get it reasonably close. He was rarely out leg before wicket or hit on the pads, as he believed in playing the ball. In all the years of watching him I cannot recall him being dismissed bat-pad off a spinner. Few other batsmen have treated a bad delivery with such disdain. One small error and a bowler would suffer, the ball inevitably being dispatched swiftly to the boundary with contemptuous ease. Pace never troubled him, and he was a master of spin. He took full advantage of his strong physique to hit with great ferocity to all quarters of the ground and, like most left-handers, particularly favoured the cover-drive and the pull. Bowlers could only beat him by placing the ball on the right spot, just too short for him to drive, or not short enough for him to pull or cut. Overall, the key to his batting was his fantastic touch, his feel for the bat and ball. I know from experience in catching practice sessions with the Springbok or Transvaal teams that this 'touch' would come through. Time and again he would hit the ball in the exact spot for a man to run and catch; here for the faster runner, and there for the slower man. None of us could emulate this uncanny placing of the ball.

It has been said so often, but it is a fact that had he been able to play a full career of international cricket, Robert Graeme Pollock would almost certainly have rewritten the record books. No wonder, as a 19-year-old playing in Australia, he drew praise from the master, Sir Donald Bradman.

Lee Irvine: He was a supreme example of a destroyer of bowling. At the peak of his career in the early 1970s it used to be said among bowlers that if Barry Richards, Graeme Pollock and Lee Irvine were each batting with 50 on the board, the player they would least like to bowl to was Lee Irvine. He was merciless. He could hit the ball harder, further, and to

182   more places than any of his contemporaries. He could be technically

perfect like Barry, or completely unorthodox like the West Indian Alvin Kallicharran. In my time, before Pollock moved to Johannesburg, Lee was undoubtedly the outstanding Transvaal batsman. He had enviable co-ordination with excellent eyesight and fine footwork and, like most men of his build, he was extremely quick between the wickets, rarely letting a chance for a quick single slip by. He had a favourite habit of killing the ball at the crease or thereabouts and calling his partner for a quick single. Fielders would be tempted to move in closer, and he would then have little trouble sending a bad delivery whizzing past them for four. He was also a fine wicket-keeper, the best for Transvaal in the era between John Waite and Ray Jennings.

Eddie Barlow: Here was a batsman with his own special and telling style. His square-on, almost two-eyed stance, with his bat far from his feet, belied his technical proficiency. His back-lift may have been slightly loopy, but the bat always came straight through towards the ball. As they say about golfer Lee Trevino's swing – it looks somewhat unorthodox, but the club face comes through to connect perfectly. Contrary to common belief, he never played across the line of the ball. He is rightly remembered for the 'Barlow cut', his penchant for deliberately cutting the ball high and hard over slips and, because he is not a tall man, like other quality players of his build, he became an expert at playing forward or back. He was a consistent scorer on both sides of the wicket, utilising to the full his powerful shoulders, arms and wrists. Highly intelligent, with his own definite views on life in general, an overriding factor of his play was his confidence, together with his enthusiasm, and his assessment of his own ability. As he walked to the crease he gave off an aura of controlled aggression. Bowlers were his arch-enemies. Often many perform worse against batsmen with such reputations because they fear them. Eddie was that kind of batsman, as his figures for South Africa, several provinces and Derbyshire indicate. A fine seam bowler and excellent slip fielder, he must rank among the best players South Africa has ever produced.

Kepler Wessels: Here indeed is a world-class batsman, who proved his ability when wearing Australian colours and who, had he remained in South Africa, would have been in all the Springbok sides that played in the 'rebel' series. Serious by nature, he approaches his cricket in similar vein. Even net practice has a purpose: no casual hitting for him. He works away at what he intends doing in the middle. His temperament is ideal, especially for the big occasion, as he showed as a batsman in India in 1991, and as South African captain in the World Cup in Australasia and then in the West Indies in 1992. He remains unperturbed under pressure, setting about the task at hand with calm deliberation. He is a good pacer of his innings, skilful at balancing between the run target and the available time. Always looking solid, he is usually a slow starter who likes to play himself in, build his platform, and then go for the runs. A good cutter and strong on the leg side, he also scores well through the covers and mid-on. A vastly underestimated striker of the ball, a perfect example of his prowess was the way he took on and succeeded in taming the extremely hostile West Indies attack in the Barbados Test in April 1992. As a high-order left-hander, he would be a strong contender for inclusion in any world side.

Peter Kirsten: Of similar build to Lee Irvine, he has a fine touch, is quick between the wickets and on his day can dispatch the ball wherever he wants. His favourite scoring shot is the square drive, which he has honed to perfection. Place the ball slightly outside the off-stump and it goes like a tracer bullet to the fence. This is also aligned with a delicate and effective late-cut. He also favours picking the ball up off his legs and flipping it to mid-wicket. With no apparent weakness in his game, bowlers have great difficulty in working out a method to beat him. Although small of stature, he relishes big innings, as his record of several double centuries for Derbyshire indicates. Such is his insatiable thirst for runs that, unlike so many batsmen, if he is, say, on 130, he is not content to ease up. His sights are set firmly on the double ton. A better off-spin bowler than many give him credit for, he is also a world-class fielder, especially in the covers.

Henry Fotheringham: An indication of his technical ability is reflected in the fact that he built a reputation as a very good middle-order batsman and then, on request, half-way through his career moved up to be an opener and became one of the best in the game. With excellent footwork, and consequently always a master against spin, he adapted quickly to facing the new ball and became a consistent run-maker. A free scorer who did not like to be bogged down, he was not scared to take on even the fastest men, judging to perfection whether to play back, go forward, hook or cut. Strong on both sides of the wicket, one always knew he was in form when he would, almost immediately, play a delicate late-cut to third-man. It was like a parent tapping a child on the bottom – a gentle warning. Those in the know would chuckle, as they knew trouble was at hand for the opposition. Big-hearted and encouraging at the wicket, I found it a pleasure to partner him, and it would be fair to say that some of our successful first-wicket stands over the years both for Transvaal and South Africa were to a great extent the result of Henry's positive outlook and example of how to get on with the business of accumulating runs.

Ken McEwan: A firm striker all round the wicket, his one apparent weakness was against anything short on a quick wicket. This is borne out by the fact that in England, where the ball usually does not come off as fast as in South Africa and Australia, he was more at home, becoming one of the most consistent run-makers for Essex over a number of seasons. Once he was settled in he was very difficult to dislodge. With his solid defence and free strokeplay he was rarely tied down and possessed a wide range of effective shots. He had a deceptive ability to score with apparent ease at a consistently fast rate. Another 'touch' player like Graeme Pollock, he had a knack of placing the ball exactly where he wanted it. Most batsmen strive to keep the ball on the ground, but Ken was never afraid to draw a fielder in, say, from extra-cover, and then hit the ball over his head between him and a man on the boundary. He was a great improviser in one-day cricket.

Allan Lamb: Although he has played most of his distinguished career for England and Northamptonshire, I include him because he was born in the Republic, established a growing reputation in the Cape, and still holds the Currie Cup record of 294 when guesting one season for Orange Free State. Fiercely aggressive, he can pull, cut, drive, do almost anything, and is almost unstoppable when in the mood. It could almost be said he has too many shots. He destroys any bowler who dares send down anything loose; his one weakness is perhaps that he tries to score too quickly when the situation calls for a cool head. However, so confident is he in his own ability that he probably built his game around the theory that attack is what he is best at. Certainly, over the years, he has succeeded more times than he has failed.

Kevin McKenzie: This is one of the most underrated players in the game anywhere in the past two decades. A fine, fluent, all-round striker, he played for his country in unofficial Tests and was for years a permanent member of a great Transvaal side, yet he so often appeared to have been overshadowed by others. Had he been born in another age, had Graeme Pollock not dominated the scene at number four, I am certain that Kevin's star would have shone more brightly and his ability would have been more appreciated. As it was, he came in at number six and was often called upon to get 30 or 40 in double-quick time in order to win the match or seek a declaration. Had he been with another province, or found a place higher up the order and been given the time to stretch out his innings, a far higher profile and far more high-scoring innings would have resulted. But he was such a loyal team man that he never complained and was always prepared to do what was required of him. As he was a brilliant hooker, every other bowler seemed to send down half-volleys, resulting in 185 their being smacked for four. He was one of the few modern players not to wear a helmet, saying he felt uncomfortable in one and being quite happy to rely on his quick eye and reflexes to keep him out of trouble. Yet he was perfectly at home against fast bowling: for instance, he hit a superb 84 for Transvaal against the West Indies during their first unofficial tour of South Africa. And this included taking four fours in one over against the legendary and intimidating Sylvester Clarke. I am not a great watcher of cricket, but I always tried to see Kevin batting because he was so positive and one always felt that something was going to happen. On the one occasion when he was able to go in first wicket down for Transvaal he produced the goods. Alvin Kallicharran was injured and stood down for a match against Natal in Durban. Kevin promptly scored 95 in the first innings and 164 in the second.

During my long career I have faced many talented bowlers. Many have, without much difficulty, claimed my scalp, so it is not an easy matter to choose my Top Ten South African bowlers. But in making my selection I have tended to go for consistency of performance over a period of time, rather than a one-off situation.

Vintcent van der Bijl: Without doubt, he was the best South African bowler I ever faced. I have always said that if he had played more for Transvaal than he did for Natal I might have scored many more runs in my career. Because he brought the ball down from a great height he was awkward to face, one never being sure whether one should play forward or back. Fast-medium rather than genuinely fast, usually he was short of a length and there to be hit off the front foot. But if one did go forward to drive, one would be hitting the ball on the up. And with the movement that he generated, one took the risk of getting an outside edge or being trapped between bat and pad and being bowled. He could make the ball move on the flattest of wickets, seaming or swinging just enough to be dangerous; enough to move the ball from hitting the centre of the bat to catching the edge. In difficult conditions he would bowl tight, giving away very few runs, and if the conditions suited him he was almost impossible to play. Because of the high bounce he could extract from most pitches, if connected the ball so often struck high up on the bat and as a result few batsmen were able to collar him. Graeme Pollock and some others might have done so, but I certainly was never able to. Although a big man, he had a smooth action and was happy to carry on for long spells. During that one season he played for Transvaal on the notorious Wanderers greentop he was at times frightening.

186   **Garth le Roux**: Over the years I had many fascinating duels with this

wonderful Cape Town opening bowler. The matches between Western Province and Transvaal are always something rather special, and I suppose our tussles ended with honours about even. But on the days when I was scoring and hitting him for boundaries, I knew only too well that he would keep coming back, never giving in, and scheming how to get on top. Usually he moved the ball away from the right-hander, but he had that knack of straightening up the odd delivery, so one could not assume that a delivery starting just outside the off-stump could be ignored. Traditionally, Newlands is a batsman's wicket, but Garth was able to place the ball down a channel about eight inches to a foot outside the off-stump and keep it there just short of a length and swinging away gently. Batsmen were undecided which of these balls had to be struck and which ignored, often making the wrong decision and paying the penalty. In his early years, particularly after playing in the Kerry Packer series in Australia, he had genuine pace. Always an intelligent bowler, he adapted himself wherever he played and it was no surprise that he did so well for Sussex. When weighing up potential Springbok sides, many of us automatically made Garth first choice with the new ball. A great team man, he always gave his all. He would think nothing of bowling several overs on a hot day and then, fielding at fine-leg, go haring off and diving at full length to prevent the ball going to the boundary off a fellow bowler.

Mike Procter: I faced him early in my career and his pace frightened the life out of me. The amazing thing about him was that he could generate so much pace, yet swing the ball so appreciably. He brought the ball in to the body and he was difficult to get away for one always felt cramped. If a batsman was not a good hooker he liked to let a few deliveries fly at shoulder height. He also developed a ball that used to go straight on, the batsman believing it was coming in, to get an outside edge and get caught behind. He was also very dangerous when going round the wicket, bowling across the batsman and then swinging it back in towards the stumps. Surprisingly for a man who ran in so fast and off such a long run, Mike never seemed to get injured, unlike so many modern fast bowlers. It was no wonder that, with Mike playing with Vince van der Bijl, one season Natal were able to get all 40 Currie Cup bowling points – eight matches, five points a time – and they only conceded two batting points.

And, of course, Mike was a genuine allrounder, sharing with Sir Donald Bradman and C B Fry the distinction of scoring six consecutive first-class centuries.

Allan Donald: Even when he first came on the scene as a gangling teenager with the Orange Free State in the mid-1980s he was very quick. He did not have the control then, and the more experienced players could

187

handle him. He might have remained more of a 'space' than pace bowler with promise had he not gone to Britain to join Warwickshire. There, under the expert eye of Bob Cottam, he tightened up his game and became so accurate that he is without doubt one of the best, if not the best, genuinely fast bowlers in the game today. In his early days he usually brought the ball in, and then, playing against him in the 1991 season in England, I noticed him swinging it away. I realised then what a handful he had become. If a batsman is in the wrong position and Allan swings the ball only slightly at such pace, he has little chance to readjust. On a personal note, in all the years I have faced him in England and South Africa, I have never heard Allan say a bad word. Like Sylvester Clarke, he relies on the ball to do the talking for him. For this quality and, of course, for his ability with the ball, I have the utmost respect.

Clive Rice: Here is a competitor de luxe. In his early years with Transvaal he was a medium-paced bowler. But when he joined the Packer series he realised he could not survive unless he moved up a gear or two. He returned to South Africa as quick as anyone, but as the years have passed and he has slowed down he has replaced speed with incredible guile. As I have indicated throughout this book, I have enormous regard for him both as a man and as a player, and the way he has compensated for age with skill and application underlines the character of the man. Few can use the ball with such cunning. Always utilising the crease to the best advantage and trying something new, he is quick to sum up a batsman's strengths and weaknesses and play them accordingly, working the ball off the seam at medium pace into the areas where he knows he stands the best chance of breaking through.

He has been able to bowl so consistently for so many years because he has such a good action. He has a lovely spring in his step, with a smooth, forward release. He thumps the ball into the pitch very hard, and that is why, even in his 40s, he is difficult to score off. If I, as a captain, found myself in a position where, with one over to go and the other side needing a few runs for victory, he would be the one man to whom I would happily toss the ball. His knack of placing delivery after delivery with pin-point accuracy into the block hole is uncanny. For example, Clive will always be remembered for the famous Currie Cup match at Newlands in 1977 when Western Province needed 8 runs in the last over to win. Clive had been injured and had bowled very little. But our captain, David Dyer, had such faith in him that he handed him the ball to bowl the 18th and 20th of the compulsory last 20 overs. He got a wicket and 5 runs were needed. Le Roux came in for the second last ball. It hit him on the pad and he and Drummond ran a leg-bye. Drummond faced the last ball. He did not even try to hit it to the boundary, Clive yorked him and Transvaal were victors by 4 runs.

A fine aggressive batsman, excellent fielder and captain, I will always be grateful that I played my career with and not against him.

Don Mackay-Coghill: A marvellous left-arm seamer, he was decidedly unlucky never to have played for his country. His stock ball was the inswinger to the right-hander, but he also had the one that ran straight on across the body. A batsman was never too sure whether to play the ball in case he was trapped leg-before, or leave it to pass by. He was able to disguise this variation and was just quick enough to keep one guessing. A tribute to his skill is reflected in the fact that he was able to get Barry Richards out more often than any other bowler. A fine worker of the ball, he was always confident of his ability, a characteristic which would lead to his being such a success in the business world. He also had that knack of breaking through at the required time, scooping up a hatful of wickets and turning a possible draw into victory. He did this on numerous occasions.

Rupert Hanley: He was a fine bowler to have in the side to play as a foil to a quicker and apparently more hostile partner like Sylvester Clarke or Vince van der Bijl. A batsman would often survive unscathed after a torrid time with one of them and then either relax slightly or try to attack 'Spook'. This would be a grave mistake. He had firm control of line and length, and was never happier than at the Wanderers where he would place the ball just outside the off-stump and swinging away. In his younger days he was quick, but later substituted greater accuracy for speed. He was a particular asset in one-day games when he would often be told to bowl his ten overs in a row and, because of his remarkable accuracy, often finish with 20 or fewer runs scored off him. This in turn put great pressure on the batsmen to take risks and attack the other bowlers in order to increase the run-rate. His best Test performance was in a one-day game in Pretoria against the West Indies, when he took 6 for 20. He also registered a hat-trick at the Wanderers against Rowe's side.

As a team man he was invaluable. During one match against Northern Transvaal he was out late partying, and on his return to his hotel his room-mate happened to be his rather annoyed captain Clive Rice. 'Right, Spook,' he said, 'you are going to work hard tomorrow.' Hanley took his admonishment well, and went out the next day and skittled the opposition cheaply.

Stephen Jefferies: A fine left-arm in-swing seamer, he looked the type one could score off, but time and again he returned excellent figures. Once he bowled out the Orange Free State, taking all 10 wickets for 59. 189

He had the ability to produce the unplayable ball that could completely deceive even the best batsman who had settled in and was scoring freely. The ball would be coming in to the right-hander, who might decide to let it pass through to the 'keeper. Suddenly it would straighten up and rap him on the pads plumb in front of his wicket. Stephen might have ended up with better figures against the West Indies if there had not been the experience of the tourists' game against Western Province. He trapped two leg before wicket as they followed their habit of shuffling across the wicket. They complained, and from then on the umpires in that series were reluctant to give Stephen LBW decisions which were rightfully his. A man who bowled many long spells into the wind at Newlands, he was an ideal partner for Garth le Roux.

Alan Kourie: Undoubtedly he was the best slow bowler in South Africa during the 1980s. Never a great turner of the ball, his control was uncanny. An exploiter of the crease, he could place the ball on the same spot for over after over, varying his flight and direction as he teased, tempted and bluffed in his desire to beat the batsman. His two arm balls, one that was obvious and the other well disguised, was another profitable ploy. A burly man who could be quite intimidating if the mood suited him, he was a past master at gamesmanship and enjoyed getting under a batsman's skin by way of facial expressions or the odd aside. He consistently produced good figures at the Wanderers, a ground which traditionally suited seamers. Many an inexperienced batsman fell to his baiting, as well as some who should have known better. Despite his size, Alan was remarkably agile, being a superb catcher off his own bowling. And I can think of no better slip fielder when he was around. He was a good batsman, scoring freely on numerous occasions and defending patiently and grimly if need be.

Denys Hobson: Leg-break and googly bowling is, regrettably, almost a dying art world-wide, which is a pity for these bowlers are always exciting to watch. They usually either produce a crop of wickets or get badly mauled. Denys had his blue days, but at times he was gloriously successful, particularly at home on the Newlands wicket. There was always the worry for a visiting captain of finding his team with 5 wickets down and needing 80 or so to win, and on would come Hobson with a mean look in his eye and take 5 for next to nothing. No floater, he delivered with some pace and his googly was well disguised. That is, until his final years when we Transvalers learned to pick out the googly by the way he held the ball. Whether other provinces did so I would not know. Not since Rhodesia's Jack du Preez a decade earlier had South Africa produced such a competitor and craftsman.

As an armchair selector given the task of choosing 14 for a hypothetical World Cup from my 20-odd years in first-class cricket, these are my players: Barry Richards, Eddie Barlow, Graeme Pollock, Henry Fotheringham, Lee Irvine, Kepler Wessels, Peter Kirsten, Clive Rice, Mike Procter, Vince van der Bijl, Allan Donald, Garth le Roux, Ray Jennings (wicket-keeper), and Alan Kourie. It must be obvious that, having selected these 14, there are so many others who would never have disgraced themselves in any South African side, and to all of them I extend my warmest appreciation of all the hours we have spent playing with or against each other.

One of the many blessings of my three years with Somerset was the opportunity to meet and compete with some of the best cricketers in the world. A high percentage of players who reach international standard are contracted to county clubs or play them on tour, and selecting a 14-man squad for my World Eleven was not easy. My criterion was that I had to have played with or against my candidates, so others seen on television or read about – and there were many – do not qualify. As it is, there is such an abundance of talent on display that limiting my shortlist to 14 was a major problem.

For example, at first I had the current West Indian captain, Richie Richardson, among the six batsmen. Then I realised that I had forgotten Mike Gatting of Middlesex and England, and I had to include the latter because I had seen him close up both in England and South Africa far more often. There was David Gower, the former England captain, a superb player who is often accused of not taking his cricket seriously, of relaxing when around 60 or 70 and not dedicated enough to care about getting his hundred. But the fact that this wonderfully stylish left-hander has scored nearly 8 000 Test runs somewhat belies that casual reputation. If he never plays international cricket again it will be England's loss.

I cannot find room either for the gifted Zimbabwean Graeme Hick who, in 1989 and 1990, was in a class of his own. Then there is my former Transvaal team-mate, West Indian Alvin Kallicharran; my former Somerset skipper Chris Tavare; Neil Fairbrother of Lancashire; and Allan Border of Australia, among others, let alone several Pakistani and Indian batsmen like Javed Miandad and Sachin Tendulkar.

So, my final 14 reads:

Batsmen

Graham Gooch (England): I first saw him when he brought the unofficial English side to South Africa in 1982, and at first sight I realised that here indeed was a batsman out of the ordinary. Like Clive Rice, and 191 subsequently many others, his stance is unorthodox in that when taking guard he holds his bat in the air behind him at an angle. I was not impressed at first, but concluded later that it made much sense in that this is the position from which one actually plays the ball, not where it is grounded. However, I still prefer to keep the bat just off the ground near my back foot. Whatever his stance, he knows his business of accumulating runs as his incredibly consistent record for England and Essex over the past decade indicates. His innings at Port Elizabeth at the beginning of that 1982 tour was an early eye-opener for me. Having seen off the South African opening bowlers Garth le Roux and Mike Procter (then a little past his best), the burly Englishman next faced Vince van der Bijl, at his peak and always in my book a bowler against whom a batsman has to pass muster. Gooch scratched a bit at the Natalian's first over, then went to town and scored a superb 114. He also took a memorable 136 off Transvaal that season, and I needed no further convincing. A good hooker and cutter, he is strong all round the wicket, particularly off the front foot, and is a fierce competitor against any kind of bowling. Like me, Graham is near the 40 mark, but I believe he still has several more good seasons left in him. An outstanding captain, a proud man with a great heart, and a truly gifted batsman.

Desmond Haynes (West Indies): A characteristic of his play is the apparent abundance of time which he appears to have to play his shots. All great batsmen have this attribute, but it is more obvious in this likeable man. As with Barry Richards, at times one forms the impression that he and the bowler have agreed where each ball is going to land and he is there ready and waiting to dispatch it . . . short outside the off-stump, pitched up to leg, it does not matter . . . Haynes is untroubled. Strong and particularly firm on the leg side, he is equally at home in one-day or five-day cricket. I remember being injured when batting in a match against Middlesex at Uxbridge and was thus able to study him carefully from the stand as he scored a fine century and set his team on the road to a last-over victory. Even though Somerset was at the receiving end, I thoroughly enjoyed the craftsmanship of the man.

Mike Gatting (England): Along with Graeme Pollock he is the best player of spin bowling I have ever seen. His short legs are no handicap as his footwork is faultless, rarely failing to get to the pitch of the ball and dispatching it with punchy shots from firm wrist work. A good runner between the wickets who is always encouraging to his partner, he thirsts for runs the moment he arrives at the crease, and it is a pity that the suspension he and other 'rebels' received for touring South Africa deprived his country and the world of a truly class-performer. He succeeded Mike Brearley as captain of Middlesex and England, and there can be few better leaders of men in the game today. As a cricketer and as a man, he is out of the top drawer.

Robin Smith (England): I was critical of him when he first played for Natal as a youngster and had reservations as to whether he would make the grade. But his going to play for Hampshire, and subsequently for England, soon caused me to re-evaluate him. If there is a harder striker of the ball than Robin Smith, I have yet to see him. He is a powerful, muscular man and he hits the ball ferociously to all quarters. In a match at Southampton he scored an 80 and a century, and I noticed that if he placed the ball only a metre from a fielder, it was invariably going at such a pace that it was destined for the boundary. The West Indians often made the mistake of pitching the ball just short outside his off-stump, and he was then able to indulge in his favourite shot, a vicious cut. His temperament is ideal, scoring quickly, or playing patiently if the occasion demands it. It is no wonder that he is a permanent fixture in the English squad for one- and five-day matches.

Viv Richards (West Indies): I did not see much of him, but enough to recognise a master batsman. He is the type who can play unorthodoxly like Alvin Kallicharran and turn a ball from off-stump to mid-wicket, or play down the line as prescribed in the textbook. All depends on his mood and the requirements of the day. His record of 49 centuries for Somerset reflects the class of the man. To this day Taunton supporters speak of him almost with reverence. In one game against Warwickshire which started at 11 a.m., he began batting at noon and by the time he was out at around 5.30 p.m. he had 322 on the board. He looks arrogant as he walks to the wicket and plays his shots with apparent disdain, but in reality he is a kind, modest man and I had many a long conversation with him about batsmanship and the game in general.

Martin Crowe (New Zealand): I played with him in two World XI games and was able to see him close up. We played an England side at Jesmond near Newcastle, lost the first one-day game, but put England out for 180 in the second match. Gordon Greenidge decided not to open, so Martin partnered me. He scored a wonderful century as between us we passed the home total. A good improviser, as we saw in the World Cup and as I saw in the New Zealand/Somerset match in 1990, by nature he is stylish and conventional. Like all good players, he is hard to pin down once he gets going and has no apparent weaknesses. He is a worthy successor to other great New Zealand batsmen like Martin Donnolly, Bert Sutcliffe, John Reid and Glen Turner.

193

Bowlers

Curtly Ambrose (West Indies): Using his height to full advantage, he does not bowl particularly short but extracts great lift, making it difficult for the batsman to come forward with any confidence and drive him. A product of that almost endless line of Caribbean pacemen, he combines speed with a highly intelligent approach to his bowling, invariably placing the ball exactly where he wants it. Judging from the times I faced him, he is certainly one of the best in the business today. In combat, I often felt I should be pulling or hooking the balls I was playing at chest height, but on inspection of where these deliveries were landing, they were certainly not short enough to play such strokes, and thus one was generally forced to play most of his deliveries defensively.

Malcolm Marshall (West Indies): He had probably lost a yard or two of pace when I played against him, but the quality was still there. One of those players who always gives his best, he swings it both ways, has a vicious cutter, and was still quick enough to pin a batsman on the back foot. Undoubtedly he is a world-class bowler who knows exactly what he is trying to do with each delivery and is quick to work out a batsman's strengths and weaknesses. Most knowledgeable about the game, I enjoyed my numerous talks and duels with him. He is the kind of man I would love to have teaching his craft in the cricket academy I would like to establish one day.

Wasim Akram (Pakistan): Before I faced this outstanding seam bowler our Somerset manager Jack Birkenshaw warned me: 'When you think he is going to bowl, be ready two seconds beforehand. This is because at times he comes ambling in and you may be inclined to think you can play him with ease. Then, suddenly, the ball hits the bat. He has a very fast arm action and often you are caught playing him too late, when the ball is already through you.' Jack was so right. Usually Akram bowls left-arm over and swings it in to the right-hander, and when he wants to he runs it across your body. He also goes around the wicket, swings the ball in and, as a variation, then straightens it out. He did this with great effect against England in the World Cup final in Australia in 1992. He has a deceptive change of pace and often traps batsmen who go looking to hook him. Rightly, much of the credit for Pakistan's winning the World Cup trophy can be attributed to his brilliance. He is what I like to call a serious bowler.

Waqar Younis (Pakistan): He emerged a year or two ago from the Surrey nursery to become an almost overnight sensation with his incredible pace, only Allan Donald being his current equal. I faced him quite a bit in England and developed a healthy respect for him. Unlike Wasim

Akram and his gentle run-up, Waqar really charges in and then unleashes himself like a coiled spring. He sends down few short deliveries. Like Brian Statham and Neil Adcock of an earlier generation, he is of the school whose prime target is the stumps – hit them as often as possible, or at least trap your man leg before wicket. Occasionally he does give you a half-volley and is smacked away to mid-off, cover or mid-wicket, but one has to be certain of connecting, or pay the price. His greatest asset is his late swing either way at pace, very much like Mike Procter. His tendency is to utilise his swing when the ball has lost shine on one side. Playing Somerset once at Weston-super-Mare, he sent two balls in succession just outside the off-stump to my partner Peter Roebuck. The third delivery appeared to be similar. It swung in so viciously that it hit Peter on the left heel and took his feet out from under him. I played his in-swingers for a while and then he had me caught behind with a ball that left me. And this was after I had a half-century on the board. Because he puts so much effort into his bowling there is enormous strain on his back, and it was no wonder he missed the World Cup. Like all genuine fast bowlers, he is best used in short, sharp spells, otherwise his career could be short-lived.

Sylvester Clarke (West Indies): Having played against and with him so often in South Africa, I had every opportunity to study this great bowler over a period of time. It is only because the Caribbean produces so many good seam bowlers that he has been somewhat overshadowed, but this does not detract one iota from his talent. With his big in-swinger and leg-cutter, he was the kind who could sweep through a side like a cyclone and time and again produce remarkable figures. Such was his pace and guile during the two unofficial West Indian tours of South Africa, that 5 or so wickets an innings was the norm. He was in such control of his game that he would tell his captain exactly where he wanted his fielders placed, and was rarely wrong. Using his massive back and powerful arms to the full, he relished nothing more than bowling at full pace. Even at net practice for Transvaal, he would amble up and send down scorchers off only a three-yard run. He put the fear of the Almighty in many a batsman, even when he was past his best in his period with the Orange Free State.

Michael Holding (West Indies): I only faced him twice, but was mesmerised by the quality of his bowling. He had probably begun to slow down, but his action was as smooth as silk as he ran in from only 15 paces and manoeuvred the ball at will, with in-swingers, out-swingers, leg-cutters, probing constantly for weakness. His athleticism was also a feature of his game. One might push a delivery from him firmly to mid-on, and more often than not he would be there to field it himself and cut off the run.

One of my great regrets is that I never faced the game's leading international wicket-taker, Sir Richard Hadlee. He rested when New Zealand played Somerset at Taunton and I told him how much I would have loved to test myself against him. But as the spearhead of their attack he had to have time off somewhere on the tour. Two other West Indian fast bowlers whom I faced, Courtney Walsh and Franklyn Stephenson, would be close for inclusion in my World Squad, as would be another whom I did not meet, Ian Bishop, as well as India's Kapil Dev and England's Phil De Freitas, Neil Foster, David Lawrence and Angus Fraser.

My World Squad slow bowler has to be England and Middlesex off-spinner **John Emburey**. At his best he was real class, a genuine spinner who varied his pace to suit the situation or the wicket. He could bowl economically in a one-day game and was not afraid to be hit in a three-day match to gain valuable wickets. He prefers a wicket that bounces more than one that turns. This is because he favours pitching the ball with it going past the batsman at knee height, knowing that if there is a bat-pad chance it would stay in the air for a while to give close-in fielders catching opportunities. He had the knack of appearing to hang in the air when delivering, watching which way the batsman was shaping up and reacting accordingly. His captain Mike Gatting has such faith in his ability that he is never scared to bowl him at the end of a one-day innings, even if he has precious few runs with which to work. Overall, a shrewd man and a clever cricketer.

My World Squad wicket-keeper is **Jack Russell** of Gloucestershire and England, a highly competent and consistently clean taker of the ball when up to the wicket or standing back. It is not always appreciated how much a good wicket-keeper instils confidence into the rest of a fielding side, and Jack is in that mould. In addition he is, of course, a batsman of some quality, with several high Test scores to his credit. It is never easy to keep wicket day-in and day-out through the long English season but Jack, with his incredible fitness, is always enthusiastic and ready to pounce on that half-chance when it comes his way.

14

ADMINISTRATORS, GROUNDS, AND UMPIRES

Now that South African cricket has emerged from the dark shadow of isolation, it is fitting that tribute should be paid to the three men who, for more than a decade, did so much to maintain and promote interest in the game in this country. For years, almost without a break, Dr Ali Bacher, Joe Pamensky and Geoff Dakin devoted their energies to several objectives: modernising the sport to cope with the demands of a changing society (ie introducing sponsorship and one-day limited-over tournaments), eliminating all vestiges of racial discrimination in constitutions from national to club level, embarking on a massive development scheme to propagate the game among all sections of the community, and trying to regain recognition and respectability among fellow cricketing nations.

The unofficial, or so-called 'rebel' tours by English, Sri Lankan, West Indian and Australian teams during the 1980s attracted much media speculation and controversy, but critics are inclined to overlook the fact that this trio of administrators and their many able colleagues were so successful in their modernisation programme that today the United Cricket Board of South Africa is rightly recognised as one of the most efficient and progressive administrations in any sport anywhere.

The result of this hard work is easy to see. Cricket is more popular than ever before, is widely supported by major commercial interests – ensuring that financial worries are minimal – and the standard of the game is remarkably high, despite two decades of isolation. For the national team to reach the semi-finals of the World Cup after suddenly being thrown back into the cauldron of international competition speaks for itself, and there is every reason to agree with optimists who say that possibly within two or three years, South Africa will be the major power she was on the verge of becoming in 1970 after thrashing the Australians for two series in a row.

Dr Aaron (Ali) Bacher has been at the heart of this dramatic, disheartening and, finally, exciting metamorphosis. Born half a century ago near Johannesburg, he showed ability as a player and leader at an early age, captaining Transvaal and then the Springboks when barely into his majority. He was not a gifted batsman; he was, rather, a solid technician who utilised his ability to the fullest advantage. Although never scoring a Test century, he did once take 235 runs for Transvaal off the Australians. But it was his captaincy which first earmarked his emergence as a national figure. Blessed with a first-class brain and steeped in knowledge of the game, he handled players superbly, motivating and encouraging them and using his tactical skills to win more matches than he lost at any level.

Although he qualified as a medical doctor, his love for the game drew 199 him into administration as managing director for Transvaal, and eventually for the former South African Cricket Union and now the United Cricket Board of South Africa. His reputation, industriousness, imagination and diplomacy saw him at the centre of the 'rebel' tours controversy. When his board decided that these tours were vital to maintain playing standards and public interest, it was Bacher who travelled widely, signing up players whose trust in him was never misplaced. It was only after the 1990 Gatting tour went sour and was cancelled half-way through that he confessed: 'It was the first time in my life that I lost confidence in myself. When the tour was called off it was seen as capitulation.'

But he soon recovered from this débâcle, was one of the first to realise that it was better to work with the so-called 'enemy' – the African National Congress and other 'radical' political groups – and thus was formed a friendship with another remarkable conciliator, former Robben Island prisoner Steve Tshwete, that was to evolve into a fruitful partnership and play a major role in getting South Africa back into international cricket. South Africa is indeed fortunate to have had, and still have, such a man at this period in its cricket history.

Joe Pamensky earned his laurels off the field. A chartered accountant by training, one of the most successful businessmen in the country, and a diplomat by instinct, he achieved his initial success in cricket as the financial power behind the throne, for Transvaal and then for South Africa. All schemes and ideas had to be run past his acute mind before being accepted. His skill and popularity saw him propelled into the presidency of the SACU, and it was with this authority that he led his team of Ali Bacher and Geoff Dakin through most of those tumultuous years of reorganisation. Wise, loyal, and a conciliator of integrity, so highly regarded is he that his provincial peers elected him Transvaal Cricket Administrator of the Century, and in 1984 he won the South African Sports Merit Award. The supreme accolade in the sport he loves so much came when he was made one of only 180 non-cricketing personalities to be given an honorary life membership of the Marylebone Cricket Club.

Geoff Dakin was one of many former players who moved eagerly into administration of the game he loved. A long-time opening batsman, he still shares with Colin Rushmere the Eastern Province first-wicket record of 312, against Western Province at Newlands in 1962/63. As he moved through the administrative ranks he concluded that as things stood in a nation where the policy of apartheid still prevailed, getting back into international cricket was a pipe-dream. So, in his own way, he set out to
play his part in bringing about change. He saw cricket as an ideal way to

do this, and must have derived much satisfaction when that change materialised.

Burly in build, tough-minded, a realist and a solid negotiator, Geoff is at times inclined to be more outspoken than his colleagues, but his heart is in the right place and his firm leadership as president of the United Cricket Board of South Africa in times of stress should not be overlooked. Speaking of his job as national cricket leader, he once confessed: 'I would not mind going over the same route again. I found it exciting. I am the sort of person who enjoys a bit of excitement in life – a bit of an adventure.' He certainly got plenty of that.

The key personality in the modernising of the administrative side of the game in South Africa has undoubtedly been Ali Bacher. In other times, when it was a strictly amateur sport, when costs were not crippling, and when there was no television to tempt people to watch matches from the comfort of their living-rooms, those who ran the game did a pretty good job. But it was most fortunate that the 'Doc' came along to put a firm commercial hand on the tiller at a provincial and then national level.

There is a full-time, highly efficient staff to run what is now a big business, one which is certain to grow even more as South Africa plugs back into the full international circuit, with countries queuing to tour and wanting return tours by the South Africans. Such major companies as South African Breweries, Panasonic, Benson and Hedges, Nissan, Yellow Pages and BP see cricket as a perfect promotional vehicle, but they would not commit themselves to a large financial input if they were not satisfied with the administration.

All the tournaments are run like clockwork, and I am particularly pleased to note that our premier tournament, the Castle Cup (formerly the Currie Cup) has been settled to be a four-day affair. At first I was concerned in case players were unable to take the extra time off work for matches, but although some may have problems, it does seem that employers are treating the matter sympathetically. Those who are self-employed believe the sacrifice is worth it. From the purely cricketing aspect, the four-day game can only improve the standard of play and the quality of pitches. And above all, the chances of that irritating practice of contrived results are lessened. So often in three-day games, with good wickets, a team may score, say, 400-odd for 3 or 4 wickets and then declare; the other side matches that figure and then ensues the circus of making ridiculous declarations in order to get a result. This can lead to the situation of a side obtaining a victory in a match which it did not dominate and which it did not deserve to win. Certainly this happened many times in England, and for that reason they, too, are moving to the four-day fixture.

Another factor in three-day games, in England at least, was that bad pitches were being prepared to suit the bowlers in order to get results. This was obviously to the detriment of the batsmen. And of course the four-day fixture is good training for aspiring Test batsmen and bowlers. Batsmen can learn to build an innings, seam bowlers get to pace themselves even better and to hone techniques, while there is more room for spinners to come in and make use of a worn strip. There will be those who claim that the three-day match was good enough before to produce great matches and players. But this is a fallacious argument when one considers how many more great players might have evolved from the four-day game and how many three-day matches ended in fruitless draws.

Of course the one-day games have their place. They are proved money-spinners wherever they are played. The public loves them, be they 40, 50 or 55 overs, day or day/night fixtures. Kerry Packer did cricket a great service when he introduced the concept in the late 1970s. Look how the World Cup has taken a grip among people, even those who normally do not watch 'ordinary' cricket. We live in a fast, exciting, television-orientated world and if the limited-over game had not been born, it is questionable whether the traditional game would have boomed as it has done. Certainly, as a batsman, I thoroughly enjoy them, and there is nothing more exhilarating than to have a ground packed with happy spectators cheering as runs are accumulated and wickets fall, often at a breathtaking rate. It goes without saying that it is vital that one-day games must be played on true wickets, otherwise they can degenerate into a farce. There must also be the fixture balance, and recent history has proved that there is room for both types of cricket.

I have lost count of the number of grounds on which I have played during the 30 years since my first tentative efforts as a schoolboy in short pants. The difference at a senior representative level between England and South Africa is that in the Republic we tend to play in the big stadiums – the Wanderers, Newlands, Kingsmead, Springbok Park, St George's Park, Centurion Park – whereas the bulk of English fixtures are played at smaller places of great character, with grassy banks, plenty of tents, trees and, frequently, rickety old stands. Of course the county sides do play at the famous large Test grounds like Lord's, the Oval, Edgbaston, Headingley, Trent Bridge and Old Trafford, and it is a privilege to do so. When these big grounds, like those in South Africa, are full, they have a special, heady atmosphere of their own. Conversely, when they are empty, or near-empty, it is somewhat depressing.

The lasting and most favourable impression I have of playing in England is of the intimate grounds like that of Somerset's headquarters at Taunton, with its view of church spires and the River Tone flowing nearby. Along with Cape Town's Newlands, this is my favourite venue. There is a real family atmosphere, games are well supported, even though victories for Somerset in recent years have been sparse. But the people know their cricket, applaud and appreciate skill from either side, and there settles over the place an air of satisfaction and pleasure. Somerset's other home grounds of Weston-super-Mare and Bath are turned into semi-tented stadiums for the week's cricket and at these two, with the festival spirit generated by the occasion, one cannot but enjoy oneself – even though the outfield at Bath is rough and the changing facilities a bit primitive.

I also very much liked playing at Worcester, with its famous cathedral gazing somewhat imperiously over the scene; Canterbury, with its lovely trees; Hampshire's ground at Southampton, and so on. There are some stark, rather featureless grounds, but they are few and far between. With a game like cricket, character, tradition and history can do wonders for even the most Spartan facilities.

The quality of playing pitches in England varies of course, while in South Africa it was noticeable during the years of isolation that we became very provincial-minded. With no official Test matches, winning the Currie Cup became all-important and pitches were often prepared to suit home teams. For example, in the Transvaal, because of the frequency of rain during a highveld summer, our wickets at the Wanderers were usually prepared to give a result in only two and a half days, making it very difficult for batsmen. It was a lottery, with sides often being shot out for under a hundred. Bowling out the opposition cheaply and ensuring we got maximum points was given top priority. Sure, our batsmen would also have to work for runs, but in the era of the 'Mean Machine' there were usually enough to get winning scores – Pollock, Fotheringham, Kallicharran, Rice, McKenzie, Jennings, Kourie, and yours truly, if it was my day. It was great to win points but, overall, not good for the game. Those were glory days for Transvaal, but provincial sides are so much more evenly balanced today that even a Wanderers greentop is no guarantee that the Transvaal lion will give its victory roar.

Newlands used to be a featherbed, a batsman's paradise, but then the authorities in other provinces realised that the only way to halt Transvaal was to play them at their own game and prepare wickets that helped the bowlers. And this they did, leaving more grass than before. The balance began to swing towards the bowlers, and very often they only needed to run up and land the ball and sooner or later they got a victim. I like to think that wickets are now prepared more evenly, with a 60/40 per cent ratio in favour of the batsman. I say this because it makes for a better game of cricket. On good pitches the quality of the top batsmen will emerge and they will score their hundreds, while the best bowlers will get their share of wickets.

In England in 1990, when the wickets generally favoured the batsmen too much, the best bowlers, seamers and spinners, invariably showed their class and got wickets. I was told that for years before the pitches usually favoured bowlers. In 1991, however, I think the balance was just right. In particular, I like to see the way the spinner is returning to English cricket, even that long-forgotten artist, the leg-spinner. What a difference, and what a pleasure, it was to play on those English wickets where I knew that, if I had played myself in, I stood a good chance of controlling the situation, whereas at Wanderers it was often a case of getting runs while one could because trouble was lurking somewhere.

Newlands is my favourite South African ground. With the backdrop of Table Mountain and the famous oaks, the ambience of the place is unbeatable – even when it is a Transvaal-Western Province game. We are traditional rivals and therefore our encounters usually draw the best out of us. We 'Vaalies' can be needled mercilessly and regrettably a good performance at times goes unappreciated. I recall Graeme Pollock scoring a double century there in his first season for us, and there was barely a handclap in the ground. Imagine! A Pollock double hundred was something of a wonder, a glorious moment of cricket, yet petty local prejudice prevailed on that occasion. Conversely, I would have enjoyed a typical Peter Kirsten double hundred, even though it might not have been good for Transvaal. Usually, however, the ribbing from Cape Town spectators is lighthearted, the Province players themselves are good sports, and it is rare for me not to enjoy being at this famous ground.

I used to hate St George's Park. But since it has been radically modernised I have grown to like it very much and the pitch there certainly does give batsmen a lot of confidence. Durban's Kingsmead wicket used to terrify most batsmen and it was many years before I reached three figures there. Now it is a good wicket and once a batsman has settled in there is every reason for him to get a good score. At the same time, it also gives both seamers and spinners a chance. Centurion Park in Verwoerdburg is a fine cricket stadium, having a choice of big grandstand for those who like to watch in a more formal way, and grass banks and trees and room for umbrellas and braais for those who prefer the picnic style of enjoying the match. As it is a new ground the wicket will take some time to settle and develop its own character, although the present tendency is to leave enough grass to suit the seamers.

A famous English football referee once said that the finest compliment ever paid to him after handling an FA Cup Final was that he was hardly noticed. That is, he ran the game with such proficiency that there were no controversial or questionable decisions, no errors of judgement which caused him to be a focus of attention. The game ran smoothly and efficiently. The same criteria can be applied to cricket umpires. If they do their job correctly, they are hardly given a second glance, and everyone is grateful. But should they fall down on the job, the knives are out.

In years gone by umpires were rarely involved in controversy. Questionable decisions seemed to be minimal and players usually accepted the so-called rough with the smooth. But nowadays, because the sport at senior representative level has become so commercialised and players' livelihoods are involved, pressure has increased to such an extent that 'neutral' umpires are being used more often. Of course, all umpires are strictly speaking neutral, but accusations of bias are on the increase and it is felt that the best solution is, where possible, to bring in men from outside countries, provinces, counties and states. This immediately negates any possibility of accusations of prejudice from players, officials, the media and the public.

Umpires may or may not welcome this trend. As it is, they have enough of a job on their hands ruling on incidents which are often over in a second or two and with cameras and television monitors ever present to catch them out. The players and/or the media who are often critical of umpiring decisions have probably never umpired at any great level and thus are not really in a position to question decisions. I believe the game would be much better in South Africa if more former players started to don the white coat. A 'feel' of the game is always an enormous help, and people who have played at a fairly high level will be able to sort out the genuine appeal from the 'con'.

The standard of umpiring has improved very much in South Africa in recent years, but without doubt the best umpires are in England. At Test and county level they are usually seasoned professionals and former players who know the laws thoroughly and also know the players and how their minds work. In 1991, of the 24 on the English umpires panel, 21 had played first-class or even Test cricket. They are part of the circuit scene, eat and drink with the teams, and are accepted accordingly. It is   205 hard to fool them and few try. Barry Meyer, David Shepherd, Ken Palmer, Barry Dudleston, John Hampshire, John Holder, Mervin Kitchen and Dickie Bird and their colleagues are a credit to the game.

If personal experience is any criterion, in nearly 200 innings I played in England during my three years there, if I got three bad decisions it was a lot.

Everyone feels comfortable when these men are officiating. They stamp their personalities on the match with quiet authority from the outset. My first encounter with Barry Meyer was a Transvaal-Western Province match over New Year. I had never set eyes on him before. Yet, as I asked for 'one leg', he replied: 'That's one leg, Jimmy'. He called Henry Fotheringham 'Fothers' when giving him guard, and when Garth le Roux finished the first over, Barry said to him: 'Garth, you're running on the wicket, keep off'. Typically, before the game he had taken the trouble to find out the names and to identify the players on both sides, thus being able to strike up an immediate rapport with them. My reaction was: 'Now we have an umpire. This is great.' And throughout the match he exerted firm but unobtrusive control. It is no wonder he commands such respect. He has also done much to improve the standard of South African umpiring, and both players and umpires owe him a big debt of gratitude for the wonderful work he has done.

Because of the high standard which these umpires impart to the game, there is little or no dissension among the county professionals. There is disappointment and the odd niggle and, being only human, some players do let off a bit of steam, but the serious questioning of decisions is rare and not tolerated. Intimidation by opponents still occurs to a certain extent in both England and South Africa, but seldom gets out of hand and is fading. Certainly I do not condone or practise it.

One of the most satisfying aspects of South African cricket these days is the way it has been taken up by our African youngsters. In the early days when I was a schoolmaster at Fairways Primary School in Johannesburg, we used to play against under-12 and under-13 sides from Alexandra. The enthusiasm was there and they did produce some reasonable bowlers, but they were hopeless when it came to batting. They would run down the wicket and swing wildly, more in hope than good judgement. As natural athletes they soon picked up the knack of bowling and are fine fielders, but no one had bothered to teach them batting discipline and technique. And of course they were badly beaten.

But things have changed now. They are getting good coaching in all
aspects of the game. Much money is being poured into coaching schemes

throughout the country, and I am certain that the time is not far off when our first African Test cricketer will emerge, probably a bowler. Now that South Africa is once more playing international cricket there is every incentive for all our aspiring young players to work at and develop their game. I have plans to open a coaching academy when I retire, and hopefully I will be training our international cricketers of the future.

APPENDIX

APPENDIX

Jimmy Caps The Lot

by Jack Bannister
BBC Radio and TV Commentator

The time is 3.40 p.m. on Wednesday, 18th September, 1991, the place is Taunton, and the occasion is the tea interval on the second day of the four-day Britannic Assurance County Championship match between Somerset and Warwickshire. Somerset were batting and Jimmy was 79 not out – and desperately keen to score the 11th hundred which would break the previous seasonal record for the county, held by the watching Bill Alley since 1961.

I had vacated our homely Press Box on the other side of the ground from the handsome new pavilion, to walk round to have a word with Umpire David Shepherd as he followed the players off for his 'cuppa'. Jimmy naturally walked off first, to a huge and warm round of applause, and I stepped back to let him make the most of his precious few minutes' rest. I played the game long enough to know that there are times when even friends should not speak to a cricketer, and this was one of those times.

It was a hot day, and Jimmy walked off in a cocoon of concentration, still wearing his batting gloves, and obviously keen to reach the haven of the dressing room. Suddenly, a lady member pushed past me and thrust an autograph book towards her hero, with a request that he personalise the signature with a message to her.

If ever a request was badly timed in the wrong place, this was it, and I shut my eyes in embarrassment.

I should have known better. Jimmy snapped out of his concentration, smiled as he peeled off his gloves and took great care in giving the lady exactly what she wanted as his team mates overtook him. Most cricketers, understandably, would have either walked on without a glance or word, or refused the request with one of their own to try again after play.

It is the measure of Cook the man, that he did not even think that the request was an imposition – and that is why he leaves Taunton after three happy years with a greater two-way rapport of affection, pride and respect, than any other overseas player I have ever known in the 23 seasons since Greg Chappell was Somerset's first specially registered overseas player.

211

Usually, after-dinner speakers feel they have been coerced into singing for their supper, and a feeling of total enjoyment of such an evening is as rare as a Somerset win against Warwickshire. (It is my article and I'll write what I want.)

But I can honestly say that the special farewell Dinner organised by supporters for Jimmy on Saturday, 14th September, 1991, gave me more pleasure than any function I have attended in a long time. I made one mistake – forgetting that with Stephen James Cook the final speaker, the absence of any right to reply should have made me more careful when I preceded him.

As any of the 193 people know, who made the evening in the Pavilion such a great one, I waded in head first about Warwickshire's prospects for the following week when they played the final game of the season. I promised Jimmy a working over from Allan Donald, and made other references to what an unsuccessful signing-off game it would be for him.

His reply made no mention of the sheer cheek of the 'Brummie' to come West and bite the hands that had fed him. Until the end – just before he movingly read out the poem he had composed to express his feelings after three years with Somerset.

He said: 'I must end on a sad note by referring to the divorce case you all read about in the western press recently'. I thought 'funny, what has this got to do with cricket?'

On went 'Cookie'. 'The judge had a difficult custody problem of the eight-year-old boy to resolve, and decided he would be guided by the answer of the lad to the question about which parent he would like to live with. "Do you want to live with your mother?" "Oh no sir, please no. You see she beats me."'

A sympathetic 'aah' went round the Somerset members, with an even more puzzled J.D.B. wondering what was the point of the story.

'Right, then you want to live with your father? "Definitely not sir. You see, he beats me as well." I have got to ensure that you live with someone. If it is not your mother or father, who on earth DO you want to live with?'

Just like when Colin McCool used to bowl me out within a few minutes, I never saw the googly coming.

'PLEASE SIR, CAN I GO TO LIVE WITH WARWICKSHIRE? THEY NEVER BEAT ANYBODY.'

Thanks, Jim. In fact thanks for everything you have given me so far. Unlike Somerset supporters, I shall see more of South Africa's leading batsman, because I shall broadcast and write on his first competitive appearance in world cricket for his country – wherever and whenever that is.

212

Jimmy expressed doubts about his ability to last much longer, but I believe that such is the ability and fitness of the man, that it is not impossible he will tour England in 1994, the proud wearer of that Springbok cap he wants so badly it hurts.

A Test match is just that. A test of the best by the best. Jimmy ranks with anyone in world cricket, and he deserves that test in a Test.

In this appreciation of a gentleman who is a gentle man, I have deliberately eschewed the use of statistics for several reasons. They are bound to be chronicled elsewhere in this publication, and I dare not risk the wrath of David Oldham by getting one wrong. But the real reason is that Jimmy Cook is much more than a run-machine. Much more than a recital of admittedly magnificent figures earned in a wonderful career of 20 years.

Occasionally a journalist finds the right phrases to express himself, and I am content that I did that with my closing remarks at that memorable evening in the Pavilion last September.

I finished by saying to Jimmy: 'I want to pay you three compliments and, knowing you, I know which one will give you greatest pleasure. Throughout your career, you have been a credit to yourself. A credit to the game of cricket, and A CREDIT TO YOUR COUNTRY.' I like to think that Jimmy liked that.

Jimmy Cook: Career averages 1972-1992

Year	Team	M	I	No	R	HS	Ave	100	50	C	R	W	Ave	BB
1972/73	Tvl	7	13	1	345	64*	28,75	–	2	1	–	–	–	–
1973/74	Tvl/Tvl	8	14	1	226	53	17,38	–	1	3	16	0	–	–
1974/75	Tvl	11	18	1	613	104	36,06	1	3	8	–	–	–	–
1975/76	Tvl/Tvl B	9	16	2	526	136*	37,57	1	3	7	15	1	15,00	1/15
1976/77	Tvl/Tvl B	7	14	2	375	105	31,25	1	1	12	2	0	–	–
1977/78	Tvl/Tvl B	6	11	1	519	146	51,90	2	2	3	–	–	–	–
1978/79	Tvl/Tvl B	7	11	1	415	179*	41,50	1	1	4	–	–	–	–
1979/80	Tvl	3	5	1	132	68	33,00	–	1	2	–	–	–	–
1980/81	Tvl	8	14	1	581	126	44,69	1	5	4	–	–	–	–
1981/82	Tvl/SA	11	19	3	576	114	36,00	1	3	8	–	–	–	–
1982/83	Tvl/SA	13	21	2	1 142	201*	60,11	4	5	11	–	–	–	–
1983/84	Tvl/SA	11	21	3	1 016	166	56,44	2	6	3	–	–	–	–
1984/85	Tvl	11	16	0	782	140	48,88	2	5	5	–	–	–	–
1985/86	Tvl/SA	11	20	1	840	124	44,21	2	5	7	–	–	–	–
1986/87	Tvl/SA	10	18	2	748	110	46,75	3	2	3	1	0	–	–
1987/88	Tvl	8	16	5	422	159	38,36	1	1	4	–	–	–	–
1988/89	Tvl	8	14	1	721	180*	55,46	3	2	–	–	–	–	–
1989/Som		23	41	4	2 241	156	60,57	8	8	13	–	–	–	–
1989/90	Tvl/SA	9	16	1	566	111*	37,73	1	2	2	5	0	–	–
1990/Som		24	41	7	2 608	313*	76,71	9	11	10	42	2	21,00	2/25
1990/91	Tvl	10	20	1	547	109	28,79	1	2	5	–	–	–	–
1991/Som		24	42	8	2 755	210*	81,03	11	8	16	26	0	–	–
1991/92	Tvl	4	7	0	250	88	35,71	–	1	4	–	–	–	–
Total		243	428	49	18 946	313*	49,99	55	80	135	107	3	35,67	2/25

	M	I	No	R	HS	Ave	100	50	C
Benson & Hedges Career Averages	71	71	7	2 197	116	34,32	3	15	14
Nissan Shield Career Averages	69	66	7	2 952	164*	50,03	9	17	19
Unofficial One-Day Internationals	7	37	1	1 356	131	37,66	2	8	13
Unofficial Test Matches	19	34	3	1 320	169	42,58	3	7	8
Official One-Day Internationals	3	3	0	52	35	17,33			1

(Statistics by Frank Heydenrych)

214

STEPHEN JAMES COOK

Educated at Hyde Park H.S., Witwatersrand University

R.H.B., S.R.A.   Born Johannesburg, S.A., 31.7.1953

First Class Match Statistics For Somerset

Years	Capt	M	Inns	NO	Runs	HS	100s	50s	Cts	Ov	Mdns	Runs	Wkts	Avge	5 Wkts	B-B
1989		23	41	4	2241	156	8	8	13	8		42	2	21.00		2-25
1990		24	41	7	2608	313*	9	11	10	4		26	0			
1991	1	24	42	8	2755	210*	11	8	16							
1989-91	1	71	124	19	7604	313*	28	27	39	12		68	2	34.00		2-25

HS 313* v Glamorgan (Cardiff) 1990. **B-B** 2-25 v Derbyshire (Taunton) 1990. **Big Partnerships:** 3rd wicket 285* runs, S.J.C. (313*) & C. J. Tavare (120*) v Glamorgan (Cardiff) 1990; 3rd wicket 276 runs, S.J.C. (156) & C. J. Tavare (153) v Lancashire (Taunton) 1989. **Other first class centuries** (27): 156 v Lancashire (Taunton) 1989; 147 v Essex (Chelmsford) 1989; 147 v Gloucestershire (Bath) 1989; 105 v Surrey (Guildford) 1989; 120* & 131* v Nottinghamshire (Trent Bridge) 1989; 148 v Leicestershire (Taunton) 1989; 130 v Sussex (Hove) 1989; 117* v New Zealanders (Taunton) 1990; 197 v Sussex (Taunton) 1990; 112* ret hurt v Northamptonshire (Taunton) 1990; 137 v Warwickshire (Taunton) 1990; 152 v Middlesex (Uxbridge) 1990; 116* v Surrey (W-s-M) 1990; 114 v Hampshire (Taunton) 1990; 143 v Worcestershire (Taunton) 1990; 162* v West Indians (Taunton) 1991; 152 v Glamorgan (Swansea) 1991; 107* v Hampshire (Bath) 1991; 131 v Lancashire (Taunton) 1991; 193* v Essex (Southend) 1991; 210* v Northamptonshire (Northampton) 1991; 126 v Kent (Taunton) 1991; 209* v Sri Lankans (Taunton) 1991; 197 & 115* ret hurt v Hampshire (Southampton) 1991; 127 v Warwickshire (Taunton) 1991. **County record:** 11 centuries in a season (1991).

Limited Overs Match Statistics

Refuge Assurance League

For Somerset

Years	Capt	M	Inns	NO	Runs	HS	Avge	100s	50s	6s	Ov	Runs	Wkts	Rs/Wkt	Rs/Ov	B-B	Cts
1989-91		47	47	4	2004	136*	46.60	7	9	10							17

Centuries (7): 123 v Lancashire (Taunton) 1989; 124* v Gloucestershire (Bath) 1989; 114 v Glamorgan (Taunton) 1990; 136* v Hampshire (Taunton) 1990; 132 v Hampshire (Taunton) 1990; 112* v Warwickshire (W-s-M) 1990; 129* v Worcestershire (Worcester) 1991. Only Somerset batsman to score three centuries in a season. 902 runs in 1990 created a new League record for the most runs in a season (this was exceeded by T. M. Moody [Worcestershire] in 1991). **County record partnerships:** 1st wicket 176 runs, S.J.C. (114) & P. M. Roebuck (63) v Glamorgan (Taunton) 1989; 3rd wicket 223 runs, S.J.C. (136*) & G. D. Rose (148) v Glamorgan (Neath) 1990 (League Record).

Benson and Hedges Cup

Years	Capt	M	Inns	NO	Runs	HS	Avge	100s	50s	6s	Ov	Runs	Wkts	Rs/Wkt	Rs/Ov	B-B	Cts
1989-91		16	16	0	854	177	53.37	1	7								6

HS & Gold Award 177 v Sussex (Hove) 1990. Gold Award v Surrey (Taunton) 1991. HS by a Somerset batsman in the Benson and Hedges Cup.

NatWest Trophy

Years	Capt	M	Inns	NO	Runs	HS	Avge	100s	50s	6s	Ov	Runs	Wkts	Rs/Wkt	Rs/Ov	B-B	Cts
1989-91		7	7	0	177	45	25.28										3

HS 45 v Worcestershire (Taunton) 1990.

All Limited Overs Matches (3 competitions plus matches against Sri Lanka and Sussex)

Years	Capt	M	Inns	NO	Runs	HS	Avge	100s	50s	6s	Ov	Runs	Wkts	Rs/Wkt	Rs/Ov	B-B	Cts
1989-91	1	72	72	0	3048	177	42.33	8	16	DID NOT BOWL							28

Index

217

220